Best Wishes,

Annette Bird
Sept 16, 1994
West Point

SO PROUDLY HE SERVED

The Sam Bird Story

by

Annette Bird and Tim Prouty

Edited by Joan Pollack

OKARCHE
BOOKS
Wichita, Kansas

First printing 1993

ISBN 0-9635542-4-7

LCCN 92-83081

Editing, design, typesetting, and printing services provided by About Books, Inc., 425 Cedar Street, Buena Vista, CO 81211, 800-548-1876.

ATTENTION CORPORATIONS, COLLEGES, AND PROFESSIONAL ORGANIZATIONS: Quantity discounts are available on bulk purchases of this book for educational purposes or fund raising. Special books or book excerpts can also be created to fit specific needs. For information, please contact Okarche Books, P.O. Box 782076, Wichita, Kansas 67278-2076 or call 316-687-0049.

Dedication

In loving memory of Brien Thomas Collins
1940 - 1993
reunited again with the "old man."

Acknowledgments

The authors wish to express their heartfelt gratitude to the following, who contributed their recollections to the telling of this story: Kevin T. Almeroth, John Barrier, CWO George A. Barnum (Ret.), Hazel M. Bird, Richard E. Bird, Jr., Claudine Talbott, CSM David L. Bost (Ret.), George C. Bruce, Robert Bruce, Wilson Cadman, Jim M. Cherry, Jr., Patricia H. Clarke, B.T. Collins, COL Joe B. Conmy, Jr. (Ret.), LTC T. Nugent Courvoisie (Ret.), Dr. Ray Cook, M.D., Gary Davis, Mrs. R.J. Davis, MAJ Tommye H. Davis (Ret.), Vincent F. Dattoli, Dennis J. Deal, Jerry J. Diamond, Jim Drennan, Samuel D. Draper, Ed Drum, Pat Drum, David P. Easterling, James L. Felder, Joey D. Forgione, Charlotte Gable, Jack Gable, COL Mark D. Gatanas (Ret.), Richard E. Gaudreau, COL John W. Gorn (Ret.), SSG Max T. Hanning (Ret.), Richard A. Harrison, Jr., Robert J. Houston, Chaplain John E. Keplinger, J.R. Koontz, LTC Ben W. Lagare (Ret.), Bill Laundy, Bob Lawson, Hank W. Link, LTGEN William J. McCaffery (Ret.), Julie McCarthy, James T. McDonald, Doris McKibbin, Paul C. Miller, Jack B. Morgan, COL Tom Muller (Ret.), Eileen O'Hara, LTC Dean L. Parker (Ret.), David P. Porreca, Pam Porvaznik, COL James A.W. Rembert, Bruce Roberts, Laurie Roberts, Joe D. Romagnoli, Jim W. Rone, Ann Rowland, Richard A. Scott, Cy Shearer, Dr. John P. Slater, Freddie "T.J." Slaughter, LTC B. Larkin Spivey (USMC) (Ret.), C. Alex Spivey, J. Burnam Taylor, Jr., Kurt Tegtmeier, Eric D. Thibodeau, COL Henry Tufts (Ret.), R. John Turnbull, Deanna Vanderhoofven, John White, COL Bruce Wilson (Ret.), GEN James K. Woolnough (Ret.), and Eugene C. Zabel.

We are grateful to Penny Shaida, Pat Whitley and David Synstergard for all their help and a very special thank you to Ann Rowland and Joan Pollack for their encouragement and inspiration.

The authors are grateful to William Manchester for his kind permission to use extended extracts from *The Death of a President*, New York: Harper and Row, 1967 (these excerpts are in bold print throughout the book), and his letter to Paula on the 28th of March, 1967.

The photographs contained in this book are taken from the Annette Bird Collection unless otherwise specified.

Finally, we owe a special debt of gratitude to Marilyn, Tom and their wonderful staff at About Books, Inc. for moving heaven and earth to get this book out by Memorial Day. They are true professionals!

Table of Contents

PART V: CLASS REUNION

PART VI: IN GOD WE TRUST

PART VII: AUTUMN SHADES

PART VIII: SUNSET

HOUSTON-BIRD

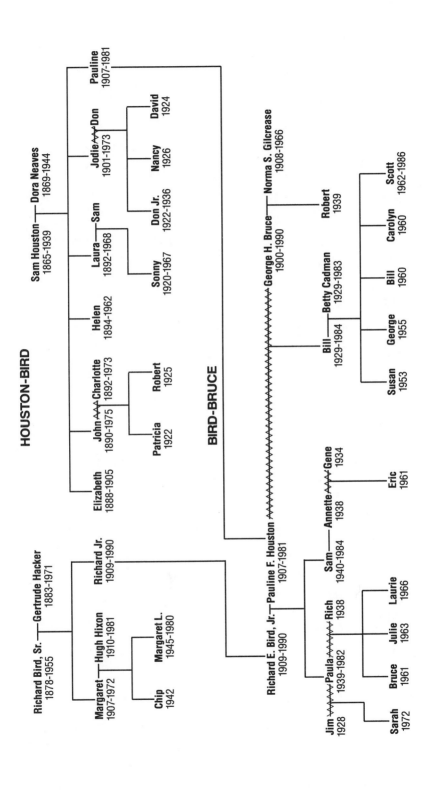

BIRD-BRUCE

To Dick, who loved his son.

"I ran into a captain . . . and we got to talking and he asked me a couple of routine questions like where I went to college and I said I started at The Citadel, and that stopped the conversation. He said, 'Did you know Sam Bird?' I told him that I didn't know Sam Bird but I certainly knew who he was . . . and the man . . . and I don't remember his name and there's no way I will ever remember it . . . he had served with Sam somewhere.

We talked for a long time . . . and I told him that I never knew him; I never shook his hand. I never even got close to Sam Bird.

We talked, some twenty-four years ago. We must have talked for two hours. He wanted to know every single thing that I knew about Sam Bird; which was precious, precious little.

But this guy had a way . . . a way of saying, *Sam*. He said it—almost in awe. I mean, here was this guy, a peer, at least on the books totally equal to Sam Bird . . . but this guy respected him so much. I can't even begin to convey the respect he had. And he told me . . . specifically told me, everybody who came into contact with Sam Bird; whether it was superior, a peer or a subordinate . . . They all felt the same way."

Dennis Deal
Veteran of the Ia Drang Valley

1

Prologue

Richard Ely Bird, Sr. was born in Cincinnati and came to Wichita, Kansas, with his parents in 1890 when it was still a rough and ready, frontier cattle town. Thirteen years later he married the pretty, but altogether no-nonsense daughter of a wealthy, pioneer Wichita family. Gertrude Hacker had a delicate kind of beauty that belied her forceful nature.

The couple had two children. Margaret Cordelia, the elder by two years always appeared to her little brother to be the focus of their parents' attention. That brother, Richard Theodore, was born in 1909. Around the time of his fourteenth birthday, Dick obtained his father's permission to change his own middle name to Ely so he could become "Jr."

The family occupied a fairly substantial, two-story town house at 1120 North Market Street, not far from the business district. The home was comfortable but there was no danger anyone would consider it ostentatious. The senior Bird made it a fundamental tenet *never* to own anything that could just as easily be rented or borrowed. This gave rise to a number of situations that produced their own discomforts.

An innocuous task that developed into near epic proportions visited itself upon Dick and his mother with relentless regularity through spring, summer and fall. This was the weekly Saturday afternoon ritual of mowing the lawn. Dick was spared the initial neighborhood excursion in search of an available lawn mower. That particular chore fell to his mother. Her Saturday afternoon walk became synonymous to many with the predatory encircling of a pair of Jehovah's Witnesses. Whole families might be seen diving for cover on sighting the purposeful-looking Gertrude executing the final turn up the path to their door.

Of course, there were some among them who treated the whole situation with philosophical resignation—as long as they weren't singled out on a regular basis. Yet even those with irritable natures found themselves deferring to Gertrude, for she had a knack of disarming hostility in people. The malicious jibes and insults to his father were reserved for Dick, Jr., whose job it was to return the lawn mower when the chore was done. Such remarks burrowed deep and indelibly.

By the time he was twenty-four, much of his life had been spent in the shadow of his father. Richard Ely Bird Senior was a crusty, bespectacled curmudgeon. He held sway over the district court in Wichita before going on to become the Republican Member of Congress for the Eighth District of Kansas from 1920-22, and Masonic Grand Master for Kansas the following year.

Dick, Jr. left home in 1933 for the University of Kansas at Lawrence and completed his law degree at Washburn Law School where, it appears, he spent a mite more time *in* the bar than actually studying to become a member of it. On obtaining his L.B.S., he returned home to Wichita to live with his parents and take up the position of associate with his father's law firm.

At first glance, Dick was handsome: tall, lean and rangy with large, dark, brooding eyes that pre-empted the less flattering features of a slightly bulbous nose and receding hairline. Always impeccably attired, each time he stood up a tiny ripple would be set in motion down the razor-sharp crease in his trousers. As a rule, women did not find themselves instantly attracted to him. So far he had led a singularly unremarkable life. It wasn't so much that the fledgling attorney had disappointed people in their expectations of him. He simply hadn't enraptured many of them either.

Friends and family alike were caught off guard by the sudden, surprise announcement of his marriage in Eureka, Kansas, (some 45 miles east of Wichita) to Pauline Frances Houston Bruce—the inordinately beautiful, twice-married daughter of Samuel J.

Houston. Her father was a local civic leader of prominence, notoriety and great wealth. He was a distant relative of his namesake, the 19th Century American frontier hero and Texas statesman.

Dick and Pauline had begun dating just that spring. Their romance began in an open air ballroom on the west side of town. Pauline was a scintillating dancer.

The wedding coincided with Dick's twenty-ninth birthday on June 14th, 1938, though the first inkling their respective families had of what had taken place came upon the happy couple's return to Wichita the following day. Apparently matters had come to a head in Eureka's Blue Lantern Tea Room. The town was conveniently able to provide a quickie marriage service and the moment was sealed. This induced a volcanic reaction in Samuel J. Houston, Dick's newly acquired father-in-law, and in his own father as well.

The reason behind the apparent swiftness of events would all become clear eight months later. And from that day forward Pauline adamantly refused to acknowledge the anniversary of her wedding day!

★　　★　　★

Pauline was the youngest of the six children of Dora and Sam Houston. The eldest was Elizabeth. Then came John, Laura, Helen, and Josephine. In 1905, at the age of seventeen, Elizabeth shocked everybody by running off with a suspected small-time thief. Sam Houston was furious. "How could this wanton child selfishly bring such shame upon the family?"

He acted decisively and without compromise. Elizabeth was effectively excommunicated. The mere mention of her name aroused such ire in him the rest of the family were made to feel as though they were committing blasphemy by simply enquiring about her well-being. Dora, however, refused to break contact with her eldest daughter.

Once a week without fail, loaded up with as much food as she could carry, Dora would slip out of the family home and hurry to a secret liaison. This continued without incident until one such occasion when Elizabeth failed to meet her as arranged. Dora finally decided to take the food over to her daughter's house, which was located on the other side of town in a so-called "unsavory neighborhood."

Nothing about the squalor of the urine-soaked alleyways could have prepared her for what lay beyond the threshold as she awkwardly prized open her daughter's kitchen door. Before she could put the food down on the kitchen sideboard, she was overwhelmed by an acrid, sickly-sweet stench. On the floor in front of her lay the two-day-old corpse of her daughter bludgeoned almost beyond recognition.

The man had left town, never to be seen or heard from again. Charges were never filed. Elizabeth was buried in an unmarked grave and the record of her burial disappeared without trace.

Dora became pregnant again shortly afterwards. Pauline was born on September 3rd, 1907, when her mother was thirty-eight. From the moment she made her boisterous entrance into the world with round blue eyes and an extravagant shock of blonde hair already in place, there was little doubt that Pauline Frances Houston was going to be the apple of her father's eye.

As Pauline's tenth birthday approached, the family was making preparations to move to the A.C. Parks Mansion at 1111 North Lawrence, later renamed North Broadway, in Wichita. It had been built in 1900 at a cost of fifty thousand dollars. The centerpiece of the view from the road was an imperious gable atop six sturdy white columns, beneath which sat an impressive balcony that could have doubled admirably as a presidential reviewing stand. An awning kept the early morning sun from the veranda, which led to an oak door the size of a small portcullis. The entire facade was lavishly festooned with a variety of intertwining trees and shrubbery. It helped to partially offset an air of gaudy pomp suggested by the buttresses, balustrades and extravagant-looking cornices.

But no architectural excess could really detract from the majestic splendor of 1111 North Lawrence. It was a striking monument to Sam Houston's swift rise to wealth and status. Gone was the gauche farm boy who rode into the small Kansas

6

town of McPherson aboard a two-wheel cart with twenty-five cents to his name. He was one of the first to purchase office space in Wichita's earliest skyscraper.

Having accumulated substantial wealth from a business empire stretching over three states and with majority stock holdings in more than forty lumber yards, Sam Houston turned his attention to the establishment of a political power base. He became chairman of the committee to elect Bill Ayers, Democratic congressman for the 5th District of Kansas. In addition he was active in several secret fraternal orders, rising to become Potentate of the Midian Shrine Temple and Master of Wichita's Masonic Lodge No. 99.

Everything about Sam Houston and his family *appeared* to embody the essence of the American Dream.

On the other side of the ledger from a highly touted list of business, political and civic accomplishments was a certain notoriety that he had gained as a prolific womanizer. Certainly, in the early years, his exploits were viewed at the very least with covert envy from the male dominated, smoke-filled rooms of the local business, political and fraternal organizations to which he belonged. Over the years, however, as the incidents became more frequent and more blatant in their disregard for any sort of propriety whatsoever (discretion had never been one of his stronger suits), even his closest business and political allies became more reticent about referring to his "colorful image" and began treating him as something of a social outcast.

All through this time Dora seethed. Quietly at first, and then not so quietly. Their home became a battleground. Dora was a formidable and fiercely independent woman whose mercurial mood swings compounded her unpredictability. Immensely proud, some went so far as to say she was conceited, even arrogant.

Sam and Dora's public appearances together dwindled to a weekly card game with the local mortician and his wife, who lived across the street. They became total strangers to one another.

Dora's staunchest ally in the bitter war with her husband was her daughter, Helen. Of all the daughters, Helen bore the closest visual resemblance to her mother, although her features didn't hold the same soft allure. There was a haunting, faraway look in her eyes, hinting perhaps at some deep, unresolved inner turmoil. Her persona appeared to mirror the clothes she wore—starched and stiff. She was generally humorless. Strong-willed and defiant like her mother, there was a conspicuously androgynous air about her. She was married once for a short time and adopted a child. The marriage ended quickly and the child was promptly returned to the orphanage.

Helen felt her mother's pain deeply and bitterly resented her father's behavior. In fact, there was a rumor among the household servants that she was secretly plotting his demise. The rumor attained near-hysterical proportions when the family chauffeur, while carrying out a minor repair in Helen's bedroom, came across a large hatchet hidden beneath her mattress.

She was seen as something of an eccentric, although many went so far as to label her insane. Ironically, she spent much of her life before World War II working tirelessly for the Democratic Party of Kansas alongside her father and older brother, John. She became the party vice-chairman and was a member of the Democratic National Committee for several years. She was a luncheon guest of Eleanor Roosevelt at the White House on a number of occasions.

Of the six children of Sam and Dora Houston, Helen was unquestionably the most enigmatic and ultimately perhaps, the most tragic of them all.

As with so many middle children, Laura, the oldest remaining daughter, suffered both scorn and disaffection at the hands of her parents. Like her sister, Helen, she was plain-looking and headstrong. Her willfulness generally guaranteed that, far from flinching from the family fray, she was often to be found right in the middle of it. However, when the opportunity presented itself in the form of a wealthy banker named Sam Brown, she didn't hesitate to leave home and her parents.

Unlike Helen and Laura, Jodie (Josephine) had no appetite for embroiling herself in a family ruckus. Pretty and ineffectual, she married Don Carqueville, a truck driver. This mortified both parents, who hadn't put her through finishing school to "slum it" with the likes of such people. On the other hand, it did mean they could retain more direct control over their daughter's life.

When Sam Houston purchased 1111 North Broadway in 1917, he acquired with it two homes on the adjoining lot behind the property. One of them, 1116 North Market, was a small, white bungalow. Coincidentally, the other, 1120 North Market, had been the home of Richard E. Bird, Sr. until he became the Republican Member of Congress for the 8th District of Kansas in 1920. After their marriage, Don and Jodie were installed in the larger of the two homes, the two-story town house at 1120 North Market.

Both Laura and Jodie gave birth to children who were to some degree afflicted by problems. Jodie had a son, Don Jr., who became his grandfather's pride and joy, a girl, Nancy, and another boy, David. Don Jr. died from pneumonia and pleurisy at the age of fourteen. Soon after her children were born, Jodie's husband deserted the family and she was left to raise the three children alone.

No one was quite sure what was the matter with Laura's only child, known as Sonny. It was rumored Helen had dropped him on his head several times shortly after he was born. Sonny, whose real name was Houston, possessed the strength of an ox despite his average frame. Unfortunately, he seemed to lack the ability to moderate its use. His cousins could readily attest to this, often finding themselves hurtling through the air like bread rolls at a fraternity house dinner party when Sonny insisted on being allowed to join their games.

In addition, there was his unnerving tendency of going up to people he'd never met before, giving them a lusty slap on the back and crying out, "Long-time, no-see!" Sonny really meant no harm by this. He was a kindly soul who was just trying to be friendly. But, he was often loud and obstinate. In addition, his speech was slightly slurred, often making him sound like he was growling. He ended up alienating those he tried most to befriend—especially the long-suffering members of his own family, who treated him as an embarrassing appendage.

The affection Sam Houston accorded each of his daughters appeared to correspond directly to their respective ages and physical attributes. Pauline was his favorite.

Like any parents, Sam and Dora wanted to imbue their children with something they found lacking in themselves. Refinement seemed their most obvious missing element. When it came time, all the daughters were dispatched to finishing schools. The most eagerly awaited "finished product" was Pauline.

It was 1925 when the eighteen-year-old prodigy returned to her jubilant parents. She was their baby, the consummation of their dreams. They saw to it that she wanted for nothing. In a strange way, she brought them together when all else seemed to drive a deeper wedge between them.

To look at Pauline was to feast on an exquisite visual banquet. She was a beauty with moony blue eyes, short hair styled in fashionable sunsilk blonde waves and a mannequin-like figure, which she dressed in an impeccably coordinated wardrobe. Yet what really set her apart was the subtle implication of melancholy behind her air of gaiety. She was a woman of her time and her time had arrived.

On November 22nd, 1927, in Wichita's undisputed wedding of the year, Pauline was married to George Hickman Bruce. He was a handsome young geologist, hot off the polo fields of Stanford, who possessed matinee-idol looks that belied the boundless ambition of a hard-driven, relentless man.

He was co-founder of Aladdin Petroleum, an oil exploration company in which Sam Houston held a minor stake.

The glittering newlyweds honeymooned in Acapulco and returned to set up housekeeping in the other Houston residency at 1116 North Market. It was a neat, compact, white bungalow nestled alongside Jodie's more substantial two-story home.

Despite having blown into Wichita like an irrepressible whirlwind, George Bruce had yet to amass the kind of fortune sufficient to keep Pauline in her accustomed lifestyle. Though he was clearly uncomfortable with the arrangement, there was little he could do about it at the time. Meanwhile, Pauline applied the soothing syrup of her charm to her husband's wounds and for the time being at least, life was as normal as it could be under the circumstances. For Sam and Dora, the view from the back of 1111 North Broadway had never looked so fair!

On June 25th, 1929, Pauline gave birth to a son, George William. That very same year, the seminal issue of *Who's Who in Wichita* was published with the dashing, young vice-president of Aladdin Petroleum gracing its hallowed pages. He was in the august company of the first aircraft pioneers and other stalwarts of the business and political community. Conspicuous by its absence, as though it were some kind of dirty little secret, was any reference to Samuel J. Houston.

The following year a bizarre kidnapping plot threatened to wreak tragedy on 1116 North Market. Someone broke in during the night while everyone was asleep and plucked young Billy from his crib. George awoke in time to startle the intruder, causing him to panic and flee, leaving Billy on the front porch.

By now, the aspiring oil magnate had accumulated enough money to support the move to a larger house beyond his in-laws' sphere of influence. The extent to which this move precipitated the end of the marriage is not clear. Accounts of what led to the final breakup varied. The Bruce family held that George had reached the point where he could no longer abide his overbearing father-in-law or the expectations of his pampered wife. Her demands had begun to exert an intolerable pressure on his ability to function competently as a businessman.

Others, notably the Houstons, contended that George was involved with another woman and that when Sam Houston learned of the alleged indiscretion, the marriage was effectively doomed. Whatever the reason, the divorce was pushed through quickly without giving either party much room to ponder the idea of reconciliation. The courts did not hesitate in awarding custody of Billy to Pauline.

Pauline would marry again twice—the next time to a lawyer almost twice her age. That marriage was short-lived and Pauline returned home making allegations of emotional and physical cruelty and claiming her husband hung snakes from the branches

11

of trees in their back garden in order to frighten her. She told of being threatened at gunpoint and being locked in her bedroom for hours at a time.

★   ★   ★

Dick Bird and Pauline had first met as children at a birthday party for the "10th Street Gang." Her family had recently moved into the Parks Mansion and he was then living at 1120 North Market. Dick was eight years old. Pauline was ten. He thought she was the prettiest girl he'd ever seen. The unspoken certitude of the time was that she lay far beyond his reach—an unattainable jewel. But years later, after her two divorces, it was an even match.

When it came to drive and ambition, Dick was a shadow of George Bruce, appearing almost inert by comparison. But Pauline didn't need a rollercoaster—stability was her magnet now.

Richard Ely Bird, Sr. was adamant that his son should not enter into a preposterous marriage with this woman. There was the well-known history of mental illness which ran through her family, not to mention her two failed marriages. For perhaps the first and only time in his life, Dick went directly against the wishes of his father.

Following their elopement in Eureka, Dick and Pauline moved into the bungalow at 1116 North Market where George Bruce had found it so difficult to live. Dick had no such qualms. He stopped practicing law with his father and began driving a delivery truck for the Houston-Doughty Lumber Company. Pauline brought an unintentionally comic aspect to the situation when she hired a housekeeper whose husband was a chauffeur to live in their basement. In addition to chauffeuring Pauline to her appointments, ironically the man's other job was to drive Dick to his delivery truck in the mornings and retrieve him in the evenings.

On February 12th, 1939, almost eight months to the day after their wedding—and the reason she would not celebrate her anniversary—Pauline gave birth to a baby daughter, Paula Joanne. Shortly afterwards, the family, including Bill, moved to an impressive, white, colonial-style house at 231 North Terrace.

No sooner had they moved than Pauline became pregnant once again—much to the displeasure of her father. Sam lambasted his son-in-law for his "irresponsible behavior," threatening Dick with a fecundity of unspeakable fates. How much of this latest outburst was due to downright vindictiveness on Sam Houston's part and how much was attributable to illness was open to question.

About a year earlier he'd been diagnosed with terminal cancer. By the latter part of September 1939, he was confined to his bed. The entire family was there, gathered around his bedside, at ten past three in the afternoon on Friday, December 15th, when he met his death.

Unsuitable as he may have been deemed for the hallowed pages of *Who's Who in Wichita,* his death upstaged the war in Europe in both the *Wichita Eagle* and *Beacon* newspapers. His obituary was a rousing and fitting epitaph for a truly self-made man who had epitomized the essence of the American Dream.

PART I

NOT SO HUMBLE BEGINNINGS

Chapter One

Babe and Dood

Wichita, Kansas. The name has a familiar ring to it nowadays, although most people would be hard pressed to pinpoint its exact location on a map. The river city with its modest skyline, clearly upstaged by a surrounding legion of gigantic grain elevators, is situated little more than a hundred miles to the southeast of the geographical center of the United States. A sprawling island in a virtually unbroken sea of wheat, Wichita often lies under shimmering, crystal-clear skies that give way in the evening to the descent of clouds in the west and some of the country's most spectacular sunsets. The scene is enhanced daily by the awesome B1 Bomber in its black, death-invoking majesty, arching skyward through early evening twilight, disgorging plumes of incandescent blue with an earth-shaking roar above East Wichita's stately homes.

Traveling about the city, one is struck by its freedom from claustrophobia—a lack of oppressiveness that contributes to its small town feel. This feeling is heightened by the genuine hospitality of its inhabitants, most of whom wear their hearts unpretentiously on rolled-up shirt sleeves. Wichita is one of those places where guilelessness and integrity tend to play better to an audience than subtlety and sophistication, where a sense of community generally takes precedence over individual action and where most people place their trust in God to take care of life's larger issues. The city's population of three hundred thousand,

17

relatively small by American standards, has stayed constant over the last 10 years.

★   ★   ★

Six weeks after Sam Houston's death, at 6:44 in the evening of January 27, 1940, Pauline gave birth to a seven pound, six and a quarter ounce, bonny baby boy with a wisp of blond hair sticking up from his head. Samuel Richard Bird entered the world with a polite gurgle on a cold, clear day in Kansas—a day that was nevertheless clouded by the war hanging over most of the world. Franklin D. Roosevelt was quoted by the *New York Times* as saying in a letter:

> *"While the armed forces of so many countries are engaged in active hostilities, we are profoundly grateful, as we prepare for this year's observance of Army Day in America, that our Army is occupied with peace time training."*

The 1940 census reported Wichita's population at 133,144, fueled by the war-booming aircraft industry, whose worthy artisans were largely responsible for defining the character of the city as it is today. Then, as now, the center of town sat astride the confluence of the two Arkansas rivers.

At the time, Pauline's elder brother, John, was serving his second term as Democratic congressman for the Fifth District of Kansas, dominated by the city of Wichita. Suavity and eloquent oratory were two of his main trademarks, which clearly did not strike a particularly strong chord with the predominantly blue-collar population. His election was generally considered the legacy of the influence and straightforward, earthy appeal of his father.

The onset of 1941 brought with it the final settlement of Sam Houston's will. Each child received substantial sums. Since there was no written stipulation to the contrary, Dora and Helen assumed control of the lumber company. John Houston was considerably miffed by this. He had taken it for granted his father would leave the controlling interest to him.

Meanwhile, Pauline and Dick used a part of the proceeds from her inheritance to purchase an imperious, albeit slightly rigid, red brick, colonial-style home with white trim and manicured lawn in the exclusive Eastborough community, known as the "City" of Eastborough.

The 1941 move to 18 Lakeside Drive at the corner of Peach Tree Lane—with its emphatic white stone pillars; symmetrical shrubbery; sundry cooks, maids, housekeepers and prestigious neighbors—seemed to have elevated Dick and Pauline, super-ficially anyway, to an elite echelon among Wichitans. For Pauline it represented a kind of rebirth, a re-emergence into the refined air of "Wichita Society." She reveled, temporarily at least, in a regular round of afternoon social engagements. She was active in the Junior League. Her high point may have been reached as early as September 13th, 1942, with a photograph on the society page of the *Wichita Beacon*.

The caption read: "Against a backdrop of fleecy clouds, Wichita socialite, Mrs. R.E. Bird, Jr., poses in a colorful fall fashion from a smart downtown mart . . . in an ensemble of cranberry red and black with black marten tuxedo collar . . . Mrs. Bird is a woman with an unusually wide acquaintance in Wichita."

Pauline's other great passion was the stock market.

For Dick it was different. He had taken a shortcut to some-thing for which he appeared willing to pay the price. That Pauline exerted total financial control over his life was something he would never be allowed to forget.

Thus the move to 18 Lakeside Drive set the tone for their marriage. In Dick's case, for the time being at least, it entailed a life of going through the motions. Nothing could have more aptly symbolized this situation than the daily chauffeur-driven limousine rides to and from his delivery truck.

Eastborough and its arena of privilege provided a lavish back-drop to the unfolding formative years of Sammy and Paula Bird. For a full four years, however, Paula was confused. She could not understand why the person whom she perceived to be her mother had black skin when her skin and Sammy's was white.

19

All the diapering, feeding and care-giving was carried out by either the housekeeper or the maid and when neither was on duty, it was Dick who attended to the children's needs. When Sammy's crying got too much for everyone, the vacuum cleaner was turned on to drown the noise. The majority of Pauline's time spent with the children was limited to carefully selected outings and photo opportunities.

A more angelic-looking, dimple-cheeked pair of tots than Paula and Sammy Bird you never did see. They could have graced baby food and diaper commercials with their cherubic mischief. Paula possessed many, though not all, of her father's features: dark hair, large round, brown eyes and something her father did not possess—a smile that came at you from every-where. Sam, on the other hand, was the very image of his mother: fair skin, sparkling blue eyes and silky blond hair that gleamed in the sunlight. Together though, they were like two drops of water—obvious siblings.

Sam was his father's pride and joy. Paula, on the other hand, had to fight for her father's grudging attention. She was so eager to please him, always trying to engage his attention, yet so often encountering chill indifference. Pauline, because of her varied social and financial interests, had little time for her children during the day and the maids were busy with housework. Therefore, each morning after breakfast, Sammy and Paula would mount their tricycles and pedal "line astern" over to their Uncle John Houston's house at 27 Willowbrook, just around the corner from 18 Lakeside.

After parking their tricycles neatly in the driveway they would scurry round the back of the house to the kitchen, knock on the door and ask their Aunt Charlotte if she could come out to play with them. She usually indulged them for about half an hour before patting them both on the backside and sending them back home. They were a curiosity to their cousin, Patricia, who had just turned twenty.

Paula and Sam grew rapidly and a playhouse was constructed for them in the large back garden. But this was no ordinary play-house. It was somewhere between a garden shed and a small bungalow. Authentic wooden shutters and flower boxes adorned each of the multi-paned windows. The roof was asphalt and the main frame and sides had been put together using the finest quality lumber. The net result was that the potentially grating presence of the children was effectively exported out of the house during the day.

Of course their half-brother, Bill Bruce, was also a member of the household but he was some ten years older. In his case, matters were taken a stage further. One day, he and a friend, Buster Lassen, were discovered imbibing generous quantities of Kentucky bourbon at a local cinema, when they should've been at school. The solution to the problem came in the form of military school. The two miscreants were sent off to separate academies in the summer of 1943. Bill went to the Missouri Military Academy (MMA), a medium-sized school set in the heart of a sleepy, north-central Missouri town called Mexico.

★   ★   ★

One of the few occasions when Sammy and Paula were permitted to accompany their mother on an outing was the regular monthly visit to the "old sick lady" who lived in a ramshackle ranch house about 10 miles east of town. The routine was the same each month. A picnic lunch would be loaded into the trunk of her neighbor's Packard and Pauline and her friend would set off with the children in the back seat. They would head for a small open field about a mile from the "old sick lady's" home. The four of them would eat lunch under the shade of a cottonwood tree and then drive the remaining mile or so to the lady's home. The children were instructed to remain in the car while the two women went in for a very brief visit. After about five minutes, they would emerge lugging a large wooden crate which they would proceed to load into the trunk. It was some years before Paula and Sam would learn they had played their own unwitting part in ensuring the bar at 18 Lakeside remained handsomely stocked. Although the 18th Amendment was repealed in 1933, Kansas was still a dry state.

Next to the stock market, Pauline's greatest passion was dancing. Saturday nights were reserved for dancing. Normally Dick and Pauline wouldn't return home until the early hours of Sunday morning while the children were fast asleep. On one occasion, however, Sammy and Paula were awakened by the loud slam of the front door and the sound of arguing filtering up from the hallway. Paula slipped into Sammy's room, clasped him by the hand and led him gingerly out to the landing at the top of the stairs. The two children sat huddled together, watching everything unfold: wide-eyed, tight-lipped and terrified.

As Pauline's derisive taunts escalated into blood-curdling shrieks, they struggled to make sense out of what was going on. They sat transfixed as their mother disappeared into the living room. Seconds later, a substantial (but cheap) piece of china came hurtling through the doorway, cleared Dick's forehead by a whisker and smashed into the wall behind him. Terrified, Sammy scampered back to his bedroom. He dived under the covers, clutched the pillow to his tiny chest and sobbed himself to sleep. At breakfast the following day, the children never breathed a word of what they'd seen and their parents carried on as if nothing had happened.

John Houston lost out in his bid for a third congressional term in 1942 after the fourth and fifth districts were amalgamated. He accepted a post with the National Labor Relations Board and his family left Eastborough and Wichita for Washington, D.C. He returned only once to Wichita, some time before the end of the decade. Back in Washington, he told of visiting Pauline and finding her with a black eye and a broken jaw. She made him promise never to speak about what he'd seen.

John's daughter, Patricia, said once when referring to Dick, "I never could figure out why she married that ugly man.

"I don't think he was a man with ambition . . . for anything. He never impressed me, period. From the time I first met him I didn't like him . . . and I can't put my finger on it. He had no sense of humor and no conversation. He was a manipulator. Money attracted him however he could get it—whether it was through her or through her family."

As Sam and Paula grew, the differences in their personalities began to emerge. Where Paula was loud and boisterous, Sam appeared quiet and reflective. Where Paula bubbled over with exuberance, never shrinking from the spotlight, Sam appeared shy and content to wander off on his own. Paula was quicksilver, always ready with a reply. Sam appeared slow and ponderous by comparison. Paula had charisma. Sam seemed an ordinary little boy.

The older Paula got, the more frustrated she became in her attempts to elicit her father's attention. Dick's interest was unquestionably focused on his son. This was especially apparent when he took Sam on regular trips down to New Mexico to purchase lumber in one of the lumber company's trucks, Old Whitey. At the breakfast table before each trip, Paula was always trying to meet her father's eyes, waiting for an invitation that never came. Without question, his rejection represented the single overwhelming influence on her life.

Not surprisingly, Paula's jealousy often erupted into physical violence. She took to giving Sam a darn good whipping at every opportunity. At last the day came when he was capable of holding his own and fighting back. *Then* Dick came to the defense of his daughter, admonishing his son sternly, "Boys don't hit girls."

Sam certainly seemed enamored of his half-brother, Bill. Particularly since Bill had begun to attend military school. From the very first visit with his parents to see Bill at the MMA, Sam, a cute and slightly chubby three-year-old, saw magic in the place. The sight and sound of hundreds of boys in uniform marching in unison to the beat of a military band held him spellbound. He pleaded for a set of toy soldiers when they returned home.

During the first of their trips, a porter at the local airport in Mexico, Missouri, inadvertently helped to coin nicknames that became a special part of family communication. "Steady there, Babe," he said with a smile as Pauline descended the steps from the aircraft. And, "That's okay, Dude, I'll take those," he said to Dick as he followed his wife down with a couple of carry-on bags.

Sam and Paula giggled to one another and started addressing their parents as "Babe" and "Dood." This practice continued for the rest of their lives.

The other person besides Bill for whom Sam conceived a special affection at that time was his Aunt Helen. She entered the Women's Army Corps as part of the first all-Kansas unit on October 21, 1943, at Topeka. The sight of Helen in uniform was formidable. After completing her basic training at Fort Oglethorpe in Georgia, she joined the U.S. Army recruiting service at Watertown, New York.

"Army life from a woman's point of view is a wonderful experience," she declared. "It's something that any girl who is eligible should be happy to do." Such sentiments were perhaps not entirely shared by her sister, Pauline.

Throughout her service with the Army, Helen retained the position of vice-president with the Houston-Doughty Lumber Company. That is, until her mother Dora died a year to the day after Helen had enlisted in the Army. Thereupon, Helen assumed the controlling interest.

The phenomenal success of the Houston-Doughty lumber empire had been due in no small part to Dora's drive and business acumen. Some said she was more powerful than her husband. Indeed, the business world may have provided the perfect niche for her glacial personality. In one last vengeful act before her death, she halved Dick's salary and those of two of her husband's long-time trusted lieutenants.

Helen returned home to be with her mother just before she died. Dick brought Pauline and the children over for regular visits. Helen would greet the two children warmly and whisk them off for entertaining stories about army life in New York. Meanwhile Dick and Pauline visited the ailing Dora, lying prostrate on the sofa. Sam seemed entranced by his Aunt Helen—by her upright bearing and the fierceness with which she extolled the virtues of patriotism.

After her mother's death, Helen left the Army, took over the day to day running of the lumber company and stayed on alone at 1111 North Broadway. Dick and Pauline maintained a close relationship with Helen. Dick, in particular, went out of his way to treat her with respect and deference, despite the fact that rumors of her mental instability were beginning to surface from every quarter. Before leaving the Army, she'd undergone shock treatment in Alabama for depression. She confided to Dick and Pauline that it had been the most debilitating experience of her life.

The startling decline of the Houston-Doughty Lumber Company can be traced from that time forward. Pauline began to selectively accumulate certain lumber yards as they were liquidated. A new yard at 6601 East Kellog was constructed for Dick to manage, barely a quarter of a mile south of their Lakeside Drive home.

Dick and Pauline were preoccupied with money—saving it in particular. Shortly before each Christmas they'd lay out a variety of "presents" *they* had bought on their bed. Paula and Sam would be summoned in separately to choose which present each wanted to "give" to their parents. The child would select the present and hand the money over to Dick and Pauline. The present was then wrapped and placed under the tree. Paula grew up thinking this was how all families celebrated Christmas.

Dick and Pauline selected presents for others from items in the home they themselves had grown tired of, had no further use for, or gifts they'd received that they didn't like in the first place.

Sam followed Paula to College Hill Elementary School where, in the words of his teachers, Myrtle Thompson and Mildred Brown, "Sammy tries so hard to do everything just right. We are working on his voice and think in time we'll get it up as it should be. Sometimes with a voice as low as his, it takes as long as two years to do it." In fact, as he grew up, Sam's voice would grow deeper and more resonant and become something of a hallmark.

A flat voice though, was the least of Sam's woes at a time when he could only look on in hapless bemusement as his body deserted him with astonishing rapidity. In the space of three years, the cherubic and slightly chubby little boy acquired the endomorphic physique of a well-ripened pear. His hips and backside filled out but his chest failed to respond in kind. The most embarrassing aspect of all this for the self-conscious seven-year-old was the phenomenon causing his trousers to ride up around his sternum as he walked. However, he remained as gentle and affable as ever.

The exception came in athletics when his growing ungainliness began to cause him considerable embarrassment. The real reason, however, for his aversion to sports and gym had less to do with his clumsiness than with a big brown mole the size of a dime which had taken up residence in the center of his chest. A tight fitting tee shirt made it seem as though he had a third nipple. (Puberty and chest hair had never been so keenly awaited!) Yet the other boys never so much as made reference to it.

Sam continued to be content, in the main, with his own company, although he seemed to display an inclination toward befriending lost sheep. One such child was Russell Ketteman, a local baker's son who'd recently lost his mother to cancer. Most of the class had difficulty knowing what to say to Russell or how to act around him so they chose to steer clear. Sam's sunny, unaffected persona seemed to be the perfect antidote to any awkwardness and the two became the best of friends. Russell was one of the few childhood friends to visit 18 Lakeside. Paula had a close friend, Claudine Talbott, who stayed at the house for six months and Robert Bruce (Bill's half brother—George's son by his second marriage to Norma Smallwood Gilcrease, Miss America 1926) became a regular playmate. Robert was the same age as Sam. The one thing that always struck all three children as strange was the invariable absence of Sam and Paula's parents.

Sam listed his favorite hobbies as trains, drums and guns—in that order. He had a large model train set all laid out in the basement. Later he received a drum set which he battered mercilessly behind the double-glazed windows and closed door of his bedroom. He never betrayed so much as a suspicion of rhythm or timing. For the Christmas before his tenth birthday, Sam was delighted to receive a BB gun. Dick looked at his son through his camera lens as Sam posed awkwardly for photographs with the gun in his hands. Dick was struck by the incongruity of the image. "Well, one thing's for sure," he said to Pauline, "Sam'll never make a soldier."

★   ★   ★

In 1950 the residents of Eastborough came to an agreement with the county educational district. They agreed to sink their substantial collective wealth into a joint project for the construction of a new all-in-one elementary and grade school across from the existing small country school. Thus the modern Minneha Grade School was born. For Sam and Paula, this meant leaving College Hill and the city school system that fall for Minneha and the country.

For much of that first year, there was an awkwardness at Minneha as the children from the country districts eyed their wealthy counterparts as an exotic species. It took about a year for the ritual of mutual acceptance to play itself out, but by the time Sam had moved up to the seventh grade, things had started to settle down.

A unique aspect of Minneha as a part city, part country school was the melding of different curriculums as well as different cultural backgrounds. A tradition retained from the original country school was Friday afternoon sports in spring and fall. Girls were allowed to wear jeans on this occasion only—a heady privilege. Of course, there was really only one sport then—baseball.

There are certain children who are destined to hold center stage on such occasions. Paula was such a child. A baseball glove had been an extension of her left hand for years but there was more to it than that. The pre-game rite of assigning players was her province and hers alone. Paula had an instinct for the subtle nuances of team selection that always prevailed. Often teams would be picked and one team captain would be gloating over the fact that he'd snagged the star hitter, and then, because he was late out of the changing room, the star pitcher as well. With a word or two and a quick gesture from Paula, the star pitcher would be traded and the previously jubilant protagonist was left with the look of all fleeting heroes. His whimpers of protest were

27

of no consequence. This was Pill's (as Sam always called her in Grade School) domain. She was the "wheeler-dealer" here.

Sam was always the last choice. When it came to baseball, he had all the hand-eye co-ordination and stature of a demented seal pup. The sight of Sam standing alone at the end of the selection process drew a wince, or a sigh of relief, depending on your team and who had the last pick. Not surprisingly, he came to loathe the sport.

Fortunately, there was a way of avoiding the cruel humiliation of a Friday afternoon for the likes of Sam. Deliverance came in the form of a "Choate pass." Miss Anne Choate was an unlikely heroine. A strict, elfin-like music teacher with a tart tongue, she issued passes to those in the school band who wanted time alone to practice with their instruments instead of participating in sports. The band room thus became a haven for those like Sam who sought refuge from the visitation of baseball on Friday afternoons.

It would be wrong, however, to infer that Sam didn't possess a genuine interest in music. Even though his sense of tone wasn't all it could've been—he couldn't, bless him, sing a note—he could march in spite of his general lack of coordination. Boy, could Sam march! Ann Choate could be venomous in the way she singled out those band members with even the slightest hiccup in their cadence. Throughout the entire time he attended Minneha School, not once did Sam incur the wrath of Miss Ann Choate for being out of step.

In the music room one Friday, after securing his first Choate Pass, Sam encountered a girl with a similar ungainliness about her and an even greater loathing of physical education. Annette Okarche Blazier was one of those unfortunate, gawky-looking girls who had matured disproportionately in some noticeable areas. She was the tallest girl in the class and wore glasses. This would probably have been enough in itself to guarantee nominal notoriety, but the size of her bust garnered the merciless attention of some boys who nicknamed her "Falsies." Even though rarely uttered to her face, this sobriquet followed her around, echoing through corridors and bouncing off locker doors. As a result, she withdrew behind a wall of reticence. Like Sam, she was neither exceptionally gifted academically, nor at all slow-witted. The less-than-flattering references to her accelerated chest growth caused her to limit her participation in most classes. She would commandeer one of the back desks where she could keep a low profile.

During the first year of strained communication and distances between the two town factions, Annette often allowed her gaze to stray in Sam's direction. She noticed he wore his hair short, parted on the left side and plastered down with Brilcream. There was a stubborn tuft of hair on the crown of his head that refused to cooperate with his comb. She noticed the dark circles underneath his eyes that stood out all the more in contrast to his pudgy cheeks and fair complexion. And then there were those "husky-size" trousers he wore. They sat well above his waistline—almost around his chest. She could see this embarrassed him.

As members of the band, Sam played the drums and Annette, in a split with convention, or perhaps more accurately, in open defiance of her father's wishes, chose the trombone. She was the eldest of four children and had always had a difficult time communicating with her father. This was not particularly unusual—plenty of people experienced difficulty in communicating with Ed Blazier. It was not that he was unapproachable, but he was a stolid, unexcitable man of few words and few really close friends—his choice, not theirs. When not putting in long hours at the Beech Aircraft plant across the road from his home next to the old Minneha School, his passions were fishing, skeet shooting and listening to ball games, in that order. As a result of the constant prodding of his wife, Lois, he eventually became a member of the original Minneha School Board, which played a crucial role in the amalgamation of the two schools.

The family also owned and operated an independent gas station that was, in effect, run by Lois, whose extroverted nature was the antithesis of her husband's detachment. An unsung doer and helper, she always had time for other people and reveled in their company. When she wasn't doing the gas station's books, she was busy as president of the P.T.A. and various church groups, or ferrying her four children (after Annette came Hal, Dona and Carol) to and from ballet, music and art lessons in the well-used family station wagon. Ed and Lois Blazier epitomized the proletarian ethic of faith, hard work and community which defined much of Middle America in the 1950s. Annette's and Sam's backgrounds could hardly have been more different.

Their friendship began in the music room one Friday afternoon. They exchanged the knowing looks that barely concealed an exquisite pleasure at having circumvented the system. There was little in the way of conventional music practiced during these hours, since the heaven-sent Miss Choate had the afternoon off. The sports refugees were left to their own devices. This meant plenty of furtive chatter and perhaps an occasional melodious note.

The days passed, smiles broadened and everything led to those Friday afternoons. Soon Sam started calling Annette on the telephone after school. She in turn would dash the two blocks home from school, expending more energy than she ever did on sports, and sit by the phone, impatiently waiting for it to ring. But, to show she hadn't been waiting anxiously for his call, she'd let it ring four times before picking up the receiver. It was then a matter of whose mother's patience expired first; a cold hand would descend to pluck the receiver from a sweaty palm. In the beginning they talked about music; Sam wanted to be Buddy Rich and Annette wanted to be Tommy Dorsey. Then it was everything and nothing. At the time, Annette was struck by Sam's lack of reference to his family—except how Paula always used to beat him to a pulp and how he always used to get in trouble if he tried to fight back in self defense.

The only really serious topic of conversation revolved around the 10 to 12 weeks of instruction both of them were in the process of undergoing in order to become confirmed members of their respective churches: Sam, the Episcopal Church and Annette, the Presbyterian. Annette had always been pretty earnest when it came to religious belief but she was struck by the seriousness with which Sam approached the subject of confirmation. He was a devout member in attendance at Saint James

Episcopal Church in Wichita, despite the fact that neither of his parents were churchgoers at the time. Dick would drop Sam and Paula off at Sunday School and return to pick them up afterwards. The main influence toward the Episcopal Church came from Sam's Godparents, Pinky and Lucille Grandfield (a cheery, rotund veterinarian with perpetually flushed cheeks and his wife).

The Grandfields were Dick and Pauline's closest friends and came to play a large role in their lives and those of their children. Pinky was always jovial. Lucille was the classic socialite who became Pauline's regular drinking companion in the afternoons. As Sam's Godparents, they took an active role in his development—some would say more active than his parents. Certainly it was Lucille who cultivated Sam's participation in the church. She encouraged his and Paula's attendance. The Grandfields were present at their confirmation. From there Sam's faith and devoutness grew, essentially as a result of his own enthusiasm. Paula, however, loosened her commitment to the church as other interests caught her imagination.

By Christmas of 1952, Sam and Annette's friendship had been blossoming steadily for 18 months. Neither one had actually come out and directly acknowledged his or her feelings for the other in any frantic teenage declaration of undying love. Somehow, that would have been inappropriate. However, Sam did make the four-mile round trip into town on foot for the sole purpose of buying Annette a Christmas present. He bought her a slim, silver, surprisingly heavy 3" by 3" compact with gold-leaf floral engraving. Poor Sam had to put up with the playful jibes of his parents for a full week afterwards.

The following Valentine's Day, the children of Mrs. Skinner's class held a small party with cupcakes, ice cream and punch at their desks. Classmates also sent Valentine cards to one another, which they had deposited in a specially decorated box throughout that week, to be opened on Friday. Annette received cards from everyone in the class, including Sam, as well as an additional 24 unsigned cards. She looked across at her young soul mate whose face spread into a sheepish grin. He never actually admitted he was responsible.

Sometime during the spring that followed, Sam invited Annette over to his home for dinner after a movie matinee at the Orpheum Theater in town. It was the first time she'd set foot on Eastborough's hallowed soil, let alone had an invitation to one of its august estates. Lois Blazier gathered the two of them in the family station wagon on Saturday and took them to the bus stop outside Dockam's Drug Store on Douglas Street. From there they rode the bus downtown to the theater. Upon their return, Dick was waiting at the bus stop to take them home to dinner.

The city of Eastborough was like another world to Russell Ketteman, Annette and those like them. For that evening at least, she would be "Alice through the looking glass." She entered the front door in wonderment. She was dazzled by sumptuous wall-to-wall carpeting with pile as thick as a wheat, exotic rugs, domineering portraits and landscapes adorning the walls, demure statuettes and outlandish ornaments lavishly dispersed among the fine furniture. It was like something out of the glossy haute couture magazines she and her mother would pore over when they had time to indulge their fantasies.

At one end of an imperious mahogany dining table sat Pauline, blending perfectly with the ambient Victoriana. Dick took his seat at the other end where the meal had been placed in dishes covered by warmers. Sam and Annette were seated side by side nearest the wall.

Suddenly the front door burst open and Paula rushed in, tossed her catcher's mitt into the hallway and hurried into the dining room. Dick froze his daughter with a withering look.

"Washed our hands have we, Paula dear?" the question oozed like treacle from Pauline's lips.

"Yes Mama," Paula replied breathlessly.

Dick bowed his head. The children followed suit.

"For what we are about to receive . . ."

"Stop it!" whispered Pauline to her daughter who was fidgeting uncontrollably.

". . . may the Lord make us truly thankful." Dick punctuated his monotone with a growling "Amen."

"Amen," Sam declared in earnest.

Annette, who had been sneaking a peek at the art work and sculptures chimed in belatedly with her "Amen."

Then came the *piece de resistance* as Pauline reached down for a small hand-bell stationed beside her napkin and gave it a little ring. No sooner had she placed it back down on the table than out scurried a maid bearing plates for the meal. Annette sat, mouth agape, lost in a delicious moment of amazement.

'Isn't this the most wonderful thing?' she thought to herself, 'Just to be able to ring a bell and have everything at your finger-tips!'

"How long has your father been on the school board?" inquired Dick, with no discernible enthusiasm.

". . . Um . . . er two years, I think," replied Annette, still overcome by the spectacle around her.

When everyone had finished with the main course, Pauline rang the bell once more and the maid scurried back to remove the dishes. During dessert Pauline took out a long, sleek, ebony cigarette holder from its case and inserted one of her long, slim cigarettes.

"What are your plans for the summer?" droned Dick.

Once again, Annette was transfixed by the glamorous Pauline. ". . . Oh, I'm staying with my grandmother in Denver. She's arranged music lessons for me while I'm there."

"How absolutely marvelous," purred Pauline as she lit her cigarette. She took a deep puff and exhaled the smoke across the table. "Did you know that Sam will be going to military school this fall?"

"Er . . . yes," replied Annette, completely spellbound by such grandiloquence.

Pauline was the first to excuse herself from the table to retire upstairs. Sam looked across at his father who gave him a nod and the children got up from their chairs. Annette followed Sam's lead in sliding her chair carefully back underneath the magisterial dining table. Paula sprinted for the door.

"Paula!" roared Dick. She stopped dead in her tracks. "No running in the house!"

Sam motioned to his young companion to accompany him out onto the front porch, where he taught her how to manufacture a crude whistle out of the water succulent leaves growing up out of the step. A quarter of an hour later, Dick transported Annette back through the looking glass.

One afternoon a couple of weeks after the visit, shortly before the relentless, stifling heat of a Kansas summer drew its pall over the city for three solid months, Sam and classmate Jesse David Wall somehow managed to contrive to miss the bus home to Eastborough. Each bus departed promptly, 10 minutes after school was out. Sam was renowned for his punctuality and rarely got into trouble at school but Jesse David was another story. He was one of those exasperating, eccentric geniuses who continued to talk obliviously after the teacher had said, "Be quiet!" He was always standing up when he should've been sitting down and always in a dither when it came to where he should be for his next class. He regularly endured a barrage of taunts from the other kids and similar disdain from the teachers, who were jealous of his intellect. It wasn't that he went out of his way to attract unfavorable attention; it just seemed to be there waiting for him. Sam had become his best friend.

"Gee, I'm sorry Sam," clamored Jesse after he'd emerged running from the main door with his book bag around his neck and papers sticking out in all directions.

"That's okay."

"Hey, doesn't Annette Blazier live round here somewhere?"

"Yeah. Her folks run the gas station on the corner."

And with that, they set off.

That afternoon Lois Blazier had begun her spring cleaning and decorating in earnest. Everything in the living room, whether it moved or not, was covered in a white sheet and jagged strips of paper lay all over the floor. When the doorbell rang, Lois was half-way up a stepladder. She was sporting a pair of tattered trousers which were cut off at the knee and exposed the varicose veins on her calves, a shirt with dried paint stains from the previous spring and a bandanna fashioned out of an old dish cloth.

"I'll get it!" yelled Annette from the kitchen.

She opened the door and her mouth dropped.

"Hi!" smiled Sam.

"Hi," she quavered. Instantly, a vivid image of Pauline ringing her little bell with one hand and demurely holding the ebony cigarette holder in the other popped into her head. Here was her own mother atop a wooden stepladder, brandishing a paint stripper and looking for all the world like Barnacle Bill the Sailor.

"We missed the bus. Can I use your phone to call my mom?"

For several seconds Annette was incapable of saying anything. She yearned for the ground to open and swallow her, there and then. Instead, she found herself inviting them in and, in an involuntary reflex, offering glasses of Coke while Sam phoned his mother. The final, excruciating moment of humiliation came when the quaintly preposterous figure of her mother appeared in the doorway.

"Well, Annette . . . aren't you going to introduce me?"

Annette looked at her mother, aghast. She couldn't erase Pauline from her mind or the thought that Sam simply had to be comparing everything unfavorably with 18 Lakeside.

". . . This is Mother."

"Hello Mrs. Blazier," the boys replied enthusiastically.

"Hello boys."

"Neat outfit," quipped Jesse.

"Why thank you," Lois smiled, winking at her daughter who was dying a thousand deaths, "I selected it specially for the occasion."

Minutes later Pauline's car pulled up outside. Sam and Jesse got up to leave. Just before he reached the door, Sam turned and smiled. "Really good to meet you, Mrs. Blazier."

"Likewise, Sam. Hurry back."

Then he turned to Annette. "Thanks for the Cokes."

"Any time."

Once Sam had closed the door behind him, Annette rushed to her bedroom and slammed the door.

Later that evening Sam phoned to thank Annette once again for having gotten him out of a jam.

"I never want to see or hear from you ever again!" she cried and slammed the phone down.

Pauline looked across at her son and saw the look of stunned bewilderment that had come over his face. "I just don't understand women," he said, still somewhat shell-shocked, and wandered outside in something of a daze.

That fall of 1953, Sam followed in Bill's footsteps and entered the Missouri Military Academy. Later that year he returned to Minneha for a visit to the ninth grade class. Resplendent in his new uniform, he quickly became the center of attention. On the other side of the room, with the haunted look of someone much older than her years, Annette remained seated at her desk. She pretended to be writing, while snatching an occasional peek at Sam. 'How wonderful and handsome he looks,' she thought. And yet, for reasons much more profound and darker than false pride and teenage pettiness, she was unable to go to him.

Chapter Two

High Pockets

There are certain durable myths about military high schools that persist unto this day: The teachers and staff are made up of an assortment of fugitives from real life, including armchair-soldier disciplinarians who could never cut it themselves in the regular Army, quirky eccentrics, mad demagogues and diabolical misogynists who resent the very presence of a woman unless she happens to be over the age of sixty, wears a starched uniform, reeks of carbolic soap and works in the school sanitorium. Yet in some ways, the most persistent notion of a military school is that of educational provider of the last resort to long-suffering parents of willfully disobedient and unmanageable offspring.

In Sam's case and many like his at the MMA, nothing could have been further from the truth. Ever since his first visit to the school set in the small, sleepy town of Mexico, Missouri, some 10 years earlier when Bill was a student there, Sam had been smitten by the place.

Sam Bird and Robert Bruce, Bill's half-brother and Sam's childhood friend, enrolled at the Missouri Military Academy during the first week of September in 1953. For much of that first year, Sam's mollycoddled appearance—accentuated by a flabby, somewhat distended torso—attracted the undivided attention of the "A" Barracks bullies. And, as if his physical appearance alone didn't present his tormentors with a sufficiently enticing target, Sam had volunteered for the band. As haven to "pansies, queers and nerds," it was the single most derided institution in the

37

school. In fact, the band hadn't done much over the years to dispel this mockery from ignorant buffoons. At times, it would have been charitable to describe the end result of their collective endeavors as music.

Sam joined the band and took everything that was dished out with a kind of serene stoicism. He accepted the status quo out of the very real sense that this was where he wanted to be; this was where he was supposed to be. In that respect, his arrival at the MMA was like the link in the chain that slips onto the cog and clicks into gear; at thirteen years of age, he'd found his niche.

By the end of that first year, several classmates had begun to notice a couple of things about Sam. He did things conscientiously and scrupulously. From the beginning, all tasks and responsibilities assigned to him were treated with a kind of reverence. They were always completed promptly with the utmost meticulousness—whether or not such tasks might be considered a monumental waste of time. What struck his classmates was certainly not Sam's natural ability; he was a barely average student and definitely no athlete, as has been exhaustively documented. It was just that everything he did appeared to employ one hundred percent of his ability at all times. It was as if he had some deeply ingrained plan and come what may, was going to execute it.

At the finish of his initial year, Sam was installed as First Floor Chief in "A" Barracks. All the barracks at the MMA consisted of two-man rooms that were clean, bare and basic with a pair of bunk beds in one corner. Sam Bird was no perpetrator of such traditions as hazing and was able to be a very effective floor chief. The regular addendum to staff officers' nightly reports offered an appropriate summation of how most of them felt about him: "Bird on duty, condition good."

Painstaking attention to detail and scrupulous reverence for the system insured that Sam went the full 10 months without incurring a single demerit. Many of Sam's classmates held to the not unreasonable assumption that a nominal amount of demerits should be considered a requisite indicator of a person's membership in the human race. But, Sam was redeemed by his affable nature and a gentle air of mischief.

During 1956, his third year, Sam became the Drum Major for the band and Barracks Chief for "A" Barracks. In addition, he went another 10 months without incurring a single demerit. In his final year, the band was elevated to Company status and Sam became its Company Commander and one of the five chief subordinates to the Battalion Commander of the Cadet Corps.

★　　★　　★

Meanwhile, as 1956 drew to a close, the finishing touches were being applied to an all-new Big Six lumber yard at 6601 East Kellog. As manager of the yard, Dick was on hand to oversee every detail of its reconstruction. In that sense it had become his very own pet project. But once Eisenhower won his second term that November, Dick began to concentrate much of his attention on another project—securing the MMA Band's nomination to play at the inauguration in Washington in January. He sent out a flurry of carefully crafted letters to political acquaintances he'd built up through his father and his membership in the Republican Party in Kansas during the '30s and '40s. He concentrated his efforts on Fred Seaton, the Secretary of the Interior, whom he had come to know during those years. The reply came through at the end of November that the MMA Band had indeed beaten out the bigger and more prestigious University of Missouri Band for the nomination.

The band's performance at Eisenhower's inauguration garnered much acclaim and was a fitting crown to its metamorphosis from the rag-tag outfit Sam had joined some three and a half years earlier.

★　　★　　★

The beginning of Sam's final year at the MMA coincided with the arrival of a new Professor of Military Science and Tactics. Lieutenant Colonel Sidney P. Kersey was a graduate of The Citadel, the Military College of South Carolina. Sam's active involvement with Army ROTC and his high military standing at the MMA insured his regular contact with Lieutenant Colonel

Kersey during that last year. Kersey told Sam all about The Citadel and Sam was particularly taken by the fact the entire Citadel Band was housed in the same barracks.

Sam graduated from the MMA at the end of May 1957, a recipient of the school's highest attainable award, The Legion of Honor for industry, integrity and abiding loyalty. In some ways he received an even higher accolade from his peers, who voted him the most likely to succeed as well as the hardest working senior.

At the school's Tulip Ball that same May, Paula made it a family celebration when she was crowned Tulip Queen. She was ravishing that evening in her strapless, white ball gown, turning on a scintillating smile at every opportunity to light up the entire ballroom. At eighteen years of age, bubbling over with natural talent, exuberance and spontaneity, she was literally holding the world at bay. In many ways she was everything Sam wasn't. They were certainly very different. Yet friends sensed a powerful bond between brother and sister. And each had a similar wall of inaccessibility no one could breach.

After graduating from high school the previous year, Paula spent the next year at Lindenwood College for Young Ladies, a few miles up the road from Sam in St. Charles, Missouri. But unlike Sam, she didn't appear to take so well to being away from home and the lack of boys! So she decided to return to complete her final three years of college at Wichita State University.

Sam had quickly discovered and established his own identity at the MMA—totally embracing its ethos of regimentation and order.

Senior Walk at the MMA is a stone pathway which leads straight to a small pond and then through a thick canopy of trees to the flagpole standing in front of the main school building. After June 1985, one could read in front of the flagpole the proclamation inscribed on the plaque at its base, lovingly dedicated to Samuel R. Bird by the Class of 1957. It reads simply:

GOD WAS TRUSTED
COUNTRY WAS SERVED
DUTY WAS HONORED
MANKIND WAS LOVED

There was little doubt that had he so wished, Sam could easily have secured a congressional nomination for West Point. He chose instead to attend The Citadel, the Military College of South Carolina.

★   ★   ★

The Corps

Bastion of antiquity.
Towering bulwark of rigid discipline.
The Citadel is a unique school.
Spiritually, it cannot be transferred, modified or absorbed.
To transfer it is to kill by transplanting
what flourishes in its congenial soil.
To modify it is to break its symmetry.
To absorb it is to lose its peculiar essence.

(Extracted from *The Guidon*—"The Plebe's Bible." 1957/58)

The westward walk along Moultrie Street, in the city of Charleston, South Carolina, through a line of magnificent Spanish Oaks is a leisurely affair. Then suddenly, straight ahead, the two imperious limestone pillars of Lesesne Gate come into view. Rising up on either side, way above the trees, like colossal white ghosts, are the buildings of The Citadel.

Inside Lesesne Gate everything converges around the parade field. As dawn breaks, the low country mist hangs in layers across the vast green expanse. The morning sun rises above the chapel's tower in the east. Below, the stern admonition emblazoned in black gothic script above its front entrance reads:

"Remember Now Thy Creator in the Days of Thy Youth."

Across the field to the west from Summerall Chapel, one's gaze is instinctively drawn to the unadorned substance of

41

Barracks Row. One building with a formidable tower stands out. Two brightly polished cannons guard the main entrance. The inscription on the adjacent plaque reads:

PADGETT THOMAS BARRACKS
1922

Its tower rises up imperiously, pristine white, to crenelated battlements.

All the buildings with their stuccoed walls conform rigidly to the same Spanish Moorish design. From the pure implication of the buildings against an incandescent blue sky, to the robotic machinations of the plebes squaring off every corner, the place reverberates to an exacting symmetry, uniformity and rectitude. There is a sense of something rare, special and powerful—almost unsettling in its pervasiveness.

At the core of The Citadel lies the spirit of the Citizen Soldier and the very southern supposition of Chivalry. West Point may resound to brash proclamations of Duty, Honor and Country, but at The Citadel these philosophies seem to run much deeper. Charleston to this day remains the parochial bosom and purest distillation of the Confederate States. Its fate and that of The Citadel, it is said, will always be inextricably bound.

The *melange* of The Citadel and Charleston provides a potent draft which ought to be drunk from only by choice. A person should not enter The Citadel because of coercion by parents or anyone. Perhaps therein lies the definitive rebuttal to those who choose to heap scorn and derision on the perceived brutality and futility of the system at the school. In any event, Sam Bird most definitely *chose* to attend The Citadel.

He began his plebe year on a late August day in 1957, along with 857 others. They formed the largest Fourth Class the school had ever seen. A shade less than four years later, 311 of them would actually come to graduate; most of the attrition would occur during that plebe year.

When it comes to severity, the plebe system of the United States Military Academies ranks beyond anything else in the world. That of The Citadel is arguably the toughest of them all.

Certainly it's tougher than West Point where the pressure tends to be eased from the "knobs" after a couple of months. The passionate enactment of the plebe system at The Citadel continues throughout the entire year.

The arrival of General Mark Wayne Clark as president in March 1954 is generally credited with rescuing the school from oblivion. General Clark's arrival also provided the philosophical driving force behind the increased severity of the plebe system at The Citadel.

For many freshmen, life as a plebe provides a lurid, year-long sneak preview of purgatory. The system is consummated each year with the appropriately named "Hell Night" inside each of the four barracks, following a sardonic rendition of "No Place Like Home" on the harmonica. Yet the two hour session, which leaves a plebe's mind and limbs with the consistency of a wilted lettuce leaf, is merely an *hors d'oeuvre* for the rigors of this year. Countless inane definitions must be learned by rote; the embossed palmetto insignia on the shako (cadet's formal headgear) must be polished and ground down; the protective lacquer must be thumbtacked away from all items of brass; shoes and doorknobs must be kept constantly shined; and at the same time, the study of a full slate of academic subjects must be pursued under continuous assessment. Generally during that first year, whenever the plebe happens to be outside his room, he's expected to affect a posture known as "the brace." This is broadly defined as a constant state of attention in which the "Gauldy Knob" might consider it wise to "rack" his chin in until it has the appearance of a squashed artichoke, expand his chest until he looks as though he has just swallowed a piano and maintain the bearing of someone who has just experienced a cattle prod between the buttocks.

One of the reasons given to explain why the plebe system tends to be harsher at The Citadel than anywhere else is that cadets practically run it themselves. At West Point, for example, a proliferation of federally paid Tactical Officers has a far more conspicuous presence outside the classroom. Citadel cadets, on the other hand, tend to inherit greater power and autonomy as well as a greater opportunity to exercise responsibility. This means that although the system is generally better at fostering leadership, there also exists a greater potential for its abuse. Generally considered to be the case in Number Four Barracks during the mid-sixties, this spawned Pat Conroy's alternately acclaimed and disdained best seller, *The Lords of Discipline*.

The fundamental requisite of the plebe system at The Citadel is the development in each cadet of "qualities" deemed necessary for leadership. The Citadel is founded upon the belief that no one is fit to command who is unable to obey. This statement, of course, can come in for considerable latitude of interpretation, especially when the cadets themselves are responsible for its implementation. Therein lies one of the main reasons why its merits are so hotly debated.

"You never shit on your classmates" is an oft-quoted idiom at The Citadel. Unquestionably, this does not provide an adequate summation of the deeply ingrained love and loyalty the system nurtures. Love is the force that preserves the purity of the line. Without love, the traditions of The Citadel are corrupt and meaningless. Love can and should be the only reason why those who dish out the harshest punishment to particular individuals during their plebe year are the first to congratulate them when it's over and by so doing, merit their lifelong friendship.

What is clear as far as Sam was concerned were two things: First, he believed implicitly in the system. Second, the luxury of any rarefied discussion on the quadrangle of Padgett Thomas Barracks that late August day wasn't going to be significant, relevant, or existent.

Sam had volunteered for Band Company as a Bass Drummer, which in itself was something of an anomaly. Many of those "volunteering" for the band were attracted by such inducements as World Series tickets. These went with the band's appearance at the first two games of the 1957 World Series in New York. Other volunteers had unwittingly included some tenuous reference to music in order to bolster their original applications. Like the MMA Band, The Citadel Band came in for its fair share of ridicule—not so much for its ability, which was considerable—

but again for the kind of people it was deemed to attract. It had come to be known in some quarters as "Q" Company.

Band Company occupied the entire ground floor of Padgett Thomas Barracks. These barracks are the largest and oldest of the four cadet living quarters running parallel to the west side of the parade field. Following its construction in 1922, Padgett Thomas and its red and white checkered quadrangle drew much poetic waxing about its size, beauty and architectural proportion. Said one scholarly and literary soul:

"The twenty-six great reinforced concrete arches on the second floor gallery surmounted by more than a hundred smaller arches on the third and fourth floors gives a very impressive appearance. The semi-circular arch greets the eye everywhere; from the majestic proportions of the arches on the second floor, through all the graduating sizes down to the small arches in the balustrades of the galleries, the quadrangle can literally be called 'The Courtyard of a thousand arches.' "

However, those fourth classmen who lived inside, with bars on the windows to their rooms, might have thought of it somewhat differently. For them the staccato barking of orders (which seemed to ricochet incessantly off joyless gray walls from reveille to taps), the constant bracing, the push-ups and the recitation of inanities, especially amidst the unrelenting heat and humidity of those late summer days, might have made it more aptly termed "The Courtyard of a thousand tortures."

Whether because he'd already endured and overcome similar adversity at the MMA, whether it was his non-threatening affability or whether his own plan for life was so unshakably ingrained, Sam withstood the rigors of his plebe year with a minimum of fuss and without complaint. This was all the more noteworthy since plebes from cadet high schools received more heat than their peers and usually resented going through the system again.

Sam was a mostly unobtrusive figure during that first year. Those classmates who did come into direct contact with him then, noted a certain distinction and assurance beginning to assert itself around his unflappable presence. He was "always there," everything he did was "just right" and nothing appeared to deflect him. Many began to derive assurance themselves from this, despite the fact he still retained the ungainly shape and molly-coddled appearance that all but yelled out an invitation to anyone who had the slightest inkling of making life difficult for him. His appearance was strikingly accentuated by the white cotton trousers and gray blouse of the full dress "Salt and Pepper," clearly illuminating Sam's trousers hanging at rest a good three inches above his waist. As a consequence, Sam acquired the nickname, "High Pockets," which stuck with him throughout his time at the school.

By the end of his plebe year and following the customary vote by all the upperclassmen in Band Company, as well as his peers, Sam was selected as the senior ranking Band Company cadet from the rising freshman class and was appointed to the position of Company Clerk.

During the noon formation on the quadrangle of Padgett Thomas sometime during the fall of 1958, a junior in Echo Company allowed his gaze to wander across to a group of Band Company plebes who had formed up in the center of the quadrangle. His attention was captured by the low booming echo of a routine administrative announcement from the company clerk. The junior could not recall having heard a voice that instilled so much authority. He was even more taken aback at the notion that a mere sophomore could carry himself in such a manner. Surprised, he felt compelled to nudge a fellow member of Echo Company and to point over at Sam saying, "Now, that kid impresses me!" A senior replied, "So what else is new? That lad impresses everybody. He'll probably be Regimental Commander when he's a senior." Several heads nodded in agreement.

★   ★   ★

Meanwhile, in Wichita, Pauline had purchased the controlling interest in what was left of a rapidly disintegrating lumber empire from Helen. All the yards except "Big Six" had been allowed to run themselves into the ground through chronic neglect. Indeed, Helen's behavior was becoming more and more bizarre and unpredictable.

Some years earlier, Helen had acquired a dog and a bird from Pauline and for years had doted on these creatures. Then one morning they were both found dead. The occupants of the neighboring homes had long since become actively pre-occupied with the comings and goings at 1111 North Broadway. Helen deeply resented this. But their curiosity was really aroused one afternoon when what could only be described as a strange wailing sound began to emanate from her house. Eventually it became clear the sound was a combination of a weird incantation and singing against a background of gramophone music. These sounds continued unabated throughout the night. The following morning, Helen emerged naked through the front door onto the porch and sat down in the rocking chair. With no discernible pause in her song, she began rocking gently to and fro in the chair. This proved too much for the acute sensibilities of one of the neighbors, who went back inside her house and telephoned the police.

Helen was rocking away and still singing merrily when the police arrived. Upon seeing the police, instead of retreating back through the front door, she leapt up out of the chair and made a break for her car parked in the driveway at the front of the house. Before she had a chance to hurtle out the front gate, however, one of the officers had fired two shots into the two near-side tires.

Soon after the incident, a former housekeeper named Cecilia Dorney moved in with Helen. This appeared to exert a calming influence on matters. Cecilia worshiped Helen and events at 1111 became decidedly less titillating for the neighborhood voyeurs.

★ ★ ★

During his sophomore and junior years as company clerk, Sam shared a room with a puckish, mischievous character from Covington, Kentucky, named Jack Morgan. Like Sam, Jack had attended military high school. He had gone to the Kentucky Military Institute. But that was where any similarity between the two began and ended.

Soon after his arrival at The Citadel, Jack found he had been assigned to the Bagpipe Corps. Somewhat perplexed, he inquired, in the appropriate manner, how this unfortunate misunderstanding could have occurred. He was informed, in words possessing few syllables and perhaps an occasional delicately inserted mild expletive, that he had put down on his application that he played the piano. As a child, Jack had been "encouraged" by his parents to take some piano lessons. But before he had a chance to regret his attempt to bolster his application with such nonsense, a set of bagpipes was thrust against his choir boy's face, thus bringing the brief discussion to a close.

Jack and Sam had roomed next door to each other during their plebe year. With every single formation on the quadrangle, one or the other would murmur under his breath, "It's all going to be over today." This playful rumor became a rallying cry of mutual exaltation for each of them that entire year.

Jack, like Sam, along with most of their contemporaries and the majority of the faculty, had grown to love and revere General Clark. His arrival at the school is considered by many to be one of the defining moments in its history. Some have gone farther to suggest that he rescued The Citadel from potential oblivion. Whatever the final analysis reveals about his tenure as president and his emeritus position thereafter, the lasting impact of his presence is beyond dispute.

To many, the sight of General Clark gliding imperiously across the campus in his dress whites was the visual embodiment of the ethos of the Corps. For Sam, the general became both the symbol and the sublime guardian of his aspirations. In that respect he was Sam's father now.

His sophomore and junior years at The Citadel saw the growth of Sam's reputation. Those beyond Padgett Thomas Barracks were starting to notice the religious dedication that accompanied the execution of every task, his knack of always being able to get things done, the bearing that exuded an unmistakable air of authority and the immaculate appearance. This was manifest even on leave, in Sam's point-blank refusal to loosen the top button of his thick wool blouse while riding down King Street in the suffocating heat of a summer afternoon. Yet the pervasive sense that there was something different about Sam Bird went way beyond a perception of his total embrace of the system at The Citadel. If this respect had not existed, he would have been laughed off campus for his use of patent leather in everything from shoes and belts to cartridge boxes. Or he would have been derided and resented as a "military prick" for the gung-ho attitude that far exceeded what was required, teased for his awkwardness around women and mercilessly ridiculed for a lower torso that resembled a Mississippi Paddle Steamer. In his junior year, he began to correct the latter with daily and numerous revolutions of Hampton Park.

But Sam's difference lay more in the way he did things: the pride without the baggage of ego, the non-threatening manner, the fact that even his closest classmates could never recall his having a bad word to say about anyone. The implicit authority in everything he did seemed to stem from a willingness to stand up for principle. The combination of these facets produced an unmistakable aura that caused many of his contemporaries, even at that tender age, to talk in terms of a future military chief of staff.

Therefore, it came as something of a surprise to many, including a number of tactical officers, that he was not selected as Regimental Commander for the Corps in the spring of 1960; instead, he was chosen as Regimental Executive Officer, second-in-command.

★   ★   ★

That same spring Paula graduated from Wichita State University with honors. There had never been any question about the amount of talent with which she'd been blessed or the gusto with which she could initiate an idea. The question was always whether she had the staying power to overcome the fear of rejection and see an idea through. Certainly as legendary as her capacity to dominate any occasion was an inexplicable fickleness and insecurity when it came to the moment of truth.

Paula could look either visually stunning or utterly disheveled depending on whether her urge to impress held sway over a fear of rejection or a short attention span. Whatever the situation, it was always a matter of extremes in which dramatic statements were her forte.

Two years earlier in the fall of 1956 in her first days as a freshman at Lindenwood College, Paula quickly co-opted herself onto the Harvest Freshman Ball Committee. "She threw herself in typical Paula fashion into the planning and organization," recalled her childhood chum, Claudine.

Her ball gown was finished two weeks before the ball. It was white satin strapless, beaded with crystal. The thrill and anticipation in her eyes were evident as she spun round in front of Claudine at a special sneak preview. It was a stunning spectacle. Paula did not have "classic" looks but the combination of the gown and her unrestrained joy and exuberance elevated her to an incomparable level of beauty that morning.

Then came the phone call from her boyfriend, a high school senior back in Wichita, saying he couldn't make it to the ball. She was devastated. The following day, in what Claudine described as a "half-assed" attempt, Paula swallowed an overdose of sleeping pills. She was whisked away to the local hospital and made a complete recovery after a three day stay. "It wasn't that the jerk didn't come," she recounted later. "It was all the trouble I went to with that damn dress! That's what really got to me." She was shrewdly able to recycle the dress at the MMA Tulip Ball when Sam graduated the following spring.

Just before Paula's graduation from Wichita State, her professors summoned her into a smoke-filled office and told her they were considering giving her the "Advertising Man of the Year" award for excellence in advertising journalism. "I can still see them bumbling around, looking at their shoes," said Paula, "while they asked me if I *really* intended to go into advertising as a career—or was I just going to marry and have babies?"

She was given the award (a man's watch fob), then she got married and had babies. She married a tall, dark-haired, outrageously handsome biology graduate named Rich Roberts.

50

Certainly one part of Paula wanted to be a housewife and raise children but there was more to it than that. "She loved to be in love," said Pam Porvaznik, a close friend. "She wanted to have the feeling that comes with being in love."

Paula wanted to be taken care of. "The problem was that most of the decent men were taken in by her front of independence and capability," said another friend. "This scared them off, so she ended up dating a bunch of losers."

Rich Roberts did not the fit the image of a loser. To Paula he was a dashing knight riding up on a white charger. However, Dick and Pauline didn't want their daughter to marry him. But she went ahead with the marriage anyway. They settled in Wichita where a couple of years later she gave birth to the first of three children. On the surface at least, she appeared to have the fairy-tale marriage for which she'd always longed. Things went along happily enough for about six years with Rich supporting the family by his partnership in an interior design business.

★　　★　　★

For his final year at The Citadel as Regimental Executive Officer, Sam shared a room in the tower of Padgett Thomas Barracks with Bayliss Larkin Spivey, Jr., the Regimental Commander. He was a tall, quiet, keenly intelligent, distinguished-looking cadet from Conway, South Carolina.

In sharp contrast to the system at West Point, where the tactical officers play a significantly greater role, the day to day existence of a cadet at The Citadel is governed by the regimental staff. The situation was summed up rather succinctly by a plebe in a letter home to his parents in the early fall of 1960. ". . . It appears as though there is God, Larkin Spivey and Sam Bird; in that order!"

One of the main responsibilities of the regimental staff was, and is, the supervision of the plebe system. Their first responsibility is to arrive a week early along with the plebes and the training cadre at the beginning of the school year.

On the first afternoon in late August 1960, Dennis Deal, a young plebe in "E" Company from Pittsburgh, Pennsylvania, was

51

standing on the quadrangle of Padgett Thomas along with a couple of hundred other freshmen. They were still dressed in civilian clothes and still maintaining at least a show of innocence and a casual air of expectancy. Then Dennis caught sight of an "apparition" beneath the eastern sallyport to the barracks: tall and lean with gleaming blue eyes and the most formidably erect bearing he'd ever seen. At first sight, the chevrons on the immaculately pressed gray blouse appeared to stretch from elbow to ear lobe. He watched as this apparition strode out into the middle of the quadrangle where all the unsuspecting freshmen were milling around. There was a pause for a couple of seconds and then, sounding as though a tornado had just touched down on the quadrangle, the almighty roar of Sam's voice was followed by a series of barked commands ordering the rag-tag bunch of freshmen to form up and march to dinner. Dennis Deal decided there and then he didn't much care for Sam Bird.

One evening in early November, Sam was among the members of the senior class gathering with General Clark in the Armory to take part in a solemn rite, the celebration and receipt of The Ring. The thick, heavy band of gold bears class numerals and the prominent feature of a star above the crossed flags of the Union and the state of South Carolina. There are also six cannon balls, commemorating the shelling of the Union supply steamer, *The Star of the West*, by Citadel cadets on January 9th, 1861. This event was emblazoned in Citadel lore as the true beginning of The War Between the States. Inside the band the intricately feathered inscription of Sam's name denoted his provisional acceptance into the brotherhood of Citadel men. When eligible first classmen receive their rings in November, they wear them with the numerals of their class facing toward them, so they alone can read them. Only after graduation can the ring be turned around with the numerals facing outward, denoting a true Citadel man.

Sam graduated from The Citadel with a host of honors on a cloudless day in early June 1961. It certainly would be fair to say his four years at the school had not been marked with controversy. There was only one slightly bizarre run-in with a regular Army colonel in the Swamp Fox Room of the Francis Marion Hotel following the Band Company Christmas Party in December of 1960. The colonel took Sam to task for the way he addressed a fourth classman. (Sam had simply addressed the fourth classman in the manner prescribed for a senior to address a plebe.) The colonel went on to lambaste General Clark, the Adjutant, and The Citadel in the way they turned out "a bunch of stiff snobs." He further told Sam and a classmate they'd better pray to God they never served under him in the future. They said they would pray. Sam wrote up the incident in triplicate, and following an Army investigation, the colonel was reprimanded. The incident was made all the more bizarre by the fact that the colonel was a former graduate of The Citadel and had a son enrolled in the school at the time.

The only time Sam had incurred the disdain of any member of staff at The Citadel was when he emphasized the initials of the South Carolina Unorganized Militia, to which the majority of the tactical officers belonged, at the head of a paper he had submitted to one teacher he didn't particularly like. He duly received an F. Except for that, Sam's actions had perfectly mirrored the ethos of the school he'd come to love so deeply.

The afternoon following the graduation exercises, Larkin Spivey saw his friend of the past year striding out across the campus in his brand-new Army 2nd lieutenant's uniform. He couldn't recall a time when he had seen Sam looking more proud.

Chapter Three

Straight Arrow

Sam graduated from The Citadel on Saturday June 3rd, 1961, and by Sunday he had arrived at Fort Benning, Georgia, ready to begin the Army's Basic Officer School on Monday morning.

After completing Basic Officer School three months later, Sam headed to Eglin AFB in Florida and the Army Infantry School's 10 week Ranger Course. Ranger School generally succeeded in sorting out the loud-mouthed, would-be tough guys from those possessing *sterner stuff* by means of 10 weeks of tortuous, grisly and demanding exercises. A psychotic streak was generally considered to be something of a useful asset for the course. Certainly no one would have tagged Sam as a tough guy in the conventional mold of football players and the like. Yet as others fell by the wayside, there he was, completing another *job* without fuss or complaint.

After finishing the Ranger course it was back to Fort Benning and Airborne School—a relative breeze by comparison. Only the expression of sheer, naked fear on Sam's face prior to his first parachute jump might have indicated otherwise.

Long before graduating from The Citadel, Sam had discussed his future plans with Lieutenant Colonel Tom Muller, a tactical officer with whom he was in almost daily contact through the school's Department of Military Science and ROTC activities. That spring Muller had received orders to the 1st Cavalry Division in Korea, accompanied by a promotion to Colonel. Sam told the colonel he was going to volunteer for Korea himself and would try to join Muller's regiment. By November 1961, letters were winging their way between Colonel Muller, General Clark and the Army. Sam found out in early December that he had indeed been assigned to Colonel Muller's command as a platoon leader (in charge of about 35 men) with Company A, The 1st Battle Group, 5th Cavalry.

The Korean War had ended in July 1953. In 1961, the 1st Cavalry Division was charged with securing the uneasy peace along the so-called "Demilitarized Zone" (DMZ).

Prior to leaving for Korea, Sam was able to take a couple of weeks leave at home in Wichita with his parents. Over the preceding four and a half years or more, a fundamental change in the nature of Sam's relationship with Babe and Dood had taken place.

★   ★   ★

Addie Davis, the family's indomitable cook and housekeeper, who possessed a tongue sharp enough to fillet plywood, had watched it all unfold. In 1961, she'd been with the Birds for several years.

Addie was short and stout—compact rather than overweight. She had a sympathetic demeanor that matched her friendly voice. But she took no guff from anyone, least of all Dick, who felt the acid side of her tongue on several occasions. He was without doubt wary of her. She thought Dick was ridiculous, particularly when he went into one of his self-imposed sulks to spite Pauline, which was often. Addie was probably Pauline's best and only real friend in the whole world, though it certainly wasn't a friendship in the conventional sense.

As the children grew, and as Pauline's drinking increased, her forays into Wichita Society decreased. By the end of the decade, she and Dick appeared to be faithfully repeating the pattern of her parents.

As Addie said, "They'd just sit around and drink highballs and do jigsaw puzzles. I just wanted to chew their heads off! They'd be home so much. I'd be so glad when the summer came because they'd like to go out in the garden then."

56

Pauline's one real passion, besides partaking of liberal quantities of bourbon, was still the stock market.

Addie went on, "He (Dick)'d sit down there and play solitaire, and she'd be right there playin' the market. Ooooh did she ever play that market!"

According to Addie, one day in the early '60s, Dick bought a boat. "It was the biggest thing I've ever seen in my life! Mrs. Bird was scared to death to ride in it, but she did! I told her, 'Never would I. If I was afraid to ride in that darn boat,' I said, 'I wouldn't go.'

" 'Ooh, Dick want me to go.' I said, 'If Dick wanted to kill you, you'd go!' Then she went and drank like a fish and got in the boat."

His parents' reliance on alcohol clearly offended Sam, and like many children in similar circumstances, he became an overachiever, particularly when it came to discipline and order. He took to the strict regimen at both military institutions like no one else.

The one comment repeated time and again by those who knew the family was "How on earth could such parents produce such exceptional children?" But the fact is, Sam and Paula survived to succeed in spite of, not because of, their parents.

Now whenever Sam came home on leave, Addie noticed a dramatic "about face" in Dick and Pauline's behavior. When Sam was away, Dick and Pauline would freely indulge their intemperate love of alcohol within the walls of 18 Lakeside; they had begun to withdraw from socializing outside the home. Pauline drank particularly heavily when one of her drinking cohorts came over for the afternoon.

Once, she ordered Addie to fix drinks for her and a friend and see to it the glasses were replenished whenever they became empty. Addie didn't consider this part of her regular duties and was not enraptured with the idea. In addition, she strongly disapproved of alcohol in any shape or form. However, in a rare departure from custom, Addie held her tongue. Instead, she proceeded to mix two decidedly potent highballs for the ladies' pleasure. Shortly after imbibing a couple of Addie's special concoctions, the two women were flat on their backs and failed to come to dinner. Although the scheme succeeded in insuring that Addie was never again called upon to serve drinks in the afternoon, it had no overall effect on the rate at which Dick and Pauline drank. The only person who was capable of changing that was Sam, and he did it with his mere presence in the house.

When Sam was home on leave, Dick and Pauline might have an occasional highball before dinner but that would be all. To Addie, they were like different people when their son was around. The atmosphere often appeared strained and awkward; they were like children cowering from a strict father, only Sam had become the father.

It should be noted that Addie's feelings for Sam did not exactly mirror the adulation of his parents, or the admiration of many at The Citadel. She saw only his strictness and solemnity. And she couldn't for the life of her understand why he insisted on washing (in the family machine) and ironing his own clothes. The only time she saw a smile spread across his face was when he passed a platter of oatmeal cookies she would bake specially for him and leave on the sideboard. It was a given that each day by the middle of the afternoon the platter would be empty.

Although Sam's sense of humor was not the sort to make Addie laugh, there were a number of occasions during that Christmas leave when his actions made her giggle. Since Sam had been home last, Dick and Pauline had purchased a magnificent sculpture of a nude woman and positioned it for all to see—on the hearth of the dining room fireplace, a foot above the floor. It was a four-foot tall, silky-smooth wooden sculpture. The slender, attractive woman stood with her legs together, hands behind her back and head on one shoulder. She had a serene aura of innocence.

Each morning Addie made a point of peeking through the serving hatch as Sam came into the dining room. He was always the first down to breakfast. Every morning without fail, before sitting down at the table, he would stride purposefully over to the hearth and turn the sculpture around so it faced the fireplace. About an hour later Pauline would enter the dining room. Before sitting down, without uttering a word, she would glide over to the hearth and turn the sculpture back around so it was once again facing into the room. This early morning ritual continued for the entire two weeks of Christmas leave without a single word passing between Sam and his mother about it.

Also since the last time Sam had been home, a painting that depicted two semi-naked women laying opposite one another in a meadow, flaunting mildly suggestive expressions, had materialized above one of the sofas in the sitting room. Seeing the abject look of disapproval on Sam's face as she came into the room with a plate of cookies, Addie thought she'd have a little fun with him.

"What do you think of our new house guests then?" she asked as she offered him a cookie from the plate.

"Hmm . . . floozies," he muttered, with a wry look of contempt for the question, as he took one from the plate.

"Mighty fine lookin' paintin', I'd say."

The frown on Sam's face deepened into a scowl and Addie took her cue for a swift exit.

Each morning, however, Addie inquired of Sam whether he'd developed a better appreciation of the picture. Each time he would start muttering about floozies. He was unable to turn the picture around though, since there was no way to rehang it. Some days later, however, a large paper plate was found wedged in front of the offending area!

Outside of the home, Sam never lost his ability to laugh at himself and have fun, particularly with Paula and his half-brother, Bill. Inside his parents' home, however, he retained the demeanor of the strict "father." And Dick and Pauline (if not Addie) always fell into line.

★   ★   ★

A short time after his arrival in Korea, toward the latter part of January 1962, Sam was notified by Colonel Muller that he'd been selected as Junior Aide de Camp to General Woolnough, the division commander. Sam's first reaction was somewhat muted, since he'd been eager to "soldier" during the early part of his career. The colonel too, was ambivalent. He had begun to treat Sam like a second son and really wanted to nurture his young platoon leader himself. The colonel was quick to rationalize the situation though, and placated Sam with the reasoning that soldiers learned to become generals by working with, and learning from, great generals. He thought General Woolnough was destined to become a four-star general. Sam, as always, said, "Yes Sir!" and so the colonel lost his protege, as he'd always known in the back of his mind he would.

★　　★　　★

The morning after his twenty-second birthday, Sam retrieved a letter out of his mailbox from Paula. He thought it a little strange to be receiving two letters in such close succession, since she'd sent one with his birthday card a couple of days earlier.

Saturday Evening - Wichita Time

January 20th, 1962.

Dear Sam,

I'm afraid this letter isn't as cheerful as the last one, but I've got bad news. Aunt Helen passed away this morning. It's hard to believe, I know. I guess I really don't believe it myself. I volunteered to write you to help Babe & Dood out. They hated to upset you with a short wire, and I thought you might rather hear it from me, 'cause we probably feel about the same. I will really miss her, in spite of our teasing, but she wasn't in good health, and it may be for the best. She hasn't been her old self lately, especially since you left. The story is that she was looking for her cat outside and, suffering from low blood sugar, probably passed out and never woke up again, because of the snow and cold. How true it really is, you'll have to decide for yourself—I haven't really been filled in yet, but I believe she made her own decision. Cecilia (her companion/housekeeper) *found her and called Mama, but she was dead when the ambulance came . . .*

Paula was right. Helen had taken her own life. The media was given the impression she had gone out to look for her cat and frozen to death—not an unlikely story given the fact that the temperature was ten degrees below zero at the time.

> *... Babe's taking it as well as could be expected. She might feel worse later tho'—or show it more. She just seems "numb." (Doing well with the arranging of every-thing though.) 'Course, Pinky and Lou were there when I was, so it's hard to tell.*
>
> *Please don't feel like there's anything you can do. There's nothing I can do, and I'm here. Babe's sending flowers for you to the funeral. So don't worry about a thing. You're really lucky to be where you are. Jodie may come but nothing definite yet. Uncle John is sick and can't.*
>
> *Don't let it bother you. It's all past and for the best or it wouldn't have happened.*

Sam received a second letter from Paula, a couple of days later:

January 23rd

Dear Sam,

> *The weekend and yesterday have been very sad, but it's had its lighter moments too, as Helen would have wanted.*
>
> *Jodie came flying in Sunday, but can't stay long because the tax men are after her! She has been with Laura (Pauline's other sister) since she came, but today, she is going to visit with Babe and us. She looks real well. Older, but still pretty. Lots of gray in her hair—but same 'ol laughin' Jod.*
>
> *Bill, Mom and Dood went down to see Helen in the "slumber room," the day before the funeral. To make a long story short, Babe led them into the wrong room! ... and you just don't do that in these places. She kept talking until lo and behold, there lay somebody else "slumbering!" Poor old Bill about died getting out of the mortuary! ...*

Helen Houston was laid to rest in Wichita's Old Mission Mausoleum along with her mother, father and nephew (Jodie's son, Don) at eleven o'clock on the Monday morning following her death. She had directed the executor to particularly avoid "any unseemly waste, in vain show or pompous ceremony."

. . . Aunt Helen wanted a private service so all her neighbors wouldn't come "out of curiosity" to see what she looked like dead.

The service was nice and pretty with a Christian Science reader. The casket was closed and I was glad, not being a "very good funeral goer." Sonny, Laura, Jodie, Cozetta (Wofford, another housekeeper of Helen's and neighbor and friend of Addie Davis—"She was the one who got me tangled up with them Birds in the first place!"), *Cecilia, Bill & Betty, Babe & Dood, Uncle Sam* (Laura's husband), *Pinky and Lou: The whole gang was there! . . . and there weren't any fisticuffs, believe it or not. We couldn't keep Sonny from Rich any longer. I had to introduce them. You can probably guess what Sonny came out with: "Long-time, no-see!" I bet you didn't know that Sonny's real name is Houston Brown. I about died! Aunt Laura kept calling him "Houston" throughout the whole ordeal . . .*

Helen's will was read at 3:30 that same afternoon.

. . . The reading of the will is just "indescribable." It's the one thing you shouldn't have missed. Tickets were selling at $100 up! Laura announced that she wasn't going— but of course she did—no need tho'—as she didn't get nothin'. Hold on to your hat . . .

After reading the first two standard boiler plate paragraphs of the will, the executor cleared his throat and went on:

"I hereby give, devise and bequeath to my sister, PAULINE HOUSTON BIRD, an undivided one-half of all my property of every kind and character . . ."

. . . The room just shook, it was so quiet! Babe's mouth hit the floor! Oh, if you could have been there! . . .

Helen had left one-eighteenth each to nine others: including Sam, Paula and Dick (whom, she stated in her will, had always treated her with courtesy and respect) and Jodie and her two children. Laura received nothing. Not because of, ". . . *any lack of interest or feeling of kindness toward her, but because she already has more of 'this world's goods' than she will ever need or use and any gift from me would only add to her problems.*" Sonny, however, was one of those designated to receive one-eighteenth. John Houston received $100. Yet perhaps the most intriguing bequest, of $1,000, was set aside for any niece or nephew who would name "*any issue from their body,*" Helen. The offer was never taken up.

In addition to the cash sum, Sam was left a pair of diamond earrings to give to his future bride. Pauline promised to keep them in safe custody until that day arrived.

Laura had no intention of letting the will stand. She had many reasons for her feelings—deep-seated resentment that Pauline had always been treated better than the other children, the bitter estrangement in her own relationship with her parents or simply another example of Sam and Dora's legacy of confrontation. During the car journey to the will reading she told the executor about a long, impassioned telephone conversation she'd had with Helen on the evening before her death. Laura alleged that Helen was so disturbed over Pauline's purchase of a new home at 609 Rutland Avenue that year (1962), which she thought beyond her means, that she was going to change her will and give Pauline's share to Jodie. In fact, despite their move to this luxurious, ranch style bungalow, Dick and Pauline were scaling down considerably from 18 Lakeside.

The will itself had been carefully drawn and executed in anticipation of some such attempt by Laura to break it. Helen had also drawn up a will with her attorney in which "*none of the kinfolk would get anything.*" The details of this will were never disclosed. In any case, all remained quiet after the reading and both Laura and Jodie appeared cordial. The first sign of discord did not emerge until Jodie left for Albuquerque without saying goodbye to Pauline.

On the surface, things remained quiet until the documents were drawn up for probate. Signatures from the heirs and legatees were sought for a "waiver of notice" and this culminated in a torrid telephone exchange between Laura and Pauline. Laura accused her sister of being responsible for Helen's death and went on to tell her that she aimed to see to it Pauline was cut out of the will. Described by the executor as being, "In true Houston fashion," Pauline "volleyed the ball back, repeatedly!" So when the executor tried to placate Laura, it was, as he put it, "Like petting a wounded lion."

When the hearing for probate came up, the judge, instead of accepting the written depositions of the two witness doctors, had them brought in for his personal examination. This followed a telephone conversation with Laura, who told the judge Helen was insane and had been for years and hadn't been competent when the will was drawn up. Laura also informed the judge that Helen had been induced by Pauline to make the will and that the doctors who'd witnessed it had actually killed her with drugs on Pauline's say so. Since the charges were wholly untrue, Paul White, the attorney and executor, had little trouble establishing the will. However, after that, the court reported that Laura intended to contest.

By now Sam was becoming rather upset about the toll all this was taking on his mother. But there was little he could do from Korea besides writing to the attorney. White wrote back to say that since the doctors had made it known they were considering taking legal action against Laura for her slanderous telephone conversation with the judge, she had for the time being at least, "quieted down."

Laura's contest insured the will wasn't settled until June of 1963. The grand old house at 1111 North Broadway was liquidated as part of Helen's estate. It had been built at a cost of $50,000 in 1900 but was sold for a mere $25,000 in 1962.

★   ★   ★

Colonel Henry Tufts, a venerable and loquacious man with a distinctive drawl, took over as Provost Marshall of the 1st

Cavalry Division at Camp Howze in Korea in May of 1962. He had barely been there a couple of days and was still trying to locate a suitable place to call home when Sam told him that he and the other two aides to General Woolnough had a rather elegant room on the end of their quonset hut. Without further ado, the colonel moved in beside Sam, the 1st lieutenant and the captain.

Tufts, as commander of over three hundred military police, was referred to as "The Sheriff." He had now taken over what was potentially the most difficult job in the division. The 1st Cavalry Division was positioned along the DMZ as the mainstay of a force designed to secure the uneasy peace that had reigned since the July 1953 armistice. All told there were some 23,000 Americans in the area who were supposed to act as a deterrent and as a ready reaction force against any potential North Korean incursion or fighting force along the DMZ. The task of the military police was to make certain, through the enforcement of law, that the division remained at a maximum state of readiness and effectiveness to carry out its job. Therein lay the problem; the eight-and-a-half years following the armistice had witnessed a marked decline in the U.S. Army's ability to do just that.

As long as there is an extreme potential for conflict in an area, it's a generally accepted notion that soldiers should be there to prevent the situation from deteriorating into civil war. When American soldiers (the highest federally paid soldiers in the world) happen to occupy an area, it's a generally accepted notion that such an area will represent a fertile domain for prostitution. For many of those who professed to represent the so-called "Vanguard of Liberty," Korea had become an oasis for formerly repressed sexual appetites.

The problem in Korea in 1962 was that the situation was way out of control and had been so for a number of years. In 1962, the venereal disease rate among the officers and enlisted men was 500 cases per 1000 men per year. In a somewhat dubiously fitting commentary on the situation at the time, venereal disease was considered "line of duty."

There were over 3,500 prostitutes operating from the quaintly named Tea Rooms. And these were just the registered ones. Korean farmers would bring their daughters to sell at the main gate of the base every day. The economy had become so depressed in the area, most of the young women couldn't make a living except by selling their bodies.

In an attempt to redress the problem, a curfew had been imposed after eleven o'clock, when every American serviceman was supposed to be in his compound. However, the curfew merely succeeded in giving rise to a rash of comical episodes after 11:00 P.M. in which a whole range of colonels, captains, sergeants and privates could be seen scampering out of prostitutes' hootches in their underwear, followed by MP's in hot pursuit.

One particularly enterprising lieutenant colonel decided it was too much trouble to travel into the local town of Song Jung Gol, so he set up his own brothel in the Joint Service Area of the base. He was soon dispatched back to the U.S., although such audacious entrepreneurial activity was only an indication of the way things were. In addition to prostitution, some officers and senior NCO's were regularly found drunk on duty and the stealing of Army property was rampant. Up to this time, theft had been conveniently and exclusively laid at the door of the derisively named "slicky boys" of the local population.

The attention of the new commanding general, Clifton Von Kann, had recently been drawn to an opinion poll conducted in the U.S. among former Army personnel. The large majority had a negative attitude toward the Army in Korea. Von Kann was determined to do something about the situation.

At Officers' Call on the mornings of November 16th and 17th, 1962, Von Kann delivered a verbal lambasting to the officer corps of the 1st Cavalry Division, accusing them of an overall lack of leadership and questioning their worthiness to wear the division colors. At the end of his withering denouncement, he asked, "Are you willing to stand up and be counted?"

Some completely ignored the question and carried on as if nothing had happened. For the majority of those present it meant keeping heads down for a couple of weeks, perhaps a month, until the general's little fit of pique could subside and he mellowed and overlooked the prevailing conditions; but then, there was Sam.

As junior aide to the general, Sam's job during the day was not too arduous, so he volunteered for duty with Tufts and his MP's at night to help enforce the eleven o'clock curfew. He was deputized as an MP and accompanied the colonel on sweeps through the red-light district, often until three or four o'clock in the morning. Sam referred to it as "stick time" since the policemen normally carried night sticks, although he never carried one himself.

Most of the activity following curfew began when Sam accompanied Tufts and his MP's into the Tea Rooms for the ensuing shake-down. They consistently found soldiers of all ranks; yet whether it was a colonel, sergeant or private, Sam gave no leeway whatsoever. Over and again, he could be heard to say, "There's only one road to follow and that's the straight and narrow."

As much as anyone whom Tufts had ever run across, that was Sam's code: "You do what you're supposed to do, and if the rule says you don't do it, you just don't do it." The term, "Straight Arrow," had long been around in the Army to describe someone who went by the book, but Tufts had never met anyone to whom the nickname could be more aptly applied.

Sam took great delight in loading the offenders onto the waiting truck, but he always did it with the utmost respect and courtesy; that is, unless any of them became belligerent. In that case he'd simply put his Ranger School training into effect.

Tufts felt Sam never turned it into a moral crusade. Whatever went on before eleven o'clock wasn't his business. Sam even had his own favorite little prostitute who always wore an orange bikini. Whenever he and the colonel were inside her Tea Room, the call would go up for her to perform the limbo. Each time she would oblige, and each time Sam and the colonel would applaud and leave the Limbo Club for new pastures. No, as far as the colonel was concerned, it was a straightforward matter of "The

Rule" with Sam. Whenever he was on duty, he retained maximum self-discipline so there could never be any question of a double standard.

When he was off-duty, Tufts saw a different side of Sam. They always had to stop at the bakery on their way back to camp and consume about half a dozen sugar doughnuts, but it was in the bar where Sam's sense of humor really seemed to emerge. "He'd belly up to the bar with the rest of them," said the colonel, "though never to excess, just a couple of drinks. Everything would have a funny side to it when he was off-duty. We'd often find ourselves asking, 'What the hell are you laughing at, Straight Arrow?'"

As far as the colonel was concerned, one of the uncanny aspects to it all was how Sam appeared to manage to do everything without rubbing people the wrong way—particularly his contemporaries, who might've had good reason to resent his actions. The simple explanation lay in the underlying authenticity of his personality. He had a facility of mixing with generals and colonels but seemed to be more at home with the troops. He could walk into a room where a group of enlisted men were gathered without anyone raising an eyelid. He'd sit down and be offered a cup of coffee and would join in the conversation wherever it was. Most enlisted men could smell an officer with an ulterior motive at a thousand yards, but Sam had no falseness about him and they picked up on that right away. He often said no more than a soft spoken, "How's it going?" or, "What do you hear from your wife?" but it meant something to them because they could sense his honesty. They knew Sam respected them, not because of who they were, but because they were human beings. He was, as William Manchester would later say, a "square, unsophisticated patriot."

One other thing that struck the colonel about Sam was the fondness with which he spoke about his parents; his feelings for them were obviously very deep.

★　　★　　★

In January of 1963, Sam found out he would be joining the Old Guard, the elite ceremonial unit located just outside Washington, D.C., after his tour in Korea was over.

Sam arrived at Fort Myer, Virginia, in March 1963 and reported in as a platoon leader to Company A, the 1st Battle Group of the 3rd Infantry—the Old Guard. In July he was transferred to the Honor Guard, whose exclusive job it was to handle military funerals.

In early autumn, as part of a joint service casket team, he took part in a series of rehearsals for the perceived impending funeral of President Hoover, who after suffering a long illness, was considered close to death. Later, on Veterans' Day, November 11, Sam was on duty at the Tomb of the Unknown Soldier for the wreath-laying ceremony carried out by President John F. Kennedy, who paused to exchange a couple of words with the young 1st lieutenant. Of course, Sam was a staunch Republican, but ever since marching in the young president's inaugural parade as a Citadel cadet two-and-a-half years earlier, he had conceived something of a warm regard for his commander-in-chief.

PART II

NOVEMBER 22 - 25, 1963

Chapter Four

"Something Terribly Wrong"

It was Monday evening, November 25th, 1963, and Sam had just returned to his bachelor officer quarters at Fort Myer where he had spent less than six of the preceding 84 hours. He switched on his television set for the CBS summary of the events of the previous four days. He was about to sit down to watch when it occurred to him that he ought to place a brand new reel of tape on his large, unwieldy tape recorder sitting on his desk and start recording. Supplemented with his own commentary, the finished product turned out also to be a three hour audio memento of appreciation for the eight other men who, along with him, had just witnessed history and been a part of its making.

★   ★   ★

A familiar collection of resonant echoes merge to form the jarring litany of that day.

"You sure can't say that Dallas doesn't love you, Mr. President."

"No you can't," he answered.

The Hertz sign on top of the Texas School Book Depository showed 12:30 P.M.

"There's something wrong on the motorcade route . . . There's something terribly wrong!"

At 12:40 P.M., Central Standard Time on November 22nd, 1963, CBS interrupted "As The World Turns" with the voice of Walter Cronkite.

"In Dallas, Texas, three shots were fired at President Kennedy's motorcade in downtown Dallas. The first reports say that President Kennedy has been seriously wounded by this shooting. More details just arrived; Mrs. Kennedy jumped up and grabbed. She called, 'Oh no!' The motorcade sped on . . . Stay tuned to CBS news for further details."

Even today, we yearn to be able to reach our hand into the infamous Zapruder footage and somehow lower the president's head below the assassin's line of fire.

Cronkite delivered the emphatic pronouncement at 2:38 P.M., Eastern Standard Time from CBS news headquarters in New York. "From Dallas, Texas. The flash, apparently official. President Kennedy died at 1:00 P.M., Central Standard Time."

★   ★   ★

At Fort Myer on November 22 when he first heard the president had been shot, Sam replied, "Oh, really?" He stepped backward and retorted, "The who?" For him, there was only one thing to do. He got into his car and drove back down Fort Myer's Avenue of Trees into Arlington National Cemetery to the Tomb of the Unknown Soldier. This place was incarnate to Sam as the most hallowed ground in the United States.

As it happened, he'd just conducted a colonel's funeral there. **The routine of a military burial was never routine to him. He treated each one with gravity and solemnity, and as taps sounded and the clock crept toward 1:30 he** [had] **watched the colonel's elderly widow slowly descend the slope beside the grave. Her two sons were assisting her. In her arms she carried the flag from the coffin, folded in its traditional triangle. One son, thinking to lighten her burden, offered to take the colors from her. Wordlessly she shook her head and hugged the banner to her breast.** [Sam had been] **proud of her.**

74

Upon re-entering the gates of Fort Myer, he saw the post's flag begin to descend. He pulled over to the curb, got out of his car and posted a rigid salute. While he was bringing his hand down sharply to his side, a captain strode up and told him to get an eight-man Army casket team together. They would be going to Andrews Air Force Base to collect the body of the slain president.

The following is based on Sam's After Action Report, first-hand accounts of other members of the Joint Services Casket Detail and the reel-to-reel tape footage from Sam's three-hour recording on the evening of November 25th.

Andrews Air Force Base, Maryland

At approximately 1700 HRS, 22 November, 1963, at Fort Myer, Sam, along with eight other members of his chosen Army casket team, the strongest, most reliable men on the post, boarded an H-21 helicopter. In the pinkish twilight of early evening, high above the ground, Sam looked down at the spectacular panorama of shimmering, dazzling lights that was the sprawling city of Washington, D.C., to the north.

He peered down on the White House, federal triangle, the memorials, the Roman complex of the Hill. This was the first time he had ever ridden over the city, and he thought its beauty breathtaking. He remembered all the tours he had taken, all the souvenirs he had bought and sent home to Kansas. None matched the splendor beneath him. The Capitol dome reflected the day's dying light . . . It was the most spectacular panorama [Sam] had ever seen. He wished this were some other day.

The helicopter touched down at Andrews just after 1730 HRS and Sam directed Sergeant James Felder, the non-commissioned officer-in-charge (NCOIC) of the Army team, to march the men over to a convenient place beyond the Air Force cordon which had been set up around the area where the presidential aircraft from Dallas was due to come in to land. Meanwhile Sam reported to Captain Patton, the special events officer of the Military District of Washington.

The captain instructed Sam to assemble a joint services team from the personnel—including those of the other services as they arrived prior to the touch down of Air Force One. The captain also informed him the aircraft had radioed ahead to say that secret service agents aboard the plane would remove the president's casket.

Sam surveyed the cordoned-off area and saw that an Air Force casket team had already formed up. He went over and asked who was in charge. A tall, rangy twenty-seven-year-old staff sergeant named Richard Gaudrea stepped forward. "Come with me," Sam told him.

As U.S. Marine, Navy and Coast Guard contingents arrived, Sam continued to form and reform his teams until he had at least one soldier, sailor, marine, airman and coast guardsman in each.

He took one team of six with him over to an enormous, garish-looking, yellow bed-lift truck. He stationed them on its platform. The other team under the command of Sergeant Felder was ranged round the platform's double braces, which formed a double X. The idea was that Team One would secure the president's remains from the aircraft and place them on the raised bed of the truck. The bed would then be lowered and Team Two would remove the casket from the truck and place it in a Navy ambulance for transfer to the helicopter. In addition, in the midst of the general pandemonium that was building, Sam detailed a joint eight-man Army/Air Force team to cordon off the area around President Johnson's helicopter.

Darkness had fallen and wispy layers of mist interwove to create the effect of a partial veil over the crescent moon when Aircraft 26000 swooped down virtually without a sound from the somber, black sky at 5:59 P.M., Eastern Standard Time. The eerie spectacle was heightened as the great beast rolled quietly to a halt, shrouded in the glare from the circle of lights that had been rigged up.

A door opened swiftly in the rear of the plane as the yellow bed-lift truck with Sam and his team aboard, the other marching alongside, edged toward it. On seeing the bronze casket in the doorway, Sam smartly raised a white gloved hand in salute. At the same time, he caught a glimpse from the corner of his eye of the enormous, hushed crowd beyond the fence. The sight took him completely by surprise, for it hadn't occurred to him that anyone else was there. His eyes filled and he choked at the sight of the bare casket, not covered by a flag. He was shocked and kicked himself for not having brought one with him.

The yellow lift came to a halt beside the plane's hatch, and Sam looked right up into the pulsing face of Brigadier General Godfrey McHugh, the late president's Air Force aide. McHugh had been described in various publications as alternately handsome, dashing and flamboyant. None of those adjectives, however, would have been used to describe him on this particular evening. Sam saluted again. Suddenly, McHugh launched into a ranting tirade climaxing with the screamed command, "Clear the area. We'll take care of the coffin!" He meant himself and the secret service agents.

With a calm assurance that belied his years, Sam instructed his men to descend from the truck by the ladder on the side. On seeing them struggle to hold the solid bronze casket steady, he had two of his men stay and assist with carrying it out of the aircraft and setting it down on the raised bed of the truck.

Unfortunately, the bed-lift truck proved alarmingly inadequate—the limit of its capacity to extend downwards was five feet short of the ground. Despite this, the second team was positioned, ready to receive the casket on the left side of the truck. However, as they moved forward to secure it, they were again waved brusquely away by a flustered McHugh bellowing, "We'll do it. We don't need you!" At the same time, a group of secret service agents barreled forward with a surge that knocked Sergeant Felder out of the way to one side. The scene was threatening to become a grotesque farce, as for a few terrible seconds the casket swung wildly between and across the agents' grasp. Three members of the second team lunged forward just in time to prevent an unthinkable catastrophe and steadied the gashed and listing casket before ensuring it was finally lowered safely into the waiting Navy ambulance.

As Staff Sergeant Richard Gaudrea stood back, away from the ambulance, he watched Jacqueline Kennedy being helped down off the truck. The sight of her rose-colored suit and nylon stockings, stained and matted with her husband's blood riveted his attention. Yet her innate dignity as she moved toward the waiting ambulance succeeded in restoring a measure of decorum to the situation. While all this transpired below, Sam and two members of the team, posting rigid salutes, remained at attention on top of the truck.

Once the casket team was secured, the two teams formed up on the left side of the ambulance and Sam joined them from the truck. As the ambulance pulled away, Sergeant Felder marched his squad of six over to the helicopter. After the ambulance left the airfield, Sam joined them and they flew directly to Bethesda Naval Hospital.

Bethesda Naval Hospital, Maryland

At 1845 HRS the banana-like H-21 helicopter carrying the team landed at the heliport beneath the hospital's soaring twin tower. The very moment Sam stepped out he was greeted by an explosion of press photographers' flash bulbs. They assumed the casket would be right behind him.

Of course, it was still en route from Andrews in the ambulance. The journey across the city was some eight or ten miles through the height of the evening rush hour. While the team waited for the casket to arrive, the lawn in front of the hospital was engulfed with an immense yet peaceful congestion of onlookers. By the time the ambulance finally arrived at the entrance to the hospital, the crowd had created a solid barrier between the team and the casket. When Sam and Major General Wehle, the commander of the Military District of Washington, eventually reached the ambulance and peered in, they discovered to their alarm the casket was no longer inside and the driver had disappeared as well.

They rushed into the lobby of the hospital to find the casket there on the floor with a sheepish-looking Air Force aide standing some yards away from it. The general and Sam instantly saw red. The Military District of Washington was the very embodiment of ceremonial perfection and for the casket to be lying there virtually unattended was a flagrant affront to every ceremonial norm there was.

Sam formed up the team of six to carry the casket into the inner hospital. Before they were able to move forward, however, Brigadier General McHugh had wrested Yeoman 2nd Class "Bud" Barnum of the Coast Guard away from it and had, according to Sam's depiction of events in his after action report, "awkwardly taken his place." Compared to the thoughts of the rest of the team at that moment, it was a charitable reference. McHugh was clearly incapable of holding his end of the casket up, which resulted in a halting, slow pace along the floor. Before they reached the end of the corridor, McHugh had capitulated and Barnum had retaken his place. Fortunately, the entire episode occurred out of public view. Once Barnum was back in position, the team proceeded quickly with the casket into the restricted mortuary area and lowered it onto a waiting gurney.

When the body was removed from the casket and taken into the autopsy room, the team assumed duties as part of the security detail. Sam took turns with Sergeant Felder and Army Specialist 4th Class Doug Mayfield in standing guard outside the door to the mortuary for the next eight hours while the autopsy and subsequent embalming of the president were carried out. This was something Sam didn't have to do. He could have spent that time with fellow officers and dignitaries upstairs instead. Indeed, Sam spent much of that time inside the mortuary witnessing the autopsy. This generated several thoughts and observations which he added to the tape recording on the following Monday evening.

"It was quite a shock to see the president; to see his naked body torn down by gunshot, his autopsy, then the restoration of a crushed individual, disfigured and dead, back to the image that we knew him as—John Fitzgerald Kennedy. He was dressed back into a blue suit, in which most official photographs portray him, and a silk shirt with the initials JFK embroidered on the sleeves. They were fold-back [cuffed] sleeves."

During the autopsy, some secret service agents went to Gawler's Funeral Parlor on Wisconsin Avenue to get a replacement casket after Sam notified General Wehle of the state of the original bronze casket from Dallas. It had been chipped, dented and had lost one of its handles during the confusion at Andrews. The agents returned with a casket made from solid, five-hundred-year-old, African mahogany.

At approximately 0400 HRS Saturday morning, one of the undertakers handed Sam a standard five-and-a-half by nine foot, Veterans' Administration issue American flag folded in its customary triangle.

Waiting there, [he] suddenly recalled the colonel's widow at Arlington the previous noon. He remembered her stumbling down the slope just before he heard the president had been shot, and how she refused to let her son relieve her of the flag. She had clutched it tight against her heart with both forearms. He realized that he was holding it the same way.

Sam knew exactly what to do, handing it from man to man, unfolding it and conducting a ceremony with the rest of the team to place it over the coffin. On completion of the solemn rite, the team saluted the flag-draped coffin, carried it back outside the hospital and slid it smoothly into the waiting Navy ambulance. The team then climbed into a limousine as part of the official entourage and escorted the remains back to the White House.

Looking out of the car during the journey, Sam noticed people from everywhere and of every kind **standing at attention beside cars at intersections. In the all-night service stations, attendants faced the ambulance with caps held over their hearts. As the slow-moving procession turned off Massachusetts onto 20th Street, Sam looked back down Embassy Row and saw the line of hundreds of automobiles following them, bumper to bumper as far back as the eye could see, their headlights flashing.**

The White House, November 23

At 0428 HRS, the cortege entered the northwest drive of the White House. The somberness of the occasion was intensified by the lighted kerosene flares lining the driveway, which in turn illuminated the throng of mourning humanity silhouetted against the White House railings. A twelve-man Marine drill team that had arrived on 20 minutes notice escorted the ambulance to the front door.

Once the ambulance halted, Sam's team left their limousine and carried the casket through the Joint Honor Cordon, between the pillars of the north portico into the White House. The actual weight of the casket remains a matter of conjecture to this day, but estimates range from eight hundred to twelve hundred pounds. What is beyond dispute is that it was proving to be too much for the six-man team on their longest carry so far. As they struggled through the narrow doorway between the cordon of servicemen on either side, it looked as if they were going to drop it. Ceremonial protocol held that the officer in charge should remain a comfortable distance away from his men; his job was simply to make sure matters of protocol were strictly observed by his team. Seeing the six men begin to lurch alarmingly, Sam disregarded standard operating procedure and stepped up swiftly from behind. He slid his fingers beneath the coffin, bracing it from the rear. A wrenching strain plunged through his arms like an electric concussion and Specialist 4th Class Mayfield rolled his eyes back and whispered imploringly, "Good God, don't let go!"

The seven men carried the coffin across the marble hall, over the red carpet into the majestic chandelier-hung East Room of the White House and lowered it gently onto a replica of the Lincoln Catafalque, used in 1958 during the ceremonies for the Unknown Soldiers of World War II and Korea.

A priest conducted a brief blessing only for the family. After Mrs. Kennedy had left the room, the Death Watch was posted. The Death Watch consisted of a detail of specially selected servicemen in their dress blues. On watch, they stood at rigid attention. Then the casket team was stood down and returned to Fort Myer.

The carry into the White House had been the first of any significant distance and they'd almost let the casket fall. Sergeant

Felder was a veteran of almost eighteen hundred military funerals with the Old Guard and he had absolutely no doubt in his mind when he told Sam they just had to have two additional men for the detail. For his part, Sam didn't hesitate to make the request and Seaman Larry Smith of the Navy and Private First Class Jerry Diamond of the Marine Corps were added to the team.

Sam had been asleep in his bachelor officer quarters for about 45 minutes when he was awakened by the sound of heavy rain against the window. He leaped out of bed. **His first thought was that he was going to get thoroughly drenched, because he was "too proud to wear a raincoat."**

Ten minutes later, along with the other members of the post, he fell in outside. There, by order of the secretary of defense, they were to be officially told of the president's death. Throughout the day, the team rehearsed and trained continuously in the rain for the forthcoming duties of the next two days. **Sam found that every man in the ranks had independently reached his own conclusion about raincoats; not a slicker was in sight.**

In the evening they assumed duty as the Death Watch for the casket in the White House. Later that night when they were relieved, Sam should have returned to his quarters for some necessary rest. Instead, he chose to spend the night **on the first floor of the mansion, wandering from hall to hall, munching sandwiches from the platters, noticing the little Kennedy touches and thinking in awe, This is the president's house; this is where he actually lives.**

November 24

At precisely 1300 HRS the following day, Sam was supposed to give the team the order to lift the casket from the catafalque and carry it outside to the empty horse-drawn caisson that had pulled up at the front door. But Mrs. Kennedy and her children had not appeared yet.

Outside, the band played "Abide With Me." Beyond them a huge multitude had gathered outside the gates, cramming along sidewalks, against buildings and on rooftops just to catch a glimpse of the procession. Then Jacqueline Kennedy emerged serenely from the front door, dressed all in black with John, Jr. and Caroline. With a sense of shock, Sam recognized them. **Young John, watching the body bearers, asked, "Mummy, what are they doing?" His mother said, "They're taking Daddy out." John asked, "But why do they do it so funny—so slow?" She said, "Because they're so sad," and Sam looked away, and forgot the clock.**

The sight of Mrs. Kennedy gave the team a tremendous lift as they brought the casket out and placed it on the caisson. Then they formed up in two ranks in front of the Presidential Colors and "Black Jack," the riderless horse, but behind the caisson. They were ready for the march to the Capitol.

The order, "Present arms!" was barked out and the cortege began to move down the driveway to the unique tattoo of muffled drums. They moved through the state and territorial flags held by an honor guard of sailors who dipped the flags as the procession passed. And then out onto Pennsylvania Avenue and past the legions of the masses lining sidewalks, rooftops and balconies for as far as the eye could see. As the procession marched down Pennsylvania Avenue, the stillness of the crowd was excruciating. Recalled Sam, **"As the guards along the curbs saluted the colors over the casket you could see the long faces of the people on the sidewalk, trying not to break down and failing over and over. An old man put his hand over his heart, and then his face screwed up and he clapped his other hand over his eyes."**

Block by block the silence became more profound while the sound of muffled drums became more pronounced. The view down Pennsylvania Avenue was awe-inspiring.

As the caisson pulled into the east plaza of the Capitol, the flag at half mast on the roof began to flutter in the breeze. The crowd strained to see, some watching from as far away as the Supreme Court, standing with telescopes and binoculars.

The United States Capitol

While the chief mourners disembarked from their vehicles and moved over beside Seaman Edward W. Nemuth and the Presidential Colors, Sam marched to the base of the Capitol steps, came to an abrupt halt and performed a flawless about turn. Simultaneously and in perfect synchronization with Sam's movements, Sergeant Felder left the remainder of the team at attention facing the casket and began to unbuckle it from the caisson. By the time he'd finished, the chief mourners were in place and Sam had marched back over behind the casket team, coming to attention beside the Presidential Colors.

An officer shouted, "Present!" Then a captain, allowing for the brief echo delay, shouted, "Fire!" In the next moment, the other officer shouted, "Arms!" and hands came up sharply in salute. Instantaneously, the first shot of a 21 gun salute thundered overhead, reverberating around the nation's Capitol. At the same split second, the first note of the Navy Band playing "Ruffles and Flourishes" could be heard. It sounded very different. When the band began to play "Hail to the Chief" it became harrowingly clear why. A tune normally played at a jaunty clip was being played in an agonizingly slow dirge. The effect was devastating.

As the poignant rendition came to a close, the remainder of the team took up their positions with Sergeant Felder beside the casket. On the first note of the seafarers' hymn, "Eternal Father Strong To Save," the team raised the casket to their shoulders to clear the caisson, then brought it around at waist height. Sam, who'd been holding his salute until that point, swung round behind them as they approached the front of the Capitol steps.

They paused briefly at the base and then on Sergeant Felder's nod began to move slowly forward, one step at a time. Four steps before the first landing, Sam sensed a slight tremor in their gait and leaned forward to brace the head of the casket by sliding his hands beneath the corners and taking the weight. Little did he realize that not only had he taken some of the strain from the other members of the team but he had also unwittingly provided a symbolic gesture of reassurance to the helpless millions holding their breaths as they watched every detail of the upward journey unfold on their television sets.

The team halted briefly on the first landing and then ascended the next 11 steps to the second landing where they paused for the last time before making the final and longest ascent. It was 16 steps to the top, and clear signs of physical distress were emerging on the faces of the entire team. Halfway up, the pace became agonizing and Sam was beset with the distinct feeling they weren't going to make it. But there was absolutely nothing he could do. From behind, everything looked perfect, but the strain of keeping the casket level, especially for those at the heavier rear end who had it raised to their shoulders, was becoming physically unbearable. Quietly they urged each other on with every last sinew of their beings, up the last few steps until somehow, they reached the top landing. The hymn was still playing in the background, which meant they still had some way to go—between the colossal stone pillars, past the television camera perched to the left that focused on their every move, and up to the great bronze doors of the Capitol. Somehow, they managed to execute a side-step through the smaller inner doorway and across the floor between the roped-off areas. Pausing briefly, they moved forward again. Expressions of fatigue and strain were scored deeply into their faces now as they swung the casket around to the right, followed by the Presidential Flag dipping below the doors behind them. As Mrs. Kennedy came through the door, the team finished their turn and placed the casket upon the Lincoln Catafalque beneath the Great Rotunda of the Capitol, stepped back and came to attention. Sam stood ramrod straight at the head of the casket.

The sight of Jacqueline Kennedy and her daughter approaching the bier and kneeling down beside it, the young widow kissing the flag while the child reached up under it to touch her father's coffin was infinitely moving. Standing some three yards away, beneath an upright veneer of composure, Sam was awash with emotion.

Mrs. Kennedy and Caroline departed, and before the eulogies were read, the team was relieved by the Death Watch. They returned to Fort Myer for more rehearsal.

At two o'clock, the gates of the Rotunda were opened to the public. Over four hundred thousand people would file past the bier by nine o'clock the following morning. At its peak, the line of mourners stretched back some three or four miles.

On that Sunday evening, the team went to Saint Matthew's Cathedral for a briefing about the following day's funeral service from Captain McNamera, the site control officer. He told Sam the team would be pre-positioned at the cathedral before the funeral procession. On the captain's command, they were to remove the casket from the caisson, hold it in place while Cardinal Cushing gave it his blessing and then carry it into the cathedral, up the aisle and place it on the catafalque before the altar. Following the service, the team was to remove the casket from the catafalque and carry it to the door—once again holding it in place while honors were rendered to it, and then descending the stairs, stopping halfway down while the cardinal blessed it again. Finally, they were to lift it up and place it back on the horse-drawn caisson.

It appeared to Sam that whoever had come up with that plan must have thought they were carrying a feather duster. Little consideration had been shown for the fact that it had required every ounce of the team's strength to carry the coffin up the Capitol steps in "an appropriate and respectful manner." He therefore recommended that a church truck (a casket-length trolley) be positioned at the entrance to the cathedral so the casket could be rolled instead of carried up the aisle. This, in addition, would obviate the need for a catafalque. Finally, the casket could remain on the truck while honors were being rendered, thus eliminating the burden of weight during that time.

It would have been of considerable comfort to the team that night to hear that Sam's recommendations had been approved. Instead, even though they had been, the team was not informed until the following morning. Sam decided their only recourse was to spend the night rehearsing.

Anyone who has carried a large, heavy, precious object between the bedroom of their house and the basement can appreciate the fact that the journey down the stairs can present greater problems than the journey up. Following their tortuous carry up the Capitol steps earlier that day, the entire team was terrified by the thought of bringing it back down again. Because of the steady stream of mourners, it was completely out of the question to use the Capitol for rehearsal. The steps leading up to the Tomb of the Unknown Soldier represented the only comparable alternative in the city and its environs.

The team drove to the Tomb that night accompanied by a regulation Army casket from Fort Myer which weighed no more than two hundred pounds. Once it had been brought to the foot of the steps, the casket was filled with sandbags to help simulate the weight. Then began what to most of the team seemed an eternity of carrying, up and down the steps of the Tomb. As midnight passed Sam remained uneasy, since in spite of the sandbags, this casket was nowhere near the weight of the real one. He knew the team desperately needed to believe in their ability to do the job the following day, so as the Tomb guards went off duty at midnight, Sam asked two of them to straddle the casket while the team carried it and them up and down the steps some more. The whole team was desperately tired by now and many were developing nasty blisters on their hands. Time and again they dropped the casket with the men on top.

As the hour of one o'clock in the morning approached, the team was completely and utterly exhausted. Sam looked over at his men and saw they were physically and mentally spent. He spoke softly. "We've done all we can do tonight fellahs," he said. "We're just not going to make it tonight. Don't worry about it. We'll get it in the morning."

Chapter Five

The Pride and the Sorrow

November 25
Capitol, Cathedral and Gravesite

Minutes before seven o'clock, the sun rose above the eastern shores of the Potomac into a cloudless sky. The morning was bright and crisp. Many of those forming the huge swath of slow-moving humanity standing in line throughout the night were still awaiting their turn to file past the bier of the president in the Rotunda.

The casket team had been at Arlington National Cemetery since five o'clock in the morning, rehearsing the graveside services for later that day.

At nine o'clock, the great bronze doors of the Capitol were closed in preparation. Accompanied by an escort from the cemetery, the team arrived at the Rotunda shortly after ten o'clock. With the moment of truth fast approaching, Sam gathered his men tightly around him in a well between the Rotunda and the old Senate Chamber.

"Bow your heads," he said softly, and they all closed their eyes. "Dear God, please give us strength to do this last thing for the president."

The men straightened up as Sam glanced at his watch.

"Let's move," he said, the authority returning to his voice.

★　　★　　★

Sam's orders were to approach the catafalque and relieve the Death Watch at 10:27. Mrs. Kennedy and the attorney general were due to arrive by car at the foot of the Capitol steps from where they would be escorted to their designated place on the plaza. After receiving the nod from Captain Smith, the Capitol site control officer on the far side of the hall, the team was to remove the casket from the catafalque to begin its final journey.

As the clock crept toward 10:40, the captain still hadn't moved. The family was 11 minutes late in arriving. Upon disembarking, Robert Kennedy indicated they would like a final moment of privacy with the coffin. Therefore, instead of the anticipated nod from the captain, Sam was greeted by the sight of Jacqueline Kennedy, flanked by her two brothers-in-law, Robert and Edward, advancing toward the bier.

For a solemn 10 minutes, the team held their positions at rigid attention while the family knelt beside the coffin. Slowly they arose and descended the marble stairs.

Moments later, the captain gave an exaggerated nod of his head and Sam boomed out the order, "Secure casket!"

The team carried the casket out through the great bronze doors, past dignitaries with hands clasped against their hearts, to the top of the Capitol steps between the great stone pillars. As the captain gave the order to present arms, Sam had Platoon Sergeant Sharpe, the NCOIC at the Rotunda who was standing guard at the top of the steps, come over and hold the foot of the casket while he braced the head—his back straight, legs slightly apart and long arms at full extension with his hands cupped around the corners. Sam and the platoon sergeant bore the brunt of the casket's weight throughout the sounding of "Ruffles and Flourishes" and "Hail to the Chief," played this time at regular tempo by the Coast Guard Band, while the rest of the team took turns letting go and relaxing their arms.

As the band struck up the first note of the hymn, "O' God of Loveliness," the team moved forward and began its descent.

To their astonishment, all the way down, it was as if the casket were floating on a magic carpet, as though the weight had been taken out of their hands. To those watching, it looked flawless—perfectly level, the base of the casket always appearing to be at exact right angles to each step.

As they moved off the bottom step, past Jacqueline Kennedy on their right, the wind billowed up beneath the flag causing it to flutter. Sergeant Felder and Lance Corporal Cheek stretched out a free hand and gently smoothed it back down.

Gliding over to the rear of the gun carriage, the team hoisted the casket to their shoulders with seemingly effortless ease and slid it faultlessly onto the caisson.

Sergeant Felder secured the flag at the foot and Sam took care of it at the head while the rest of the team buckled the casket down. As the final strains of the hymn began to fade, the horse-drawn caisson pulled away to Saint Matthew's Cathedral via the White House. Jacqueline Kennedy walked to her car. A haunting silence clung to the vast crowds while the team boarded the bus for the cathedral.

Once the band had turned up 15th Street toward the White House, they struck up Chopin's Funeral March, the most famous death march of all. Its unequivocal refrain resounded over the grounds of the executive mansion and beyond as the clanking cortege approached. The bells from the nearby Episcopal Church tolled as the Marine Honor Guard led the caisson in. Once again, the entire driveway was cordoned by Navy enlisted men, bearing state and territorial flags. The cortege came to a halt outside the White House as the family and dignitaries from all over the world left their cars and assembled behind the caisson for the walk to Saint Matthew's Cathedral. When Mrs. Kennedy came to within 10 yards of Black Jack, the Marine Platoon which had stopped at the northwest gate moved the column off. The Bagpipes of the Black Watch of the Royal Highland Regiment moved in behind them and immediately in front of the Joint Chiefs of Staff.

At this point in the tape recording, Sam broke in indignantly, "The bagpipes are not from the Black Watch; they are from the U.S. Air Force!"

Both Sam and the TV narrator were right. The Black Watch had in fact been requested by Mrs. Kennedy to march between the marines and the Joint Chiefs for the journey to Saint Matthew's; nine of them had been flown up from Knoxville, where they were touring the country at the time. In addition, four Air Force pipers were assigned to join them.

The bells of Saint Matthew's Cathedral began to ring out as the chief mourners made their way from the White House.

The caisson came to a halt just beyond the front steps of the cathedral where Cardinal Cushing, the Archbishop of Boston, was waiting in his black and red vestments and imposing white miter. The chief mourners made their way into the cathedral after being greeted by the cardinal and were escorted to their seats at the front. The team approached the casket while Sam remained at attention some 10 yards to the rear. Once the procession of mourners had been seated and honors rendered, the team moved in to lift the coffin from the caisson. At the first note of the hymn, "Prayer for the Dying," they began to carry the casket and once again Sam swung in behind them. As they began the ascent of the steps to the cathedral, the cardinal took the team completely by surprise. He materialized right in front of them with holy water, blocking the way. Sam had no choice but to halt the team halfway up the steps in the most awkward of positions. The cardinal kissed the flag and began to bless the casket as the team members strived with everything they had to retain their footing in the worst of stances and brace the casket at the same time. Once more, Sam held on for all he was worth at the rear, as the cardinal droned on and on. The whole thing was on the verge of giving way and Sam was getting ready to whisper, "Sir, you'd better move!" when His Eminence came to the latin words, "and let the perpetual light shine on him," kissed the flag again and stepped to one side.

As the team continued up the steps, Luigi Vena, a tenor, rose in the choir loft to sing "Ave Maria." The sound was heavenly. The casket was lowered onto the church truck and after removing their caps, the team rolled it down the center aisle, positioning it in front of the congregation.

At the completion of the mass, "Hail to the Chief" was played for the last time and the team shouldered the casket and proceeded down the steps to emerge into the sunlight. Fortunately, this time the cardinal waited until they'd reached the bottom before blessing the casket, sprinkling it with holy water and kissing the flag. No more than five or six yards behind Sam, in an indelible image, Jacqueline Kennedy followed with her children.

The team again slid the casket flawlessly onto the caisson and the flag was width adjusted before the straps were fastened. Once the casket was securely in place, the team positioned themselves, four on either side of the caisson with Sam in the middle at the rear. The hymn being played by the band ceased and the command to order arms was given. To the sound of muffled drums, the casket was pulled away on its final journey while John Kennedy, Jr. executed an astonishingly correct salute to his father.

The funeral procession traveled back down Connecticut Avenue and 17th Street, out onto Constitution Avenue, around the Lincoln Memorial and across the Potomac. From his car, Bishop Philip Hannan, who had spoken at the funeral, looked out over Black Jack and marveled at the team's precision. Although the gun carriage divided the two groups of four servicemen, they marched as one, with Sam maintaining his position exactly at the center, a few feet to the rear of the caisson. A slightly elevated ridge of bricks separated the lanes of the Memorial Circle. It was a mere eight inches wide, yet rather than mar the formation, Sam marched straight down the middle of it on his slick, steel-heeled shoes.

The entire route to the cemetery seemed a mass of emotional ferment. Sam could feel it from all sides but his attention was drawn to something else. He had fixed his gaze on the flag draped over the coffin. On the bunting beside the field of stars was a small label that read "Valley Forge Flag Company, Spring City, Pennsylvania."

Leaving Washington and the Lincoln Memorial behind, the head of the solemn, majestic three-mile procession passed through the gates into Arlington. As the caisson entered the cemetery, the

Colonial Fife and Drum Corps, which had a special place in Sam's own affections, could be seen in front of the fountain at the main gate. The procession advanced through a joint honor cordon, the caisson rumbling gently to the point a few yards beyond the gravesite where it stopped. Sam brought the casket team to an abrupt halt and they prepared to unload their precious burden for the last time.

Once the chief mourners had left their vehicles, the United States Marine Band sounded "Ruffles and Flourishes" and began to play "The Star-Spangled Banner." A profound hush followed the playing of the National Anthem as the Air Force Bagpipe Band swung across the lip of the hill in slow time and began to play "Mist Covered Mountain," as heartbreaking as it was beautiful. At the first sound of the pipes, Sam ordered the coffin raised from the caisson. They passed slowly through a joint cordon of Special Forces troops beneath the Custis-Lee Mansion, overlooking the scene from the brow of the hill. They deliberately overshot the grave, turned a full hundred and eighty degrees and looped back in a wide arch so the head of the deep, mahogany coffin would point to the crest of the grave facing east. The casket was placed on a lowering device about a foot above the ground and the rest of the team held the flag from Spring City taut above the grave while Sam and a cemetery employee crouched down to jockey the coffin into position from either end.

They were still bent over the grave when 50 aircraft, comprised of 30 F-105's from the Air Force and 20 F-4's from the Navy, screamed low across the skies above them. Into the void left by the two F-105's who were completing the "missing man" formation loomed a majestic bird. Aircraft 26000 dipped its wing to the left and appeared suspended, low and level above the taut flag, then dipped to the right and soared off into the distance.

While the flag was still being held rigid by the white-gloved hands of the casket team, Cardinal Cushing blessed the grave. Positioned directly behind Yeoman 2nd Class Barnum, Sam clasped his cap to his chest.

Headgear was replaced as Captain Homer Gay of the artillery shouted, "Present arms!" and the 21 gun salute thundered over the cemetery and reverberated into the distance. During the sustained salute, Sam found himself gazing directly into the attorney general's eyes until his attention was caught by General de Gaulle bringing his hand down to his side prematurely— before the last report of the guns. Once again caps were removed while Cardinal Cushing delivered his benediction.

After the chaplain had completed his prayers, the order was given for the firing party to deliver three volleys. A sergeant shouted, "Aim . . . Fire!" and the neat retort of rifles cracked across Arlington. After the third volley, the squad came to attention following the order, "Present arms!"

The first note of taps cracked, like a sob, then recovered to finish mellifluously and the troops thumped to parade rest. Following several animated attempts to attract their wandering attention, the Marine Band struck up the Navy Hymn at a harrowingly slow 80 beats per minute. Now it was Sam's team's turn. They had disregarded all shouted commands and, standing four facing four, operated on signals transmitted by tension on the flag's hem under their fingers. Sam gave Sergeant Felder a nod whereupon he tugged on the flag, and they were off. **Their arms moved like whips, folding the Colors in a triangle with great speed.**

Captured from above by television cameras, the precision was breathtaking perfection. Once the blue field was in the fold, the measure of the flag was taken and the team snapped to attention. Sergeant Felder performed a final check of the flag, smoothing it and caressing it in his hands. Assured of its faultless angularity, he passed it to Lance Corporal Cheek. It went down the line, breast to breast, to Specialist 4th Class Douglas Mayfield at the end, who executed a sharp right-face upon its receipt and handed it to Mr. Metzler, the civilian superintendent of the cemetery. Mayfield completed the maneuver by executing a perfect salute. Then the flag was presented on behalf of a grieving nation to the president's widow.

Jacqueline Kennedy lit the Eternal Flame while the team remained in place. They were to have left the site first but stayed put for a time while the chief mourners departed. Finally, the team turned and stepped off, away from the gravesite and marched down the slope.

Sam ordered, "About face!" They turned abruptly and rendered one final salute to their commander-in-chief. It was not a part of the official procedure, "But," said Sam, "We had been with him so long and loved him so much that we just wanted to do it."

From there, they walked up the hill to the Custis-Lee Mansion where a bus was waiting to return them to Fort Myer. During that journey, very little was said.

★   ★   ★

The president, Sam Bird knew, had loved American history. As a participant in this moment of history he resolved to dictate his memories of it into his tape recorder before retiring that night. He did this, he said, primarily out of the love and respect he'd developed for the other members of the casket team, as well as for the man they'd just laid to rest. However, it wasn't until he switched on the television set that evening that the full impact of what he had been a part of began to hit him. Throughout the preceding days, his mind had been focused exclusively on not making a mistake. Seeing himself on television in the midst of such an awesome spectacle, he began to appreciate for the first time the immense honor and privilege that had been accorded him. He had eight copies of the tape made, which he began in a solemn, deep and resonant voice.

"In January 1961, I had the privilege of marching in the inaugural parade of President John F. Kennedy. Little did I know that less than three years later, I would be carrying him to his place of rest on his final day in office.

"These times have been challenging, filled with sorrow and grief, but we take with us a tremendous sense of pride, representing all the members of the Armed Forces of the United States, as the flag was presented on behalf of a grateful nation.

"In every man's heart there was a very deep sense of pride, and thanks to God for giving us the ability to perform a job in a manner which John Fitzgerald Kennedy would have been proud. So with this, the closing of the day in which John

Fitzgerald Kennedy was buried and laid to rest, we thank God for the opportunity to have served him.

"To all members of the casket team—thank you all for a job tremendously and perfectly executed in a manner that the people of the United States of America can be truly proud."

Sam paused briefly, and then read aloud that which he had received hours earlier from the chief of the information department of the Army.

"News release, November 25th, United Press International:

"Servicemen from the Military District of Washington carried their Commander-in-Chief to his grave today. The bearers were chosen from all branches of the services. The nine young servicemen who guarded the body of President Kennedy and carried it to rest, performed today with flawless military precision that reflected pride in what they were doing and respect for the man they honored. The officer and eight enlisted men who acted as body bearers won the admiration of the thousands who witnessed the ceremonies here and the millions who watched on television. The nine, all in their late teens or early twenties were identified as:

ARMY
1st Lieutenant Samuel R. Bird
Sergeant James L. Felder
Specialist 4th Class Douglas A. Mayfield

USMC
Lance Corporal Timothy F. Cheek
Private 1st Class Jerry J. Diamond

NAVY
Seaman Apprentice Hubert A. Clark
Seaman Apprentice Larry B. Smith

USAF
Staff Sergeant Richard E. Gaudreau

COAST GUARD
Yeoman 2nd Class George A. Barnum"

★　　★　　★

The entire team received the Army Commendation Medal at a specially convened funeral awards ceremony on February 13, 1964, for the "outstanding manner in which they maintained dignity and solemnity by keeping the casket level and moving in cadence as a unit at all times."

In addition to numerous letters from congressmen and dignitaries congratulating him on a job well-done, Sam received a host of letters from all sections of the general public thanking him for the respect, tenderness, pride and consummate perfection with which he had performed his duties.

Early on Thanksgiving Day the Thursday following the funeral, Sam received his most treasured accolade. He was on duty at the gravesite when Jacqueline Kennedy appeared unexpectedly for a visit. She spent a minute or so chatting with Sam and finished by offering him her thanks for what he had done. Even before this brief encounter, he had conceived enormous respect and admiration for the way she'd carried herself throughout the entire ordeal. It was an impression he would never lose.

There was something else he hadn't forgotten. On December 2nd, he wrote a letter to the president of the Valley Forge Flag Company, Spring City, Pennsylvania.

Dear Sir,

I am 1st Lieutenant Samuel R. Bird, Company E (Honor Guard) 1st Battalion (Reinf.) 3rd Infantry. I had the honor of being Officer in Charge of President Kennedy's Joint Armed Forces Casket Team.

I thought you might be interested and proud to know that we placed one of your flags on top of President Kennedy's coffin early Saturday morning, 23 November 1963, before it was removed from Bethesda Naval Hospital. This flag was not removed from the coffin until it was folded at the President's grave in Arlington National Cemetery, Monday afternoon the 25th [of] November.

Sincerely yours,
SAMUEL R. BIRD
1st Lt. Infantry

It was brought to Sam's notice the following week that his letter had been published in both Spring City newspapers. As a postscript, the flag company sent each member of the team an individually engraved desk flag to commemorate their performance.

It was somewhat ironic that had the casket not been so heavy, Sam would never have appeared in the spotlight. It was not customary for the officer in charge to assist physically in carrying the casket. His should have been a purely supervisory role, remaining at some distance from the casket at all times, superfluous in most respects.

PART III

THE MEANEST MUTHAS

Chapter Six

Highway 19

Following the funeral, Sam's life at Fort Myer settled back into more familiar forms of pomp and ceremony as he became the executive officer of an also-ran company, the not-so-highly thought of C Company, in the early part of 1964.

In the summer of that year Sam informed Colonel Joseph B. Conmy, his battalion commander, of his intent to volunteer for Vietnam as his next overseas duty. The colonel had been in command of the 3rd Infantry for only about five months, but he'd kept a constant eye on Sam since his arrival, hearing of his unique reputation. He saw for himself how Sam refused to let anything stand in the way of his objectives or impede the progress of his unit.

Around the Fourth of July in 1964, Conmy, Sam and the band went up to Fort McHenry in Baltimore to do an evening show with the Fife and Drum Corps. They drove there in a bus. Upon arrival, they discovered the compartment in the back of the bus containing all the big instruments, particularly the drums, was locked. The men were in their uniforms and due to go on in a matter of minutes. They'd planned the show carefully and now, suddenly, they were without drummers. In a matter of seconds Sam worked it out. Since the pipers and buglers had carried their instruments with them, he separated them into small sections and sent them on first, a section at a time. Then he somehow managed to get hold of a fire axe and chopped the door right off the back of the bus. The men quickly unloaded the drums and went on as the final section, the effect being that of a gradual musical build-up. And five thousand people didn't know the difference. They thought that's the way it was supposed to be.

When Sam told the colonel his plans to volunteer for duty in Vietnam, the colonel became worried. He went home that evening and brooded. When his wife inquired what the matter was, he said, "I'm really worried about Sam because he's such a driven man, a forceful guy and a leader. I'm afraid he's going to come back from Vietnam in a pine box. It's just the way he is. I know that nobody's gonna get the best of him as far as he's concerned, but it frightens me to death that he won't come back."

On August 20th, 1964, half a world away in Kion Hoa Province, some 45 miles from Saigon, on a narrow strip of road about a mile from their base camp, a United States Ranger Company was ambushed by a Vietcong force. Among those killed that day in the bloody ambush was 1st Lieutenant W.D.H. (Dave) Ragin. Dave Ragin was the Provost Marshall on the regimental staff at The Citadel in 1961 when Sam was the Executive Officer of the Corps. He had married the daughter of Lieutenant General Bill McCaffery, the Commandant of Cadets at The Citadel at the time. Sam had been in their wedding party. Now at home he was assuming command of his classmate's burial detail. For Sam it was the very least he could do, and for the general and his daughter the tenderness and consideration of an old classmate provided a little solace in the midst of desperate heartbreak.

Sam was promoted to the rank of captain later that year and became commander of Company C. It was during this time he acquired the nickname, "Captain Eagle," for much the same reason he was called Straight Arrow in Korea.

An apt commentary on Sam's time with the 3rd Infantry and a strong indication of his future in the Army was given in his final report from his commanding officer on August 7th, 1965.

Captain Bird's performance of duty during the period covered by this report was outstanding in every respect. This officer is definitely general officer material and should be promoted and schooled well in advance of his contemporaries.

... I strongly recommend Captain Bird be promoted to the grade of Major at the earliest possible opportunity with an equally early assignment to the Command and General Staff College.

> *Joseph B. Conmy, Jr.*
> *Colonel, Infantry*
> *Commanding*

Sam spent the next 10 months at Fort Benning, Georgia, preparing for Vietnam with the Pathfinder and Infantry Officer's Career Course. At the beginning of July 1966, he came home for two weeks leave prior to his departure for Vietnam.

★   ★   ★

It was just after 1800 HRS local time on Tuesday, July 19th, when Sam departed Travis Air Force Base in a large silver C-141 Starlifter. The golden coast of California receded in the distance behind them as they began a westward pursuit of the sun to the Far East that would carry them the breadth of the mighty Pacific. It was the first of many paradoxes Sam would encounter during his tour.

Somewhere between the islands of Hawaii and Midway the sun finally dipped below the horizon, making off with almost an entire day. Sam gazed down at his chunky Army watch and noted it would now be approaching 2:00 A.M. in Wichita. The first leg of the flight lasted nine hours, taking them to Wake Island for a one hour refueling stop. This was followed by six more grueling hours, punctuated by fitful intermissions of sleep, before they landed at Clark Air Force Base in The Philippines.

At 0600 HRS, Thursday, July 21st, Sam was applying the finishing touches to his first letter home, where it was four o'clock the previous afternoon. The six hour lay-over in The Philippines had come as a welcome respite from the punishing effect of "time travel." In about 30 minutes they'd be taking off on the short, final leg of their journey.

They were in the air two hours after departing Clark when the sandy elbow of South Vietnam came into view. They flew over the area of coastal highlands north of the town of Qui Nhon and

105

a bustling Highway 1 before picking up the east-west artery of Highway 19. This was their main navigational mark to the small, desolate airstrip at Pleiku, situated about 270 miles northeast of Saigon and 50 miles east of the Cambodian border.

It was around 10:30 on a sultry, sunny morning when Sam and the other new arrivals wearily made their way off the aircraft. There was a brief delay before boarding a Caribou aircraft for the short flight east to Camp Radcliffe at An Khe, headquarters of the 1st Cavalry Division in Vietnam. The brief holdover allowed for an exchange of empty, derisive looks and gestures between the new arrivals and the veterans of the Ia Drang Valley who were about to board the Starlifter for their journey home.

The flight aboard the Caribou was rough, but over some of the most hauntingly beautiful country Sam had ever seen. The II Corps area itself encompassed the entire Central Highlands of South Vietnam. Below them a convoy of trucks making the journey from An Khe to Pleiku snaked its way along Highway 19 through the undulating green canopy of thick, lush jungle speckled with barren outcrops that ran down sharply into rice-paddy-quilted valleys and plateaus, draped along the contours of the rivers and their numerous tributaries.

Gathering monsoon clouds loomed as they rose up over Mang Yang Pass. They heightened the already eerie spectacle of some eighteen hundred mass graves of the French Mobile Group 100 that occupied the top of the hill. The regiment had been annihilated by the North Vietnamese in 1954.

Concealed behind the crest of the hill was a river that ran down into the small, bustling town of An Khe, located in the southwestern sector of an area known as Bin Dinh Province. Nestled on either side of Highway 19 about halfway between Pleiku and Qui Nhon, An Khe was dwarfed by the vast, sprawling tent city which lay to its south at the base of a solitary seven-hundred-foot outcrop known as Hong Kong Mountain. Adjacent to the camp lay the world's largest helipad, the "Golf Course," so-called because of its multiple assortment of bunkers and craters acquired from hostile, incoming artillery. The perimeter of the entire complex was encircled with strategically placed watchtowers—gigantic and imposing structures.

Despite the fact the entire 1st Cavalry Division was based at An Khe, the base's only permanent inhabitants were an administrative echelon and perhaps a couple of skeleton battalions that were rotating through for security duty, referred to as "manning the barrier" or "operating the green line."

Sam was processed in on the afternoon of July 21st, 1966. It was a laborious procedure, taking several hours. After that he was sent to the headquarters of the 2nd Battalion, 12th Cavalry located in the west north-west sector of the camp. He reported in to Lieutenant Colonel Otis Lynn, his battalion commander. Lynn was an experienced and highly thought of soldier who enjoyed singular respect and admiration among the troops. He was seen as something of a father-figure—the kind of person who was there to look after them. In addition, Lynn was widely regarded as possessing one of the most astute tactical brains in the division, specifically with respect to his grasp of guerilla warfare and knowledge of the enemy.

Lynn informed Sam he would be assigned to Bravo Company as its commanding officer. Despite having the same unfathomable consequences, this way of being told one's assignment didn't have quite the same random quality as the procedure for assigning the enlisted man, who was unceremoniously handed a ticket, scrawled with the letter A, B, C or D.

Afforded scant opportunity to engage in any pleasantries with the battalion staff, let alone unpack his gear, Sam hopped on a jeep and was whisked off to join his company. Bravo Company was manning the green line along a five kilometer stretch of Highway 19, a few miles west of An Khe. The term "highway" should be taken advisedly, as it applied rather loosely to a dusty strip of road that would have passed for little more than a country trail in the United States. Nevertheless, it had to withstand continuous daily pounding from both military and local traffic.

On that hot afternoon, Sam was about to join a company of men—the nucleus of which had been put through the wringer, both physically and mentally. Two months earlier, almost to the day, the men of Bravo Company found themselves in a nightmare position. Their numbers had already been depleted to 85 from almost twice that number by the scourge of malaria (largely the result of negligent leadership that had failed to insure the properly supervised taking of malaria pills and the use of other precautions). They were cut off at the top of a treacherous hill of mushy-red ooze, enveloped by rain clouds and an enemy that hopelessly outnumbered them. The enemy seemed to be in a drug-induced state of euphoria, making it seem like wave after wave of crazed dogs were coming at them, hurling potato-masher grenades.

A veritable scene from hell was approaching its catastrophic climax. The enemy was in the throes of implementing a "scorpion's claw" whereby they'd managed to maneuver a large number of their troops to Bravo Company's rear, sealing them off. They were in the process of drawing up the tail to impart its final, deadly sting. Had it not been for the dogged resistance of a few apparently doomed men, exemplified by Sergeant Jimmy G. Stewart, who was posthumously awarded the Congressional Medal of Honor for his monumental courage, and the timely arrival of a platoon from Alpha Company led by Lieutenant David Porreca, the company would, in all probability, have been wiped out. As it was, over 50 percent of the men who went up the hill were either killed or wounded. Consequently, those who came back down considered themselves seasoned veterans and had acquired a deep-rooted cynical contempt for the leadership capabilities and tactical competence of their junior officers, Lieutenant Porreca excepted. The operation had been named, appropriately, "Crazy Horse."

Meanwhile, the food the men had been receiving in the field throughout this period and right up to the 21st of July had been long range patrol rations. This dealt yet another blow to the company's morale, which had been hanging by a thread for some time. In fact, one of the men's mothers had written a vociferous letter of complaint to President Johnson about the situation. This was relayed through channels to the company commander who was furious with the soldier for his *disloyalty*. Feelings of alienation and distrust were further compounded when the same commanding officer threatened that he would personally see to it the next person who succumbed to malaria was court-martialed. The very next day, as if poetically scripted, a chopper arrived to medevac the malaria-stricken company commander himself.

When the company finally returned to An Khe, a memorial service was held for those who had died during Operation Crazy Horse. The battalion chaplain, who had been at base camp throughout, struggling to make sense out of what had happened, fell back on the brittle proclamation that this was the way it had to be; they were fighting for God and this was God's will. The transparently hollow pronouncement provided about as much comfort as a cocktail umbrella in a monsoon and simply triggered a chorus of derisive laughter.

Since the middle of May there had been a near-continuous rotation of personnel as the veterans of the 1st Cav's first year in Vietnam returned home to the United States to be replaced by an influx of mostly inexperienced troops and officers straight out of Officer Candidate School (OCS). The prevailing sentiment of those who remained after Crazy Horse was summed up by one of the platoon sergeants. "Shit," he said. "A new company commander, [he meant Sam, of course] and everybody is new, and nobody knows shit!"

The way John Turnbull, a PFC who'd joined the company at the tail-end of Crazy Horse, saw it—"The majority of the people who had gone through that operation and survived were more or less wasted. And everybody else was new and disoriented. A leadership vacuum had been created and it had reached the point where it was every man for himself." Sitting on Highway 19 that afternoon when the new commanding officer (CO) arrived, Turnbull wondered to himself, 'What the hell kind of outfit have I gotten into?'

One of the first to fix a startled gaze on the somewhat incongruous spectacle of Captain Samuel R. Bird standing ramrod straight beside the jeep he'd just dismounted, resplendent in crisply starched fatigues and gleaming toe caps that refused to acknowledge the layer of dust settling on them, was Lieutenant

Brien Thomas Collins. B.T., as he liked to be known, was the Artillery Forward Observer (FO). He had been "on loan" to the company for the past seven months. His attire, demeanor and bearing were the faithful antithesis of the new company commander's. Collins, a brash, irreverent, flame-haired Irishman from New York City was accustomed to playing by his own rules. As the FO, he was unfettered from the responsibility of men under his command and free to conduct his own private war. An overall field competence and quick wit, combined with roguish charm and oratorical bluster enabled him to pursue his lust for action with scant interference from senior officers. He was a true maverick who should've come with a government health warning stamped on his fatigues. For B.T., like Sam, the war in Vietnam proved irresistible.

Yet as B.T. made his way down the dusty road, even he was somewhat battle-weary and jaded by seven months of intensive combat. He was, however, plucked out of his stupor by the paradox of Sam standing before him.

From his vantage point in a bunker, Vincent Dattoli, a young, keen-to-impress PFC who had arrived a couple of weeks earlier, also looked on nonplussed. Further down the line a series of wise-cracks began among the men, "Starched fatigues! Spit-shined boots! This guy is gonna buy it for sure! If he keeps on lookin' like a rose, he's gonna get bumped off, 'cause Charlie's gonna say, 'There he is! There's the man!' "

Inside the Command Post (CP) sat Joey D. Forgione, one of the senior radio telephone operators (RTO's). He was an eighteen-year-old from New York City who, at 6:00 A.M. on the second morning of Crazy Horse, had seen a buddy fall into his arms with a bullet through his forehead. After coming down off that hill, Joe figured he didn't have to take orders from anyone. He was a punk kid, straight from the streets, a self-pronounced "crazy bastard" who appeared to know the refrain to only one song and drove everybody crazy by singing, "I like to be in America, OK by me in America," over and over and over. He figured he had earned his "blood stripes" during Crazy Horse and had seen everything. And then Sam walked into the CP.

110

At first Joe froze. The sight of Sam in his creased pants terrified him. Not physically, but, "This guy just had to be going to volunteer the company for some outrageous stuff!" At the first opportunity Joe slipped out of the CP and ran across to the largest gathering of troops he could see. He could barely contain himself. "Hoally shit!"

"Whaddaya mean Joe?" came the unanimous reply.

"You gotta get a gander at this guy who just walked into the CP. General-George-Armstrong-Fuckin'-*Patton* just walked in here!"

The next hour was high comedy as 30 or 40 of the troops, like mischievous schoolboys trying to sneak a peek up their teacher's skirt, came up with one spurious excuse after another to walk by the CP tent and peer inside.

"Who is this guy? Airborne wings and Ranger too. Crazy Horse wasn't enough for these ass-holes. Now they give us John Wayne marching into town."

As afternoon began to merge with evening, Sam had all the other personnel cleared out of the CP tent and gathered his officers and senior NCO's together. Many of those present, including the executive officer, were shortly due for rotation. Among them a combination of apathy and indifference was evident. They were all bracing themselves for the I've-taken-a-good-look-around-and-I-can-see-there's-a-definite-need-for-some-licking-into-shape sermon.

They were somewhat taken aback therefore, when Sam introduced himself and began in a quietly assured voice. "Gentlemen, I understand this company has been in Vietnam almost a year, and has never had a party."

The group looked at each other sheepishly. B.T. Collins, the self-appointed spokesman for situations like this, managed with some difficulty to clear his throat and articulate a reply, "Yes Sir. That's true Sir."

The group had not fully recovered from Sam's opening remarks when Sam continued, "Gentlemen, the men are going to have a party and they are not going to pay for it. Do I make myself clear?"

"Yes Sir!" was the unanimously emphatic reply.

Sam used the remainder of the meeting to impart some general views on how he intended to fight the war and to say he was keen to hear their insights.

Following the meeting the group dispersed to their respective security positions along the highway. One of their number, an older, graying veteran of more than 20 years, a sergeant who'd won a Silver Star for Gallantry in Action during the Korean War, was getting ready to rotate back to the United States and retire from the military. He made his way over to a bunch of troops where Joe Forgione was holding court. Everyone stopped what they were saying when the sergeant broke in. "Listen up you guys. There's gonna be a party over at the EM (Enlisted Men's) Club when we get back to An Khe. Oh, and Joe?"

"Yeah?"

"This new captain?"

"Yeah?"

"You ain't got nothin' to worry about."

★   ★   ★

The following day, the company returned to An Khe where Sam gathered everybody together for a formal introduction. The composition of the 160 or so men whom he called before him was now verging on 70 percent new blood. They were uninitiated, "cherries," who had arrived at the tail-end of, or just after, Crazy Horse. Most were barely out of high school, eighteen or nineteen years of age. John Turnbull had just discovered he was going to be one of the new company commander's RTO's, along with a generously proportioned individual who went by the name of "Beefsteak" Harrison. Turnbull watched Sam with a particularly close eye. Unlike Forgione and Collins, Turnbull was a more placid, easy-going individual. Nineteen years old, tall and slim, with neutral features that seemed to perfectly mirror his personality, he was struck almost instantly by Sam's aura and stature.

"The first things that imprinted themselves were the blond, close-cropped hair, and then the piercing blue eyes that would fix on you," said Turnbull. "It was uncanny, but you found yourself completely spellbound by this fellah, almost without realizing it. There was something so natural, so unforced about him. He was articulate. He began by explaining some of his views on the conflict—that in war, you were bound to incur casualties, which was greeted by a series of jeers and cynical laughter from several guys—but it was his one major goal to get everybody home alive, and he expected everybody to take care of each other, to get the job done and to get home in one piece." After this, Turnbull looked around and saw that many of the other guys, like him, appeared spellbound, magnetized.

When the company was dismissed, someone in 2nd Platoon burst forth, "My God, somebody actually gives a shit about us!"

"We'll see," came the swift rebuttal.

The party for the "grunts" at the EM Club was a bawdy affair, with beer and "bull" in plentiful supply, though not necessarily in that order.

The next day, the *realities* of Sam's leadership style were introduced to the troops. A strict regimen of weapons and fitness training was kicked off with a seven-mile run to a swimming hole in full combat gear. This provoked a small chorus of *mild, discontented inquiry.*

This feeling was especially prevalent among a few men who had been in the field for some time. The feeling was further incited by Sam's insistence on singing "Airborne" songs en route.

Max Hanning was the platoon sergeant of 2nd Platoon. He had seen combat in three wars. The Army had a special dispensation exempting anyone over the age of forty from having to endure a physical training regimen. Hanning emerged from his tent dressed in full combat gear. "If the captain's gonna do it, then I can do it."

Some men fell out along the way but Hanning made it. It nearly killed him, but he made it.

The company spent the rest of the day swimming, relaxing and washing their fatigues. Then they marched the seven miles back to base camp.

Seeing that his senior RTO didn't exactly have the air of a contented man, Sam called out to him, "Specialist Forgione, what's the matter?"

"Sir, you got us running around with Airborne songs and 'All the Way' and I don't like it! We're in Vietnam, not Fort Bragg and I can't see no reason why we have to do this crap!"

Sam looked at Joe and smiled, "Most of the company are new, and *esprit de corps* is an important thing. And maybe if they feel as though they're the meanest muthas around, then maybe, just maybe, they won't feel crushed as soon as something happens."

This did little to convince Joe, who hadn't quite finished, "And another thing. I don't see the point of taking a shower. Now, where are we? Gimmee a break!"

Sam smiled once again, stating quietly to his senior RTO, "You will, while you're with me," and walked off in the direction of his hootch.

Sam had a couple of weeks before the company was scheduled out on another operation, giving him the luxury of a honeymoon to get his own feet on the ground as well as those of his troops. During this grace period, he learned that the replacement for his outgoing executive officer (XO) would be Lieutenant Porreca, one of those responsible for averting a mass slaughter in the area known as Happy Valley. Porreca was arguably the best fighting man in the battalion. He possessed the rare combination of exuberance and thoughtful, creative intelligence. His dominant feature was an unquenchable fire that burned in his eyes. Sam had been granted a massive boost.

Like the rest of the company, Porreca watched Sam closely over the next few days. He'd seen many commanders come in, and as he put it, "exaggerate their prerogative," by throwing their weight around and trying to assert themselves in laughable displays of machismo. He saw how Sam solicited everyone's opinion on how things were done, how he sought out those with experience and tapped it. He asked the privates and specialists what they thought could be done to improve conditions. This period of grace gave Sam the time to ask questions and the opportunity to lay the foundation for a bonding process. The little

morale builders he instigated had not existed before. A cohesive-
ness began to build, almost imperceptively, during those early
days.

For John Turnbull, who remembered the state of the company
on Highway 19, it was a shot in the arm. 'This guy's gonna do
some good for us,' he thought to himself.

But of course there remained a large question mark looming
over Sam's command and everybody knew it. This was all
window dressing compared to the realities of a combat situation.
Only then would Sam have any substance.

Chapter Seven

The Chu Pongs

August 2, 1966
Commencement of Operation Paul Revere II

Bravo Company was airlifted out of An Khe with the rest of the battalion on an overcast Tuesday evening. The short flight to the airstrip at Pleiku in C-130's was marginally more comfortable than it had been in the Caribou. Darkness had fallen when they reached the airfield. A fleet of trucks was waiting to take them the short journey to an open field next to a large ARVN (Army of the Republic of South Vietnam) encampment. That night they were to form part of the battalion perimeter alongside a lake several miles south of the airstrip.

Barely had everybody taken out entrenching tools to begin digging foxholes when the rains began. Pounding, pummeling, sheeting rains soon transformed the dusty bowl of red, powder dirt into a thick, gritty, cloying stew. For most it was their first experience of trying to sleep during a monsoon, a tortured night of futile adjustments and wistful thoughts of home. The rains continued unabated until noon the following day.

The near-continuous foul weather prevented all flights, save a few essential resupply missions, from taking off through the rest of the week that followed. Thus Sam was granted precious extra time for familiarization and training with his largely untried unit, culminating on Sunday with a trek across to another open field to enable the men to discharge their weapons and pent-up frustrations simultaneously. During the drill, Sam received word that a quartermaster bath unit was in the area.

Now, deep down to the very core of his being, Sam Bird was a committed Christian who read his *Bible* every day as a primary source of inner strength. Few of the company were aware of this because he never foisted these views upon them. However, when it came to cleanliness and even the slightest opportunity for a shower, his evangelical fervor could match that of any rabid preacher.

Forgione, seeing the glint in Sam's eye upon hearing the news, made a profane attempt to avert the inevitable, "What's this rain if it isn't showers? Look sir; now where are we? I mean, I can hardly drink the shit!"

The unequivocal reply came wrapped in soothing tones. "Specialist Forgione."

"Yes Sir?"

"Go take a shower."

"Yes Sir."

On Monday, August 8th, a window of blue sky penetrated the murky shroud long enough to allow B Co (Company) to be air-assaulted out (transported by helicopter to a potentially hostile area) in a 25 ship armada of Hueys (HU-1D helicopters) down to an old French airstrip about 60 miles southwest of Pleiku, near the Cambodian border. The cool blast of air that blew through the choppers came as a welcome relief from the oppressive blanket of humidity that had them sweltering on the ground. Most of the men weren't aware of the armada's slow, raking turn to the west. The company was being diverted in midair to the aid of A Co, 1st/7th, which had been ambushed by an estimated Vietcong (VC) battalion somewhere in the lower reaches of the Chu Pong Massif, a range of mountainous high ground set against the Cambodian border a couple of miles to the south of the Ia Drang River. The entire area was bursting with dense, virgin forest, jungle foliage and razor-sharp wild elephant grass, which grew as high as 20 feet in places as it embroidered the lower reaches of the barren outcrops.

The armada of helicopters soared over the steaming green blanket to a clearing in the trees where large plumes of smoke belched skyward from an almighty barrage of friendly artillery fire which had just begun to pepper its mark.

The helicopters skirted the area by circling to the south. They put down about two kilometers from where the bulk of the action appeared to be taking place.

On disembarking from the choppers, the company formed up quickly with 2nd Platoon "up" (at the head) and Headquarters (the five or six man company nerve center) hovering around the middle of the line for the short yet grueling hump through the thick jungle and suffocating humidity, which was 10 times worse for those who had just arrived in country. Private First Class Gary Davis took the point (lead position) for 2nd Platoon. A compact, stocky youth with close-cropped blond hair, he was fresh out of Airborne School and primed for action. For Gary, volunteering for the point was the clearest possible expression of his machismo. Others thought it crass stupidity, verging on the insane. Taking the point was like the pimple on the tip of your nose; you were nearly always the first one to get popped. As he moved, he felt the adrenalin pumping freely and every sense tuned to the last hair. For those like Gary, it was the ultimate high and in a strange way made them feel more in control of their destiny.

The A Co point man didn't see Gary approaching. Careful not to make any erratic movements that might provoke the man behind him into a frenzied burst of automatic fire, Gary halted the company and waited. Finally, the man recognized Gary as an American soldier. The moment of uncertainty over, the members of A Co filed past without a word, wearing vacant, expressionless faces. This struck Gary as a trifle weird, but he wasn't immediately concerned by it, being more relieved by the fact that now he had a cleared path ahead of him.

About two hundred yards further along the trail, Gary came to a clearing with an open field. He stopped abruptly and crouched down, halting the company once more. In the middle of the field lay what appeared to be a deserted machine gun bunker. The 2nd Platoon leader, a lieutenant, made his way forward to where Gary was crouched and ordered him to go and recon the bunker while the rest of the company stayed put. This quickly relieved Gary of any residual macho glow he might still have. As he set out on the loneliest journey of his life, everything that could pucker, puckered and everything else shriveled. His mouth went completely dry. Crossing the rice-paddy, up to his knees in mud, he was totally exposed, at the mercy of a sniper or anything. He was just waiting for something to hit him smack between the eyes.

After an eternity, he approached the bunker, peered over the lip and saw it was empty except for some discarded ammo boxes and shell and cartridge casings.

Meanwhile, Headquarters Platoon emerged from the tree line and Sam immediately took the 2nd Platoon leader to one side. Once they were out of earshot of the main body of troops, Sam reprimanded the lieutenant sternly for putting his man's life needlessly on the line.

Nothing could have adequately prepared Gary Davis for the sight that met his eyes when he raised his head out of the bunker and looked in the direction of the tree line on the other side of the clearing. As he lowered his gaze to the ground, 40 yards or so in front of him, there they were. It was a couple of seconds before he grasped what this symmetrical olive-green mass actually was. Its neatness seemed to ascribe an extra dimension of obscenity to the spectacle. Uniformly laid out in rows, partially covered by ponchos billowing in the gentle breeze, lay the remains of 25 American servicemen who had been walking through a ravine, straight into the path of strategically placed heavy machine gun fire.

One group of young soldiers walked tentatively over to participate in this grim peep-show. The gentle breeze acted like a bizarre shutter mechanism, permitting five to ten second glimpses—a *generous* allowance of time for reflection. A poncho blew open to reveal the head of one soldier. The three young men standing in closest proximity trained their gaze on the single bullet hole neatly bored through the middle of the forehead. It took a couple of seconds for them to realize the whole top portion of the head had been blown off, leaving something that more closely resembled a smashed egg shell. It was too much to take in but the reality became even harsher, comprising half-bodies and hideously misshapen figures with demented expressions. The black secret was out.

"My God, these are GI's, just like me."

American GI bodies that, just like them, had been laughing, joking and breathing a mere two hours earlier. Yet, like those poor, wretched souls, they could not turn back the clock. The maidenheads of their youthful invincibility had been forever broken.

Young Vincent Dattoli and his friend, Geronimo Belamide, were spared the grim revelation. A platoon sergeant positioned them in the woods well away from the pile of bodies in the clearing. However, the sickly-sweet aroma of death was not long in reaching them.

The order came down for the company to set up a perimeter and remain in the area until morning. It was going to be a long night. The surrounding area was filled with every possible sign of a large NVA presence. Sam sent out patrols to try to pick up any wounded stragglers or remnants of the VC battalion.

On top of a small rise, overlooking the clearing, one of the patrols came across a North Vietnamese soldier slumped over a 51 caliber machine gun, his wrists manacled to the stock. A little further back down the trail leading to the machine gun position, the squad spotted half a dozen freshly dug, shallow graves, some still awaiting their occupants. Such discoveries merely served to drive home the point that Sam was at pains to impart. If anyone had been deluding himself with the notion they were dealing with a poorly-motivated bunch of incompetents, then what had happened that day should give him grim cause to reconsider. The enemy battle-plan had been excellent and the cross-fires had been astutely aligned.

Few slept easily that night. Swirling mists descended to envelop the company and globules of water built up on the leaves in the trees surrounding the clearing. Fully-laden, they dripped from tip to branch below, producing a rhythmic incessant beat. The aura of the enemy filled the air around them in this grave-yard, alongside fresh ghosts in their own image.

As the night wore on slowly, the patrols began to return. Their haul was some half-dozen wounded VC, some barely alive, who were set down with their arms tied taut at the elbow behind logs with trip wire. The result—their arms were nearly severed as the wire sliced clean through to the bone. The reasoning behind this apparent barbarism was to make sure these men would never again be capable of using a gun.

A few of the troops wandered over to the tethered prisoners. Like a shaken pop bottle, they could feel hate bubbling up inside them.

While many of his men wrestled with these emotions for the first time, Sam tried to articulate his own feelings to his parents in a taped message home.

"Something I wondered about before coming over here. How, as a combat infantryman, I would actually feel, being on the battlefield, as far as seeing other people killed and so forth. Fortunately, B Co losses have been nil to date. The losses that I have seen though, have really hit hard. To see American soldiers—young boys eighteen, nineteen, twenty years old that become casualties, in addition to the older NCO's and officers. But as far as the VC are concerned, it doesn't take long at all to build up quite a hatred for them. They're dirty. Their tactics are certainly by the book but they are quite ruthless, and it hasn't bothered me one bit to see them cut down with hot steel and hot lead. It might sound a little cruel or brutal, but it doesn't take long to realize that the chips are down over here. I don't mean to sound scary or anything. I just thought I'd mention it as something you might want to know, or wonder what was on my mind."

The damp, clammy stillness of dawn was shattered by the rhythmic thump of approaching rotor blades. The choppers landed in the clearing and the bodies of the dead GI's and wounded Vietnamese prisoners were loaded aboard for evacuation.

Later that morning, B Co was air-assaulted to the southwest where they were deposited at the head of a river valley between the mountains and the border. From there they headed north on foot, hugging the base of the mountains—first to their east and then snaking westward across a muddy tapioca field before heading to the north once again, along a river valley that drew them back into the bosom of the mountains. They hugged the base of the hill again and followed it around to the west. By nightfall they'd reached another narrow valley facing the Cambodian border, with two steep-sided mountains on either side. Here they were to dig in and act as the "cork in the bottle," sealing off the border. Other elements of the battalion would flush any remaining VC toward them.

They prepared their positions that evening on the side of the hill to the south, which gave them "ring side seats," as Sam put it, for the American fireworks display that followed on the hillside some two kilometers or so across from their position to the east. First came the pounding of over one thousand rounds of artillery (literally worth fifty dollars per round). And for the finale, F-4 Phantoms screamed in low overhead from the west and lit up the mountainside, disgorging a series of spectacular exploding fireballs. To some of the troops it resembled the climax of a Fourth of July celebration. In fact, B Co was so close to the maelstrom of fury that shell casings rained from the sky like confetti and landed around them.

The assault from the enemy never came and the company moved out on foot to the north, into the heart of the Chu Pongs, toward the Ia Drang River, to begin what would become referred to as "the dreaded days." With everybody loaded down with gear, the company began its ascent. First they traveled through thick elephant grasslands at the base of the mountain valley and then up the Razorback, through layer upon layer of thick vegetation and creeping vines. They clawed their way up past rushing rivulets and roaring torrents that temporarily drowned out the mocking of the monkeys and the buzz and hum of the bugs giving minute stabs and bites to the troops. The torrents of water only intensified the strangle-hold wrought by the suffocating heat and humidity. It was like being trapped inside a tea kettle with somebody holding a hand over the spout.

When they reached the top, gathering black monsoon clouds drew in their oppressive pall, but not enough to conceal the opposite side of the valley, maybe only half a mile across as the crow flew. But they weren't crows, so it was down once more and up the other side.

Then there were the leeches—some no bigger than a pin head—that would attach themselves to exposed arms and chests. Others inched their way toward the soldiers along the ground and crawled up around their boot tops and lower legs. They were always just a split-second too slow to brush the leeches off before they sank their teeth through the skin and embedded their heads. Sucking voraciously on the blood, they would inflate like balloons. If the soldier tried to rip them off, a portion of their jaws and head would be left under the skin. This would turn that part of the body into a septic mass of jungle rot. The only way to be rid of them was to burn them off with a cigarette or squirt them with bug repellent.

Now, there are some areas of the body you wouldn't want to touch with the hot end of a cigarette, as an unfortunate sergeant in 3rd Platoon was to discover as he made his way down into a flat, marshy expanse. His relief upon reaching level ground was short-lived. One of the more tenacious of the offenders had managed to crawl inside the most tender part of his anatomy. The man was beside himself. Nightmarish screams of agony echoed through the valley as a medic rushed to his aid. But he found that the stubborn critter was already too far embedded, beyond the scope of any bug repellent. When they radioed for medevac, someone at battalion HQ suggested they might try applying a tourniquet. Those unable to restrain themselves from exploding with laughter rushed away from the hapless, stricken man whose grisly screams continued unabated. Fortunately for the poor soul, the flat marshy ground they'd reached proved suitable for a medevac and the bizarre half hour was brought to an end.

If leeches and other forms of insect life didn't get you, the insidious effects of the monsoon did—either from the incessant, pounding rains or the constant perspiration brought on by suffocating humidity. The wetness made it impossible to determine what was water and what was sweat.

In the gathering gloom, the company established camp for the night: digging their three-man foxholes, setting up their hootches, using their ponchos and inflating their air mattresses. They set up trip flares, claymores and lines of fire. After digging his own foxhole, Sam went round to check some positions and take the opportunity to get to know something about each of his men. This left him little time to write letters home. He explained to his parents in the following tape recording:

"I apologize for not writing more often, but I feel that if I could just check one more hole, send a couple more patrols out, check on an ambush, check out reports or check over procedures—just constantly overseeing things and supervising things a little closer. This just might be the one thing that's going to save someone or going to get a man out of a tough jam if we get attacked."

Sam eventually returned to the hootch he shared with David Porreca and B.T. Collins. Throughout this operation he leaned heavily on the experience of these two men. This contributed greatly to the minuscule number of casualties sustained by the company. Also, the VC had either disappeared back over the Cambodian border or had split up into small bands, making them increasingly difficult to ferret out.

Porreca and Collins probably wished they could've slipped away over the border too. All they could do though, was try to get as far away from Sam as possible. If they didn't, he'd all but asphyxiate them with a full can of bug spray. According to Sam, this was the only way he could be sure of protecting himself sufficiently against the chance of contracting malaria. B.T. felt it probably had more to do with the fact that the insect repellent was manufactured in Neodesha, Kansas. Whatever the reason, they invariably went to sleep coughing and spluttering.

In the morning they would often awake to the grating, rasping sound of Sam shaving without any water. Yet despite his incredible fastidiousness, he never once lectured Collins or Porreca about their appearance.

The rugged terrain of the Chu Pongs meant that a suitable landing zone (LZ) couldn't always be found for hot chow to be flown in, but Sam tried to insure that B Co was in position at least once a day so choppers could reach them for that purpose alone. However, this didn't guarantee the quality of the food. By the time the company had made it into the third week of the operation, the food had plummeted to such culinary depths that eggs arrived still half-powdered at the bottom of the can. It was fast reaching the point where everybody would prefer to settle for C-rations.

One evening after yet another exasperating day of fruitless search for an elusive enemy, the company pitched camp on an area of solid low ground ideally suited for an LZ so hot chow could be flown in. Unfortunately, the coffee cake that arrived was of like consistence and could probably have supported a dozen helicopters by itself.

This was Sam's final straw. While the troops formed a line to receive their evening meal, Sam grabbed the radio telephone from Joe Forgione and patched himself directly through to the battalion commander. "Sir, you and the supply officer need to come out and taste the food, because this rifle company is not taking one step further until you do."

Everybody within earshot just stood for a second, mouths agape and dumbfounded. Some thought the company would really be in for it now.

No more than a quarter of an hour had passed when the Charlie-Charlie ship set down adjacent to those who were still standing in line. Out hopped the colonel accompanied by the S-4 logistics officer. Sam took them to the front of the chow line where they stayed and ate the meal. Meanwhile, everybody else stood there, egging Sam on—quietly!

The following day, and subsequently thereafter, full course meals were flown out regularly. The troops were beginning to get the feeling from his overall field competence and fatherly concern for their welfare that Sam possessed what was described by one of the platoon leaders as the "will" for their survival.

★　　★　　★

From this area of low ground, the company headed to the north again. They were faced with a particularly steep and arduous climb through rolling wooded terrain that veered sharply upward.

They set out in two columns, with Sam and HQ Platoon in the center. Once again they began their ascent by negotiating a swathe of tall elephant grass. As the pace began to accelerate, so did the swearing and grumbling.

Everyone was loaded down with gear and young Vincent Dattoli's keenness to impress was wearing off rapidly. When Riley Palmer, who'd just returned from the hospital for malaria treatment, asked him to carry one of his bags of M-79 grenades, Dattoli refused with uncharacteristic petulance. Gary Davis, who was walking just ahead of them, was totally exhausted and felt as though he could barely move.

Minutes later Sam came by. He looked at Gary, and said in a soft voice, "Hey, only another five K's, let's go."

Gary looked at Sam incredulously. He appeared just as fresh as could be, while Gary was dripping with perspiration.

"Would you like me to carry anything?" Sam inquired.

Gary straightened up, racked his chin back and puffed out his chest. "No Sir! Airborne Sir!"

Sam carried on ahead of him for about five yards, looked back for the last time and said, "All the way."

Meanwhile, Vincent Dattoli took the bag of grenades out of his comrade's hands and slung them over his shoulder.

As the company slogged through the jungle on these arduous treks, Sam would continually move up and down the column from front to back.

The lead platoon took the opportunity for a five minute breather. When they looked up, there was Sam, marching up the hill toward them. "How's it going men? Boy, it's hot isn't it?"

Each looked at one another and their fatigues, drenched with perspiration and then looked at Sam. Hot? He wasn't even sweating, or so it appeared. It was a mystery to everyone how he sustained himself. What special secrets did Sam possess that enabled him to conceal the pain he had to be in?

As the company made its way through a densely wooded stretch to yet another mountain outreach, they were joined by a pint-sized, French free-lance photographer. Her piercing eyes, gaunt features and flaxen locks in one long, single plait down her back presented a striking contradiction to the ludicrous sight of her size four feet swimming in size six combat boots. She was accompanied by a reporter from the Associated Press. CBS and *Time* magazine had commissioned the reporter to do a story on Sam linked to the Kennedy funeral.

Cathy Leroy's diminutive stature belied the pugnacious voracity with which she pursued her quarry. Clever, wiry and independent-minded to the point of occasional hostility, she didn't exhibit the kind of qualities or the (physical) quantities which would endear her to the American GI. In addition, she was carrying the lingering odor of someone who had not bathed in some considerable time.

Still, this was the first "round eye" the men of B Co had seen in months. Sam was courteous without being congenial, responding to her provocative line of questioning with liberal doses of "Yes Ma'am," and, "No Ma'am."

Following an afternoon of preliminary probing, she disappeared for a couple of days and then rejoined the company just as they were making camp for the night on a barren stretch of high ground randomly strewn with large boulders and lined by a few odd-looking silver and black trees.

This time it was as if she'd gathered herself for an all-out assault, attempting to exploit every aspect of her sexuality. In some ways it was like witnessing the mating dance of the black widow as she stalked Sam from every angle.

Sam meanwhile, was becoming increasingly uncomfortable. He was aware of the disruptive effect her presence was having on the troops. Her apparent economy of sex appeal had failed to prevent a group of his men huddling on the bank of a river to watch her remove her shirt before bathing.

Sam wasn't comfortable with the responsibility for a woman's safety in the field. His own experience with women had been extremely limited and had never included anyone like this aggressive French woman. The reality was, however, that he was a very attractive man—tall and distinguished with an aura that exuded confidence without ever appearing arrogant or threatening. An intoxicating combination for anyone, even a prickly French woman. Characteristically, Sam fell back on his instincts and deflected suggestive remarks from his men with Straight-Arrow neutrality.

Cathy Leroy spent the night in a hootch with the battalion chaplain (a questionable choice given future events), one of the medics and a soldier who had been allotted the name, Virgin Mary, because of his known inexperience with women.

The following morning as she was departing the company area, B.T. Collins stopped Cathy Leroy briefly and asked her whether any of the pictures she'd taken of Sam would be published.

"*Si seulement il est tué.*"

"Huh?"

"Only if he's killed," she replied curtly.

The May 1967 issue of *Life* magazine, some nine months later, contained a celebrated sequence of photographs that recorded the death of a Marine and the accompanying anguish of a medical corpsman. The photographer was Cathy Leroy.

August 24th saw the end of Operation Paul Revere II. Despite covering great expanses of ground, B Co had engaged in only minor skirmishes with the enemy and taken just a handful of prisoners. Sam lost two men during the operation; one was killed in action and the other wounded by incoming artillery.

That morning the company was flown back to Pleiku where they loaded into open-top, two-and-a-half-ton trucks for the bumpy ride back to An Khe. At several points along the route, the trucks were besieged by hordes of children with tiny, bony arms outstretched for GI's C-rations or candy. The conversations in the trucks centered largely on expectations governing upcoming visits to "Sin City," and "Boom-Boom!" in the town of An Khe, punctuated by more than a little laughter as exaggerated claim followed exaggerated claim as to each man's stallion-like libido.

After the company had returned to base camp that evening, most of the men took showers and cleaned up before wandering over to the mess tent to partake of their first full course meal with silverware for nearly a month. Once inside they were informed that because they had arrived back late, their salads had been given to Headquarters Company, the supporting rear echelon. The salad could scarcely have been termed a culinary delicacy, consisting, for the most part, of ground-up cabbage from Okinawa. But to guys who had just returned from the field it was a big deal.

Sam was sitting inside his tent, along with B.T. and Dave Porreca when he was informed of the salad expropriation. Without saying a word, he got up and marched out of the tent. B.T. picked up the look in Sam's eye and thought it might be prudent if he and Porreca followed Sam down to the mess tent where all the majors and big-bellied sergeants of the rear echelon were finishing off their meals. Sam strode into the tent and went straight over to the "old and bold" senior mess sergeant, who was sitting in the corner with some friends. The tent fell silent when Sam addressed the sergeant, "I understand that B Company did not get its salad."

"Well Sir, you didn't get here in time, so we gave it to HQ Company," the sergeant replied with an air of casual indifference that stemmed from years of putting junior officers in their place.

The exploding ferment within Sam rose and channeled itself directly into a look that bored through the sergeant's brazen assurance like a white-hot, iron rod. "If this ever happens again, you know what the consequences will be, don't you, Sergeant?"

Looking back into Sam's eyes, the sergeant saw the whole of Bravo Company in their fire. "Yes Sir!" he replied, as if someone were holding a blowtorch to his most delicate parts.

Sam turned about sharply and strode out of the tent.

Later that evening, when Lieutenant Colonel Lynn received word that Sam had simmered down, he informed Sam he'd been recommended for the Bronze Star for Meritorious Achievement in recognition of his overall field competence during Paul Revere II.

The following morning Sam gathered the entire company together on the dirt road that ran between their tents. He began by talking about how tough the infantryman's job was, and how proud he was of them, how they should always look out for one another. Then he had his 1st sergeant bring out a white shoe-box. Inside were a bunch of slender, rectangular blue badges embossed with a long silver rifle and laurel wreath, the Combat Infantryman's Badge (CIB). Officially, it signified they had served more than 30 days in combat. But more than that, it signified a passage—their coming of age as warriors. (The normal procedure would have been for those eligible to collect the slip of paper confirming their authorization, take it to the PX and purchase one.) To John Turnbull and those like him, this was a high-water mark they wouldn't have traded for anything else in the world.

For B.T. Collins, the presentation generated mixed emotions. His official title as an artilleryman meant he was ineligible. Yet, as everyone in the company knew and had come to appreciate, he'd been out there with them, putting his life on the line every day. As far as they were concerned, he was infantry all the way. Afterwards, Sam took up the issue with Battalion HQ as something of a cause celebre. He was informed, categorically, that B.T. was not entitled. Sam left the tent smoldering, but there was little he could do about the matter—or so it seemed.

Nonetheless, it was clear that a very serious mutual respect had begun to permeate not only the officers, but the entire company. All you had to do to be a part of that body of respect was do your job and do it to the best of your ability.

Chapter Eight

Bong Son

The two-and-a-half-week hiatus at base camp gave everyone a chance to rest and release tension. Sam, however, continued to enforce a strict regimen of training and weapons inspections during the day. He insisted the company maintain its discipline and preparedness at An Khe by studying tactics, reading maps and using the radio to co-ordinate direct fire support.

One morning he felt the company didn't fall out from formation smartly enough, so he had the first sergeant call everyone back to repeat the procedure, again and again. This was greeted by a series of groans from the troops—not altogether surprising, since they could generally be expected to moan about most things. However, it also drew an irksome response from most of the senior NCO's, a delegation of whom approached B.T. to ask what had gotten into the "old man." Collins, whose complexion had assumed something of an ashen pallor, was looking a little drawn. He explained to them that earlier in the morning, he and Sam had walked into the battalion chaplain's tent and caught him reading a copy of *Playboy*, which he had poorly concealed behind an edition of *Life* magazine. Sam turned to B.T. with a look resembling the one directed at the unfortunate mess sergeant, "I think we need to take the chaplain on a training run to help burn off some of his excess energy."

Collins, who hadn't returned to his hootch until four o'clock that morning, had little choice in the matter, but then, neither did the poor hypocritical chaplain.

133

Returning to base camp after a full seven miles, B.T. was exhausted but was never going to show it in front of the chaplain, who, verging on a state of delirium, was in no condition to notice anyway. If he wasn't hallucinating by then, he certainly was when they reached the entrance to the Bravo Company area. Situated to the right of the drainage ditch on the right side of the dirt road, almost directly opposite Sam's tent on the left, loomed a six foot by four foot, bright-yellow rectangular sign. It was nailed onto two sturdy posts which had been firmly driven into the ground. Emblazoned on it for all to see was the painted caricature of a GI resembling Godzilla in combat fatigues, toting an M-16 and proclaiming the identity of those therein; *"BRAVO: Though we walk through the valley of death, we will fear no evil. 'Cause we're the Meanest Muthas in the valley."* Of that, the battalion chaplain was clearly in no doubt.

Toward the end of Paul Revere II, two men arrived who would play an integral role in B Co's development as a unit. Sam narrated brief descriptions of each man on a tape recording he sent home:

"Let me tell you about my first sergeant. His name is Bost. Came in from Fort Jackson, South Carolina where he had been the first sergeant of a basic training company, a soldier who has been in the Army for 20 or more years. He's kind of the 'old school' type. The kind of first sergeant that is caricatured in comic books. A gruff type—in a way. He's a rugged, big bear of a man: six feet, four inches and 250 pounds. Every bit the soldier. He's been a tremendous help, both in helping me personally and squaring away a number of problems. The knowledge that he has acquired over the last twenty years has proved invaluable. I would say that he is just about my best asset in the company.

"My 4th Platoon leader caught malaria about the second week in the field. He was replaced by 2nd Lieutenant Dean Parker, a boyish-looking twenty-one-year-old who came over from Fort Benning, where he had just completed the mortar course. He appears competent, industrious and appears to know his job well.

"As for my 2nd Platoon leader, I didn't think he was cutting it. So, unfortunately for him, and I think, fortunately for the company, I relieved him and he was re-assigned to a desk job with the rear echelon."

Two weeks of relative inactivity passed swiftly and Sam was alerted to prepare for the company's next operation. They were due to fly out of base camp on Monday, September 12th, to an area about 50 miles east of An Khe known as Bong Son. The Central Bong Son Plain comprised a densely populated area of adjoining river deltas surrounded by high ground on three sides and bisected by the main north-south artery of Highway 1. Sam wrote to his parents just before the company's departure.

The area might present some problems, such as the steep hills and the mountainous terrain in some parts and the coastal, sand-dune type in others. It gets very hot. I think the temperature gets up as high as 120 degrees, so this is certainly going to require us to be in tip-top physical shape, in order to be able to operate effectively up there.

The other thing that's going to be difficult, is knowing the "good guys" from the "bad guys." When we were around the Chu Pong Mountains and the Ia Drang Valley, anyone that we saw who had a sloped head and slant eyes were Cong, PAVN or VC. The area that we are going to now is inhabited by "Friendlies," Neutral and VC. Of these, many are old ladies, old men and children. You don't know who to trust. So, in that respect, it will be difficult.

B Company was flown from An Khe to LZ English, head-quarters of the 40th ARVN Regiment. It was a large airstrip cum firebase tucked against Highway 1 as it dog-legged to the south-west through the heart of the Central Bong Son Plain.

The following day, the company was air-assaulted to the coast where they were to begin a sweep through coastal villages as a part of Operation Thayer I. They were to incorporate a procedure known as *Search and Destroy* as part of the 1st Cavalry Division's move to offensive operations in Bin Dinh Province. This was to become known, somewhat unfittingly, as the "Bin Dinh Pacification Campaign."

The geography within the Bong Son area varied dramatically. Along the South China Sea the terrain was predominantly flat, punctuated by an occasional densely forested area of undulating high ground. The villages in the area were separated from each other by open expanses of tapioca fields, rice paddies and thickets. Most of the villages contained anywhere from 25 to 50 separate hootches, or Vietnamese huts. Dotted among the hootches were small sheds used for the storing of crude farm implements and the fruits of harvest. The villages were often divided into sections by hedgerows or compacted mounds of dirt. Clusters of hootches were connected by a network of dirt paths and were usually bounded by bushes or bamboo stands.

Yet what enhanced these quaint, idyllic villages, trapped in time with their crude implements and almost medieval way of life, was the gentle sway of palms and banana trees lilting in the onshore breeze. Often the sunlight failed to penetrate the canopy of palms and thick vegetation shrouding the villages, creating an eeriness that was heightened on rainy and overcast days.

Search and Destroy meant invading these seemingly tranquil outposts of another time and place, so obviously without young men, to uncover rice or weapons caches. The entire Bong Son area formed part of a sophisticated supply network for the 22nd NVA Regiment, whose stronghold was the An Lao Valley to the west. Anything considered helpful to the enemy was destroyed. With Search and Destroy, all the incongruities and paradoxes of this "strange war," as Sam would call it, began to hit home for the first time.

Five days of Search and Destroy along a portion of some of the most idyllic coastline in the world had turned up nothing except a slew of raw blisters from interminable humping (slogging along) beneath a scorching sun. The ocean lapping against the shore beside them became a mocking taunt because they couldn't indulge in its cooling waters for fear of what might lie behind the next tree or the next water buffalo.

For almost two months now, the company hadn't come into direct contact with the enemy except for sporadic sniper fire. However, men were being lost to punji stakes, mines and incoming mortar fire. Each day, fear, tension and anxiety increased; the effect was cumulative. Would this be the day of the ambush? Every single village was conspicuous for its lack of military age young men.

The feeling of paranoia was noticeably more prevalent among the few "short-timers" who'd become so jumpy about their DEROS (end of tour) that, in some cases, they'd begun shooting at each other.

★   ★   ★

Around 1700 HRS on Saturday, September 17th, 1966, there was an uneasy feeling running through the company as they approached two women and an old man along the pathway toward yet another picture-postcard village by the sea.

It had been a hot and frustrating day. They hadn't come across a single man of military age in any of the villages they'd passed through. Everybody was on edge about the possibility of an ambush of company size.

The company was aligned in a box formation. A line formation was used when traveling through thick jungle or across narrow passes so the company could snake out at some length. But when they operated in a large open space, such as when crossing tapioca fields, they were more vulnerable in a line so they used a box formation instead. With Headquarters in the center, they were currently in a box formation moving toward the village. As the nerve center of the company, Headquarters included Sam and his two radio operators, Joe Forgione and Sam's top sergeant, Dave Bost. The FO, B.T. Collins, was never far away from Sam and Headquarters. The four platoons formed the four sides of the box, providing a protective perimeter around HQ.

When Sam reached the women and the old man on the pathway, he halted the company while Joe Forgione asked them if there were any mines in the area. All three shook their heads. A barbed wire fence appeared to signify the outskirts of the village, connecting with a hedgerow of cactus plants and other vegetation on either side. A dirt path wound its way through to an opening in the fence, where a small wooden gate had been erected between two posts, leading into the village.

Sam ordered a squad from the front edge of the box to move on ahead and conduct a reconnaissance of the village. The point man unlatched the gate, took one step forward and the ground exploded beneath his feet. Large, bloody chunks of flesh and bone flew in all directions, showering those close by. The man crumpled as everyone else hit the ground. Some 150 feet or so away, Joe Forgione yelled out, "Son-of-a-God-damned-bitch!" as he thought of the old man shaking his head when asked about mines in the area.

Sam radioed ahead for a situation-report. He was told that although the man was in a bad way, he was still alive. A couple of those close to the blast were also suffering from deafness and shock. A medevac was called in immediately. All that remained of the man's lower legs was mangled pulp, while a flying bone fragment had gouged out one of his eyeballs. Still alive, he was loaded onto the medevac chopper in a blood-soaked poncho.

Once the helicopter had taken off, Sam called in artillery to bracket the village with a salvo of about a hundred rounds. By now, night was closing in rapidly so he pulled the company back and erected a defensive perimeter before pondering what his next move should be. He didn't know what he had in the village, but whatever it was, he figured they didn't want anybody to go in there. Other factors, however, would play a part in his decision making process that evening.

This was the first occasion when most of the company had witnessed a severe injury, up close, inflicted on one of their own by the enemy. The feeling of violation escalated to feelings of frustration to exasperation to rage. A piece of commo wire leading back to the freshly vacated spider hole was all that remained to indicate the presence of the enemy.

A powerful lust for revenge fermented among the men. Sam felt the same. Others in HQ had noticed the look of disgust that came over his face once he realized one of his own had been badly hurt. He took it as a personal loss and became very stern, admonishing everyone to be extra careful. Beyond that, his own rage and anger was building up within. He radioed Battalion for three flame throwers to be air-lifted in the following morning, while brushfires of vengeance continued to ignite and spread throughout the company. They wanted to get into that village and "make 'em pay, do a trick on the place, waste anything that moved." Some weren't prepared to wait until morning, preferring instead that Sam call in the Air Force to wipe out the village with napalm. Others were for the oft-used procedure of applying their Zippo lighters to thatched roofs.

The sun rose slowly the following morning, a Sunday. At around 0800 HRS, three flame throwers arrived with breakfast. Sam meanwhile, took the time to begin a letter to his parents.

Dear Babe & Dood,

At about five o'clock last night, as we were entering another village, the VC detonated a mine and seriously wounded one of my troops. We dropped about a hundred rounds of artillery on the place and I've had several choppers work the area over with their machine guns this morning. I plan on moving into the village in about an hour and level it with my mortars and flame throwers.

After breakfast, the company began its move into the village. The flame throwers brought up the rear as part of Weapons Platoon. Each man felt tight, compressed and impatient, waiting for release. Moist palms stroked the stocks of locked and loaded M-16's, skittish looks flashed. With every tentative step, the pressure built and beads of sweat trickled down over veins that had begun to protrude on rigid necks. The electricity was tremendous, almost unbearable, as the company began filing through the gate to the village, past the crater made by the explosion the evening before. Twenty yards down the path, another mine was spotted, and then another. The tension was unbearable; something had to give.

The village came into view before them. A couple of dozen hootches, maybe more, goats grazing in a pen, some chickens and half a dozen emaciated old men crouched outside their dwellings, numb with fear. Inside one of the hootches a baby started to cry. The sound was muffled but another cry began almost immediately. Further on, a pitifully malnourished woman was sitting outside her hootch cradling her baby to her chest. The front of her pajama top was caked with dried vomit. She was staring vacantly at the ground, quivering involuntarily. Another open door revealed more ashen wisps of women and children huddled together shuddering.

Men from the lead platoon started to fan out—searching hootches, upsetting pots, cans and urns, spilling their contents on the ground.

Sam and Headquarters reached the village along with an interpreter (known as a Kit Carson Scout). Sam stopped for a moment and looked around. "Get me the village Chief," he said, a distinct edge in his voice. The interpreter hurried over to the woman cradling her baby and shouted at her in Vietnamese. She pointed to an old man crouched in his doorway.

Sam accompanied the interpreter as he headed toward the old man's hootch. The old man looked up as they approached. He seemed to be looking beyond them to the tree-line in the distance.

The interpreter dragged the old man roughly to his feet. "Ask him who planted the booby traps. Where are they now?" ordered Sam, holding his stare on the old man.

The interpreter rattled off the questions in a staccato fusillade of Vietnamese. Shaking involuntarily, the man delivered his reply. "He says the VC come through here gathering supplies, stealing their rice and kidnapping all their young men."

Sam had heard the same story a hundred times. Suddenly he grabbed the old man and shook him furiously, eyes blazing, before flinging him to the ground. His youngest lieutenant, Dean Parker, looked on in disbelief. The dam that had held fast all of Sam's life, restraining every frustration, every repressed emotion, had finally burst. A defining moment of his leadership, of his life, had arrived.

140

Women and children began rushing out of their hootches, pleading and begging, as 4th Platoon entered the village brandishing their flame throwers. The order erupted from Sam's mouth like a machine gun burst. "Get the medics over here!"

★　　★　　★

Once the villagers saw the medics attending to infected wounds, more began to emerge from their hiding places. There were people in wood piles, in every conceivable place. Even though they were probably kin to the enemy, it was simply heartbreaking to see people living like this. The soldiers began to distribute candy and C-rations.

By the end of the afternoon, the soldiers were sitting on porches, playing with the babies and chatting with the women and children, whom they had been stalking with fixed bayonets and flame throwers just a matter of hours before. Upon the company's return to their firebase that evening, Sam applied the finishing touches to his letter home.

It's about dinner time and we just returned from the village I wrote you about this morning. As we approached the village, we ran into a few more booby traps, but we were able to spot them and nobody got hurt. Early this morning, when we were moving into the village, we would have killed anything that moved. I certainly wanted to level the entire area; I think for spite if nothing else. However, by the middle of the afternoon, we were having our aid men trying to help the sick people. Most of the people were women and children and most of the kids were sick. Today was a good example of how mixed-up this war can get. Like I've said before, it often seems like a strange war in many ways.

The incident appeared to set the future tone for the company; seeing that the inhabitants of this village didn't pose a direct threat, no action was taken against them. From then on, they did what the situation called for. If it called for mass firepower and fixed bayonets, those were put into operation without hesitation. If a bottle of iodine and some compassion were needed, then those were put into effect instead. But Sam Bird was the arbiter. It was his most difficult and delicate task, and yet perhaps the most indelible mark of the quality of his leadership.

Following another 10 strained but largely uneventful days which turned up little in the way of direct contact with the enemy save the now customary sniper fire and booby traps, B Company was air-lifted back to An Khe. A couple of days at base camp and it was back to the monotony of securing a five to ten kilometer stretch of Highway 19.

While back at An Khe, Sam set down a prophetic reflection on his tape recorder.

"It's a funny kind of war; in that one minute you can be relaxing on an LZ in an assembly area and an hour later you can be flown in on a helicopter for a combat air assault and really be in the thick of things."

Highway security duty fell somewhere between combat operations and green line duty around An Khe. The task of securing a segment of the dusty strip of Highway 19 entailed posting guards on all bridges in addition to having troops secure potential ambush sites along the road. Patrols were also conducted a thousand meters or so on either side of the highway and ambushes were set up along the trails after dark. It was mundane and tedious work, but it required constant vigilance in order to avoid what happened to Sam's Citadel classmate, Dave Ragin. The monotony was relieved by trips back to base camp on short leave. Indeed, the situation would've been almost tolerable had it not been for the return of the rains, which came back with a vengeance.

Lieutenant Colonel Lynn rotated back to the United States on October 1st for a new assignment at the Pentagon. He was replaced by Lieutenant Colonel Jay Hatch. Before Lynn left, he called Sam into Battalion HQ and thanked him heartily for doing a fine job, telling him he was the best combat commander in the battalion. As Sam left the tent, Lynn turned to the battalion executive officer, Major Dan Rickard, and stated, "That man will be a general some day."

This statement echoed the opinions of many in B Company. Platoon Sergeant Max Hanning, one of the older men, saw Sam as a stern, yet fair man. He felt that everybody in the company respected "Captain Bird" since he hadn't heard a bad word spoken about him. Hanning was sure Sam was destined to become a chief of staff. For much of the company, whatever Sam did was right; it was as simple as that and they all knew it. They never saw any weakness. He never belittled them. His quiet observation gave them a sense of his towering strength and that in turn lifted their spirits greatly.

They were preparing for an air assault which Sam was charged with leading out of An Khe in mid-October. In the process of checking off last-minute details with his platoon leaders, Sam saw they needed a name for a particular map co-ordinate. John Turnbull happened to be in the vicinity. As often happens when a person is listening to a conversation he's not supposed to be a part of, Turnbull found himself blurting out his own answer involuntarily, "My home town is Las Vegas. How about naming it Las Vegas?" And then, realizing what he'd done, his heart sank. Before he had time to apologize for butting in, Sam turned around and fixed him with his penetrating blue eyes. He winked at the abject specialist and said, "Well, son-of-a-gun, that's it—Las Vegas!"

The young radio operator puffed up inside with pride. "This man actually gives a shit about what I have to say," he thought to himself.

Gary Davis had a hard time coming to terms with the idea that all the senior NCO's liked Sam. Steering clear of officers had been drummed into him by senior NCO's throughout Advanced Infantry Training and Airborne School: "They'll get you killed!"

When a medic named Doc Russell joined the company on Highway 19, he approached some members of 3rd Platoon and inquired in an off-hand kind of way, "Where's the Old Man's hootch?"

"We don't call him the Old Man around here," came the sharp rebuke. "Captain Bird's hootch is over there."

Skip Draper, a medical platoon leader, took a photograph of Sam on the highway one morning around breakfast time. It was the definitive picture of Sam Bird the soldier—showing the olive-green jungle sweater unbuttoned to the top of his chest; the close-cropped, sandy hair; and the strong, sinewy neck beneath an immaculately-shaved face. You are held by his gentle, reassuring gaze. There is a softness and kindness that is somehow accentuated by a backdrop of morning-blue sky, flecked with wispy white clouds come down to touch the tops of lush, green hills.

★   ★   ★

Following a brief diversion in the Pleiku area, the company found itself back in Bong Son by the 10th of November. Sam wrote:

It feels good to be back over near the coast again. Even though the rains are with us again. This area is quite beautiful. I have my command post set up in a little clearing with palm trees scattered all around. It's a small island of grass, surrounded by rice paddies. I can look way off into the distance and see the old waves hitting on the beach of the South China Sea. The troops have climbed most of the trees and knocked down coconuts. It's a real treat to munch on them for a change. A little north of here, it almost reminds me of Colorado. On top of a little peak, you can really see for miles. The surrounding terrain is really hilly and the recent rains have caused a lot of mountain streams and waterfalls. As I was looking down into the valley yesterday evening while the sun was going down, I just had to sit and gaze for a while. It looked so peaceful. I even forgot there was a war going on, until I saw some artillery shells hitting some hills in the distance, and then I was reminded of the war once again.

A couple of days later the company moved down from the high ground and began digging "Charlie" out of the hills. This resulted in some fierce yet protracted confrontations with small concentrations of enemy troops that had dug themselves in.

Since his rather inauspicious arrival Doc Russell hadn't exactly endeared himself to some members of 3rd Platoon in assuming duties as their medic. Most of them would have little to do with

144

him. They saw him as a slob with unsavory living habits and a generally sullen and slap-dash attitude. They concluded he didn't know his job and had, for the most part, ostracized him.

After his arrival things quieted down, but then suddenly there were fire fights breaking out everywhere. Doc Russell was all over: running around, tending to wounded and putting his life on the line everywhere he went. From that moment forward, he was accepted without question, by everyone.

Another incident occurred which illustrated the fateful and paradoxical nature of war. The company was ferreting out small enemy enclaves in the hills and valleys surrounding Bong Son. It was approaching sundown on one particular evening when the company pulled into a clearing to make camp for the night. As dusk fell, helicopters flew in with hot chow while the men finished digging their fox holes and setting their trip flares. B.T. was on the radio with Artillery HQ co-ordinating the alignment of their protective artillery fires for the night. B Company had made camp in an area close to a friendly battalion, so B.T. wanted to insure Artillery HQ didn't ignore their presence and set lines of fire according to the position of the battalion alone.

When most of the men had their fox holes rigged, they started forming a line by squad to receive their evening meal. As more and more of them finished, they began to bunch up around the chow line. A new sergeant E7 named Lawson had recently joined the company. He was an older man, a devout Christian who was very humble. He wasn't the typical field sergeant—more a good garrison NCO. He probably shouldn't have been out in the field but he never complained. Sam had taken a particular liking to him and tried to ease the pressure on him physically whenever possible.

As everyone was bunching up in the chow line, Sergeant Lawson started shouting, "Spread out! Spread out! One round could get you all!"

Then all of a sudden, out of nowhere came an elongated, whistle-like whine, followed by an earth-shattering eruption. Two artillery rounds crashed in, exploding about 15 meters from the chow line. The entire area was peppered with a furious burst of shrapnel. One piece, no bigger than a small fingernail, flew straight into the sergeant's jugular vein. He keeled over like a tree and bled to death before a chopper could be called to medevac him for a transfusion.

B.T. grabbed the radio. "Cease fire you murdering bastards! Cease fire!" he exclaimed. But the damage had already been done.

Apparently, the commanding artillery liaison officer for the other battalion had, for some reason, decided to ignore B Company's presence. Sam was furious but there was nothing he could do.

On November 22nd, Sam took a squad and an interpreter with him into one of the multitude of coastal villages. After reading a letter from Paula asking how the Vietnamese people felt about the war, he realized, to his embarrassment, he didn't really know. On Thursday the 24th, Thanksgiving Day, he wrote back:

> To see the conditions that the people have to endure over here, really tears at your heart. After seeing how they live and how little they have, it really makes us feel grateful.
>
> Just finished eating our Thanksgiving meal and wow, I'm really full! It makes me feel good, seeing the troops going through the chow line, heaping their plates as high as they can carry with turkey.

That evening a care package containing a large fruit cake from Dick and Pauline arrived. It was, of course, shared among the company. Second Platoon sent their very own "Jungle Thank You Card" inscribed on the back of a C-ration box. Joe Forgione and B.T. Collins set about composing their own notes of appreciation.

The following day at noon the company departed the area. They were air-assaulted to a valley some five miles to the north. Since B.T. was preparing to rotate back to the United States, Sam had an LZ named after him—LZ Collins. When they arrived, they noticed a small creek that appeared to be about waist deep running through the valley area. This valley was surrounded by mountainous high ground on all sides, although they were no more than a couple of miles in from the coast. It was a clear day when they landed, so Sam decided to make camp to give the troops a good rest before the steep climb the next day. They set up camp with Dean Parker's Mortar Platoon on one side of the creek and the rest of the company on the other.

Everyone had barely gotten their ponchos rigged when a downpour began. In a matter of minutes, the benign looking creek had become a roaring torrent and the entire area was filling up with water. Visibility was reduced to a matter of yards as the men scurried inside their ponchos for shelter. Joe Forgione could barely see the tent 10 feet away from his. It wasn't long before the water began to seep in.

"We ought'a go outside and dig a trench around this thing so we don't get flooded out," remarked someone in the hootch with Joe.

"Well, you dig and I'll watch, 'cause I ain't goin' out there!" came the swift response, in an unmistakable New York accent.

Similar "discussions" were being conducted in most of the hootches. Sam, B.T. and Porreca huddled together. It wasn't a good tactical situation because no one was guarding anything.

"I don't know what we're gonna do," moaned B.T., contemplating who would get flooded out first, as he stared at Mortar Platoon on the other side of the creek that had now become a river.

"We gotta dig a trench," Sam declared emphatically.

"Well, forget about it, Sir. We'll get out of here somehow," was B.T.'s reply, mirroring the sentiments of Joe Forgione and others.

Sam didn't say another word. He rose, put on his steel pot, picked up his entrenching tool and went out into the downpour to begin digging a trench. Other members of the company peeked out of their tents, at first looking dumbfounded at Sam in his olive-drab undershorts, boots and pot, digging away with mud spattering against his chest and steam rising off his back. Slowly, sheepishly, the GI's began to emerge from under their ponchos to start digging. Sam hadn't said a word to anyone. He never said, "Do it!" He just always did it himself.

147

Overnight, the water level in the creek rose by nine or ten feet and by morning the company was split by the river onto two islands on either side of it. At first light, choppers were flown in and B Company was extracted.

On the evening of November 30th, B.T. applied the finishing touches to his letter to Dick and Pauline.

Dear Mr. & Mrs. Bird,

The last few days have been pretty miserable, although Thanksgiving, we had an outstanding meal. The chopper was finally able to get in, and, low and behold, we were blessed with some damn fine fruit cake! Everybody in the company got a piece and it was a boost to their soggy, bedraggled morale. It's really the little things like that which do wonders for these hard-working troops over here. You certainly are very considerate and thoughtful people.

I am the FO for this company and your fine son is the fourth company commander that I have worked for; so when I talk about his abilities as a leader and his qualities as an individual, I feel that I am qualified.

To describe him gives me a lump in my throat. He worries about his men like a father, yet always accomplishes the most difficult mission. His spirit is undying, his thirst for responsibility unquenchable, and his compassion for others, unlimited.

If you could see him and the way he operates, the way he handles men, the way he stays calm under the most adverse conditions; you'd bust your buttons with pride. It's really awe-inspiring.

Working with people like Captain Bird really makes you feel like there are some good, decent people in "This Man's Army!" A couple of days ago, he was up to his knees in mud in the pouring rain, digging a drainage ditch. Yesterday, he was helping a private hold down his shelter to stop it from being blown down by a helicopter. He runs a good ship; flexible but not limp. His spirit is an example to these kids who have a miserable existence. They seem to know

148

he won't let them down. I know myself. I would follow him
through the gates of Hell and back.

Well, must close now. Thanks again for the delicious
fruit cake. Thought you would like to hear something about
your fine son, because knowing him, you'd never hear it
from his lips.

Sincerely
LT B.T. Collins

P.S. Don't tell him that I wrote about him.

The following day Brien Collins left on the evening chopper.
The company gathered around in a circle to see him off. Back
in October, when the company was at base camp, Sam had
presented him with a hand-made wooden plaque denoting the
Combat Infantryman's Badge on behalf of the entire company.
Tears rolled down B.T.'s cheeks that day and now he was having
to fight them back once more. The whole company launched into
a rousing cheer as he boarded the helicopter.

Sam did one other thing that day. Knowing how close Collins
and David Porreca were (Porreca having saved Collins' life
during Crazy Horse), Sam casually said to his executive officer
that morning, "David, you have to go and do some paperwork
back at base camp." This enabled the two of them to spend
B.T.'s last days in Vietnam together. As the helicopter lifted from
the ground, the entire company brought their hands up sharply
in salute.

Sam received word the following day that he was being
assigned to West Point after his tour, as a tactical officer. He was
ecstatic.

On December 5th, the company was flown out of Bong Son
to the west, back over to the Cambodian border again. Intelligence reports of a large enemy buildup prior to the Christmas
cease-fire proved, as usual, to be inaccurate. B Company,
therefore, spent a relatively quiet month in the "boonies"
operating out of an area known as the Oasis.

On the 26th of December, the company received word they
were to be flown back to Bong Son the following day. This was

because an LZ named Bird (Sam's company had been the first to actually land there back in September during Operation Thayer I) had been all but overrun by a Vietcong regiment. LZ Bird was situated in an area just southwest of the Central Bong Son Plain known as The Crow's Foot. It was the same area B Company had been in during Thanksgiving.

When B Co arrived on December 27th, they were greeted by a horrendous sight. Over 50 members of a company belonging to their sister battalion, 1st/12th, had been killed, along with two hundred of the enemy. Mangled bits of bodies were scattered all over. The situation had become so desperate that Bee Hive rounds had been fired for the first time during the conflict. (The 105mm howitzer Bee Hive round is formed of 8,500 flechettes, or small metal arrows. Fired at massed infantry, it has an approximately 30 degree cone of fire up to three hundred meters—creating a shotgun effect.)

Later that evening, B Co was assigned to pursue any remaining elements of the regiment that had wreaked such havoc on LZ Bird. During that pursuit the company approached a mountain pass in line formation. Strung out at the rear, the trailing platoon came under fire from a group of snipers on the ridge above them.

Bronze Star Citation

Hearing the fire to his rear and discovering that the platoon was pinned down, Captain Bird conducted a personal reconnaissance of the company's right flank in an attempt to discover the source of the enemy's fire. Recognizing the need for fire support, Captain Bird, with complete disregard for his own personal safety, crawled forward to a vantage point from where he called for and adjusted air strikes.

Sam's style was always to call in overwhelming fire support before indulging in any "death or glory" heroics. He reiterated this philosophy when he wrote home earlier that month about a captain who'd just been awarded the Silver Star.

. . . From what I could tell, the company commander of the unit that got hit, a company in the 1/5, didn't believe in walking artillery fires in front of his units, so they were caught off-guard when the PAVN's attacked. It appears to me that he was negligent by not using all the available weapons and I believe that I would have relieved him instead of giving him a Silver Star. You can rest assured that Old Sam spends lots of taxpayers' money by calling in all sorts of support to cover us, not just when we are in contact, but when we are on the move, and B Co hasn't, and won't, have the same thing happen as long as I am the commander.

It was a standing joke among the company that Sam would probably have called in air support to take care of a hostile water buffalo.

On the 28th of December, Sam composed a New Year's letter to his parents.

Dave Porreca left this morning to take over Delta Company, as their commander got sick. Colonel Hatch said I'll probably stay with Bravo for about another thirty days and then I'll be sent to join battalion staff.

The time has really flown by and it's almost hard to believe that in a couple of weeks, my year will be half over. In spite of the unpleasantness of war and some of the hardships over here, so far, I can honestly say that I have enjoyed working over here. There's no doubt in my mind though, that I'll be glad to be back home in my own "roost" soon.

I hope 1967 brings us all a lot of happiness. I'm sure the last half of the year will be a lot more enjoyable than the first half. At least as far as I am concerned.

He was wrong.

Chapter Nine

Semper Paratus

Ever since returning to Bong Son from the Oasis on the day after Christmas, Bravo Company had been in the thick of the action. The 1st Cavalry Division, in its move to offensive operations, was attempting to expunge the all-enveloping presence of the enemy from the Bong Son region and drive them back into the An Lao Valley. This large-scale, long-term operation was given the name of the Bin Dinh Pacification Campaign. Bin Dinh was the name of the coastal province that included Bong Son and the surrounding area. As with so many other aspects of this war, the name given to the operation was at variance with reality. The enemy's activities in the region were never subdued. Furthermore, nowhere was the true nature of the conflict in Vietnam typified more precisely than amongst the rich rice and tapioca bearing lands of the central coastal plain north of Bong Son. Nowhere were the tortuous complexities, bitter ironies and twisted paradoxes of the war so poignantly woven together as in the tapestry of this beguilingly beautiful segment of land north of the Lai Gang River. Girded by breath-taking legions of lush, green mountains, the whole area might be thought of as an intravenous drip to the 22nd NVA regimental stronghold in the An Lao Valley to the west.

Though occupying no more than a hundred square miles of land, the entire region was teeming with a confused and frightened populace. It was an area which, throughout much of the war, would harbor the inextricably intertwined destinies of

153

American soldiers, NVA regulars, Vietcong and countless old men, women and children.

The first two-and-a-half weeks of January 1967 had been hectic for Bravo Company. They were deployed rapidly throughout the entire area, throwing a series of hard jabs at enemy positions and capturing 50 prisoners in the process. It was a time when the company saw considerable contact with the enemy, yet Sam was happier, both with their effectiveness as a fighting force and the capacity of the unit to keep one another alive. The preceding six months had in many ways been more of a leadership challenge—things had been relatively quiet with sporadic contact with the enemy. Of course the fear was always there; a lingering presence, deep inside, the type of fear that inexorably ground men down. They could walk for days and not see anything except water buffalo, but it was the uncertainty about what lay behind the next depression, tree or hill which gnawed constantly at their vigilance and resolve. During the previous three weeks, direct contact with the enemy had been a regular feature of life. The instinct for self-preservation superseded everything. In such instances, very little external motivation was required.

With the last week of the month came a return to frustration and fatigue; days of grueling humping under incessant rains once more led to confrontation only with shadowy images. It was as if the enemy had gone to ground—the ominous sign of preparation for a big push. All of this culminated in a "hot" intelligence tip on January 21st regarding the perceived location of a forward operating base for the 22nd NVA Regiment. The ensuing encirclement of an area north of LZ English by three battalions then produced nothing except more frustration. Everyone was relieved when B Company was extracted from the field on the afternoon of the 26th in preparation for a 24 hour stand-down commencing the following day, the 27th of January.

Consolidating at LZ English after their extraction from the field, the company boarded a convoy of two-and-a-half-ton trucks for the half-mile journey south to the fire-base at LZ Dog—a barren, dusty strip of high ground which was home to a battery of 155 howitzers. When Sam gathered the company together that evening in the middle of the perimeter to confirm the impending stand-down of the following day, it came as manna from Heaven. There were to be no patrols sent out that evening. The company could remain within the relatively safe confines of the perimeter at Dog and its environs for the next 36 hours.

After Sam left the area, 1st Sergeant Bost reminded the company that as well as being a reward for a solid period of hard work, they shouldn't forget that the other reason for the stand-down was Captain Bird's 27th birthday the following day—January 27th, 1967.

Lieutenant Colonel Hatch, the battalion commander, had granted permission for a cake and cold beer to be flown in specially for the occasion. The troops were going to throw Sam a birthday party he'd never forget—a small token of their appreciation for one "Jam-up" commanding officer. They knew Sam had only a short time left with the company before being re-assigned to battalion headquarters.

For Joe Forgione, the upcoming birthday celebration held a special significance. The "punk kid" from New York had come to look upon his commanding officer from the sunny heartland of Kansas as his best friend, an older brother to look up to. Realizing he would probably never get any closer to Sam than he already was, he wanted to insure his captain never forgot him. He'd often heard Sam talk about his desire to own a Seiko watch. While on R and R in Hong Kong, Joe had bought one that he planned to present to his commanding officer the following afternoon.

The prevailing sentiment amongst the troops, however, was a sheer sense of relief bordering on euphoria, that they wouldn't be going out on a mission the following day. After the men were dismissed, they went back to rig their ponchos, establishing them a little bit more securely in the knowledge they wouldn't be tearing them down again the following morning.

A short ride by truck earlier that afternoon took the company through a small shanty town which had sprung up beside the highway, outside the entrance to LZ English. The freewheeling entrepreneurs of the local population, like countless predecessors in other times and places, had seized on the presence of American servicemen and their propensity to spend money on anything remotely resembling creature comforts.

One such aspiring *Mein Host* had erected a small bistro containing three or four tables, chairs and several buckets of ice-cold beer. Gary Davis and a couple of friends, unable to deliver themselves from that particular temptation, slipped out of the perimeter at Dog under cover of darkness, some 12 hours before the stand-down was officially scheduled to begin.

While savoring their illicit pleasure, mulling over such things as how they were going to slip back inside the perimeter without being noticed by "Top," (Dave Bost) who would no doubt take great pleasure in writing them up for an Article 15, they were besieged by two pairs of twins scuttling and scurrying in and out beneath their table. A worried-looking proprietor hurried over to shoo the children away and apologize for his mischievous off-spring. Gary and his companions assured him they were no bother and motioned him to sit down and join them for a while. The proprietor could speak very little English and the soldiers even less practical Vietnamese. However, the conversation was carried by a series of animated gestures, expressions and numerous assists from the "quicksilver twins." In any case, Americans probably appreciate better than any other people that money is the international language for beer and companionship.

When the proprietor rose from his seat to tend to some other customers, he turned almost casually to Gary and his friends as if to do them a favor and motioned frantically with his hands, pointing to the north.

"Beaucoup VC! Beaucoup VC!," he shouted.

The soldiers nodded authoritatively, assuming he was referring to the NVA stronghold in the An Lao Valley, which they knew lay to the northwest of where they were seated. Anyway, it was of no consequence to them. They were on 24 hour stand-down. Upon finishing their beers, they bid the proprietor good night. A far more pressing problem was presented by their return to LZ Dog and how they would slip back inside the perimeter undetected.

Fortunately for them, they managed it without incident and settled down for a good night's rest.

The morning of January 27th dawned crystal-clear and sunny. After several days of incessant rain, it seemed the weather was entering into the spirit of the occasion.

The company rose gradually, half-filled their steel pots with water and began shaving. A hot breakfast arrived served up on paper plates. Each man's hootch remained intact; they wouldn't have to dismantle them until the next day. A gaggle of local children emerged from their lairs. They dispersed in groups to different sectors of the perimeter where they began peddling cans of soda and fruit to the soldiers.

At around 1000 HRS, the first deuce-and-a-half (two-and-a-half-ton truck) pulled out of LZ Dog bound for the shower point. It was loaded with grubby GI's who hadn't taken a shower since before Christmas. The shower point was located two-and-a-half miles south of LZ Dog, over the river from the town of Bong Son. It was a rather elaborate arrangement by Vietnamese standards, consisting of a tent with shower nozzles that received their water from the nearby river and an adjacent laundry tent where the men could have their fatigues washed. For those in need of more basic gratification, an ample number of ladies willing to oblige for a negotiable price were on hand. As one of the men said, with dubious resignation, "They just seem to appear, everywhere we go."

A football game was begun inside the perimeter at Dog. Those who weren't participating in the game were either stringing wire around the perimeter or sitting around relaxing with a soda and a cigarette, waiting their turn for the shower point.

Shortly after lunch, Sam hopped in front of an open deuce-and-a-half and accompanied about 20 of his men down to the shower point. Everyone was in a jovial mood, chatting, wise-cracking and singing. It had just started to sink in for most of them that they wouldn't be going out on patrol that day.

Gary Davis took his camera with him. Once the group had disembarked from the truck at the shower point, he began seeking out photo opportunities. The sight of a naked GI bounding across an area of open scrub, caught his attention. As he tried to focus on the curious spectacle, a better subject came in view. John F. Bankowski, his fellow RTO, was a slim wisp of a nineteen-year-old with close-cropped blond hair, ears like trophy handles and the tiny eyes of a fox cub. The radio set strapped to his back all but dwarfed him. He was smoking a cigarette in a kind of hunched stance that appeared to offset the weight of the radio. Davis couldn't resist the shot. Back in November Bankowski had been B.T. Collins' RTO for a short time during the height of the monsoon. For an entire day while B.T. was away on assignment, he'd lain curled up with his boss's mail clutched tightly to his chest. Upon his return that evening, Collins had found his young RTO, huddled up and drenched, inside his hootch. The letters were perfectly dry.

★   ★   ★

At 1215 HRS at Battalion Headquarters, LTC Jay Hatch received a warning order over the radio from Colonel George Casey at 2nd Brigade HQ to be ready for an operation. Casey and his battalion commanders had been restless for some months because of the routine nature of operations. They were anxious for an opportunity to commence a "big" offensive.

Scattered intelligence gathered over the past two days had once again begun to point to the presence of an enemy battalion somewhere to the north of LZ English. More conclusive sightings had been reported, establishing that at least one battalion of the 22nd NVA Regiment was located in or near one of the various coastal hamlets about five miles northeast of English. A week earlier, a similar scenario had been played out. But, it had turned out to be a mirage. Casey grabbed the chance to play it out one more time, informing the assistant division commander, "I can get it!"

At 1210 HRS, the general replied, "Go!"

The operation would entail another large bull's-eye-type squeeze, a large deployment of troops would encircle the enemy, cutting off any escape routes and forcing them into a central "kill zone." Or at least, that was the idea.

158

On receipt of the warning order, Hatch relayed an immediate radio message to Bravo Company at LZ Dog, where Dean Parker, who'd taken over as the executive officer following Porreca's departure, was the officer in charge. Sam was down at the shower point soaking up his birthday wash when the order came through to Parker. However, Sam had a radio positioned outside the shower tent. He could hear everything. Once Sam realized what was going on, he ordered everyone to gather up their things in a rush and load back onto the truck.

The men's reaction was fairly predictable. Some of them broke into song, "Roll up! Roll up! It's the Magical Mystery Tour. Who cares what's the destination? It's the Magical Mystery Tour!"

Meanwhile, back at LZ Dog things were moving quickly. Dean Parker's first thought was to round up a couple of platoons and handle the impending assault by himself, so as not to bother the old man on his birthday. However, as more information became available across the radio, this was obviously going to involve more than a small air assault.

Choppers started to arrive at the LZ, coming in from all over the area. Dave Porreca, who was over at Battalion HQ, began yelling over the radio that he should lead the assault since Sam was at the shower point.

For those at Dog who had not yet made it to the shower point, it wasn't their lucky day. Instead, all they got to hear was, "Roll up your shit and saddle up! Saddle up!"

At the shower point it took about five minutes for the men to gather up half-washed fatigues and load back onto the truck. All the time, Sam continued to monitor the radio traffic. The last man flung everything onto the truck and climbed aboard as it lurched forward. The truck screamed out of the shower area onto Highway One and up over the bridge. On the other side, one of the frustrating realities of travel in Vietnam came into play. The road was crawling with every type of traffic imaginable: carts, scooters, rickshaws, cars, trolleys and hundreds of people were walking in all directions.

As the truck headed up the highway, its occupants looked on as the mighty barrels of the 155 howitzers at Dog and English

159

veered menacingly around to the northeast. The two bases erupted in a simultaneous outpouring of explosive pounding fury, clearing the proposed landing zone. Some of those on the truck felt a tinge of reassurance. At least they wouldn't have to fight their way off the choppers.

At LZ Dog everybody was scrambling onto their respective choppers. Dean Parker had just finished briefing his platoon leaders. Eighteen helicopters were all cranked up, rotors thumping—beating out a deafening roar. The last few men from the first three platoons were taking their places as Parker clambered onto the sixth chopper with newly promoted Commo (communications) Chief, Sergeant Joey Forgione. He was just about to relay to the flight commander that they were ready to rock and roll when the two-and-half-ton with Sam aboard came hurtling around the last corner into the compound. Seconds later and the lift would have been airborne.

Sam leapt from the truck, still trying to finish dressing as he charged over toward the sixth ship with Dean Parker aboard. Some distance from the skids, he began motioning vigorously for Parker and Forgione to disembark. He ordered Forgione to a separate chopper, drawing an indignant response. "I'm going with you!" Forgione declared.

"No you're not!" Sam shouted, struggling to make himself heard above the ear-splitting noise of the rotor blades.

"Well Goddamn! I've been in your chopper ever since you've been here."

"You're Commo Sergeant now and you're going with the last lift. I can't afford to risk having the whole of HQ taken out at once."

Reluctantly Joe Forgione got out as Gary Davis and John Bankowski climbed aboard.

Next, Sam had Parker give him a briefing. The lieutenant pulled out his map and pointed out the location of the proposed landing zone—LZ Trout, a large, flat clearing of high, dry ground that had once been cultivated rice and tapioca fields. The LZ was approximately three to four hundred meters to the west of a small hamlet called Bin Phu.

160

The deafening roar of the rotor blades was not exactly conducive to a thorough briefing, although Sam kept nodding his head to indicate he understood what was being said. Finally he took the map out of Parker's hand and boarded the helicopter. The lieutenant reverted to his role as the XO, which meant he would take a position on the last helicopter into the LZ.

Moments later, 18 ships carrying the first three rifle platoons were in the air. It was now 1345 HRS on January 27th. Accompanying Sam on the sixth chopper was his 1st sergeant, Dave Bost, two soldiers and the two radio men, Bankowski and Davis, carrying the company and battalion nets respectively.

LZ Trout and the associated hamlets of My An, Bin Phu and Truong Lam were no more than four miles northeast of LZ Dog, about a mile inland from the coast. The flight picked up, gained a little altitude and flew straight over in a matter of minutes. Some 70 or 80 men were in the air, forming the first lift. Twenty-four choppers had been ordered originally, 18 of which were fully operational. This meant that Mortar Platoon, with Dean Parker, would remain at LZ Dog until the first six ships of the lift returned for them.

Gary Davis was on the left side of the sixth chopper with Sam. He took out his camera and snapped a shot of his commanding officer gazing pensively out over the Song Can River meandering lazily across the Central Bong Son Plain. The high ground bordering the An Lao Valley lay in the background. On the other side of the helicopter, John Bankowski looked out at the South China Sea and the incoming waves lapping against the white, sandy shore. Local fishermen were out in force, operating elaborate bicycle-net contraptions to the rhythm of the waves, their backs turned to the congestion of palm trees lilting in the breeze.

The helicopters swung in low over the village rooftops as the LZ came into view. The 155's were pounding it to pieces. The flight looped out to the north in preparation for its short and final approach. Captain Barry Sottak, the flight commander, had just threaded them through four different tiers of gunfire support. He hadn't been informed about two of the tiers supporting the 40th

ARVN about two thousand meters north of Trout. The problem lay in the fact that nobody could tell him who was co-ordinating this support. Sottak had worked his flight plan in around the artillery target lines but the jet aircraft and naval gunfire support came as a complete surprise to him. But this was nothing to the surprise about to visit itself upon the first three platoons of Bravo Company.

Coming in on the final leg toward LZ Trout, they could see that the area was still being prepped. Shells were bursting all over the LZ. Everything looked perfect for a landing once the fire was lifted. The artillery had certainly done its job. There was no sign of activity, enemy or otherwise, anywhere near the area. What was more, the large, open LZ provided a clear view of the surrounding area and what they could expect once they hit the ground. It was the ideal scenario for a perfectly executed air assault.

Then suddenly, the ships began to flutter, going into a sharp climb to the left. In one of the choppers directly behind Sam, which had zipped around and was now almost on its side, Specialist 4th Class Joe Romagnoli echoed the sentiments of many. "What the fuck's going on!" he cried, as the right side of his helicopter became an overhead viewing window. Looking up, he could clearly make out the command helicopter of Lieutenant Colonel Hatch soaring far above them.

The pounding of LZ Trout did not cease as the helicopters broke hard to the left and swung through 180 degrees to the south.

John Turnbull, who was RTO for 3rd Platoon now, was in one of the helicopters ahead of Sam. Turnbull broke into the company net to attempt to find out what was going on. A garbled message came back that it was imperative to get everyone on the ground immediately.

On completion of their turn, the helicopters had swung around a full 320 degrees before starting on a fresh short and final approach. Again they were heading to the northeast, to an area about five hundred meters to the southeast of Trout—the original, unequivocally-prepped LZ.

Holding his gaze out of the left side of his chopper, Gary Davis noticed a village coming into view. With his head half out of the helicopter, he began shouting, "Look! We're going into the wrong LZ and it's un-prepped!"

There was a distinct absence of any sign of incoming artillery. On the chopper ahead and to the left, John Turnbull was riding in on the skid. He watched as the command helicopter made a pass ahead of him and dropped a green smoke grenade indicating the area was clear of fire. All around him below, Turnbull saw what he assumed were American GI's, scattering across the new LZ in all directions.

Gary Davis' view to his right was somewhat restricted, although he thought he could make out a tree line. Darting in and out of the alleyways between the hootches on the left, he could see men clad in the all too familiar black "pajamas;" some carried anti-aircraft weapons and others held heavy machine guns—there were literally hundreds of NVA regulars swarming all over the LZ.

Sam was no longer absorbing the scenery. He was hastily pulling down his straps, locking and loading. The pilot jerked his head around to them and screamed at the top of his voice, "It's hot! It's hot!"

Gary, meanwhile, was looking down the barrels of a group of machine guns pointing up at the helicopter.

A couple of seconds after seeing the command chopper drop its green smoke grenade, John Turnbull saw one of the first helicopters hit the ground and immediately discharge a red smoke grenade. He was just thinking to himself, 'What the hell are all these people doing?' when a flurry of slugs popped against the skids of the helicopter he was on. Suddenly the air around him was filled with the noise of what sounded like a thousand fire-crackers all going off at once. And then it dawned on him, "My God, we're in the middle of it, right now!"

The company was being dropped into an LZ that had been completely un-prepped and was crawling with NVA regulars. As they came in, they ran the gauntlet of meticulously prepared positions on either side of the LZ. Sam's visibility permitted him to see only those on the left, but there were complimentary networks of spider holes dug under hedgerows and bunkers dug into the walls of several drainage ditches for protection against indirect fires. Many of the spider holes had been dug with two entrances connected by a short tunnel. This enabled the enemy to fire on either side. A group of these spider holes were located along a hedgerow running from the center to the right side of the LZ. These were concealed from Sam's line of vision as his chopper set down on the LZ.

John Turnbull was aboard the fourth ship in. As he jumped from his helicopter, all he could see was a blur of bodies running in all directions. There was an incredible amount of gunfire. It was impossible to distinguish individual shots; it was just one loud, continuous roar. Like most of the company who'd been in-country for six months or less, this was the most terrifying thing he'd ever seen. Once he hit the ground, he scrambled to his pre-assigned position of "eleven o'clock" on the LZ, where he found himself afforded protection by a cluster of graves and a water well. He looked up after he had rolled over beside the water well at about "nine o'clock," and was greeted by the sight of a huge water buffalo glaring down at him. "It scared the hell out of me momentarily!" he recounted later.

Meanwhile, the sorties continued to land by two's and three's in the face of an increasing volume of hostile gunfire. Sam and HQ Platoon came in behind John Turnbull on the sixth ship, putting down in the southwest center of the LZ. Having concentrated their attention on the hostile activity to their left as they came in, Sam, accompanied by the first sergeant and the two radio men, moved off in front of the helicopter to the right. Heading toward the hedgerow in the center of the LZ, they were moving at a 45 degree angle to the nose of the helicopter.

Flying in behind them were two more helicopters, containing, among others, SP 4 Joe Romagnoli and SSG Max Hanning of 2nd Platoon. Now, the ships were simply coming in as low to the ground as they possibly could, dropping off their men and flying on in one continuous motion. Hanning and Romagnoli jumped out from about 10 feet and came up fighting. They hit the ground approximately 40 feet to the rear of HQ Platoon. From their vantage points they could see Sam and the RTO's moving off from their helicopter. Several yards in front of them, Gary Davis could see a seriously wounded, blond American soldier. He was being dragged across the LZ by an NVA regular who was using his body as cover.

They had made it no more than 15 feet from the nose of the helicopter when all four men hit the ground and rolled forward. Sam rose again and began moving forward. The 1st sergeant yelled, "Gook!" and rolled to his left, over to the other side of the hedgerow. There was a frenzied burst of automatic weapons fire. A spider hole no more than 20 feet ahead of them opened up with all it had.

About 40 feet to the south, Joe Romagnoli stood mesmerized for a second, as though in a dream. He heard a metallic ping and saw Sam's helmet fly up into the air.

Gary Davis hit the prone position directly behind Sam's knees. John Bankowski lay close beside him to his left, against the hedgerow. Gary looked up and trained his eyes on the tree-line, some 50 yards to their front. Another raking barrage of automatic weapons fire sprayed all around him. This time, he could see it was coming from no more than 25 feet away.

After bringing his head back down swiftly, he realized Sam was still lying prone in front of him. "C'mon Sir, we gotta move!" he yelled.

Sam lay there motionless. Then LTC Hatch broke in forcefully over the battalion net, "Where's the fire coming from? Where's Six?"

"Six has been hit! From my front!" Gary screamed.

"Which way is that?"

"I don't know!"

At this point Gary was completely disoriented. He was unable to give a coherent direction. He looked across to his left where John Bankowski had his hand on the company receiver. He was trying to establish contact with the platoon leaders. There was a sickening thud. Bankowski looked at Gary with a vacant expression. "I'm hit," he gasped, and his face flopped into the ground.

A few seconds passed before Gary heard his fellow radio operator's lungs suck in two involuntary gulps of air. He was dead. Gary reached over to try to pull the company net from his colleague's grasp. He struggled to pull Bankowski's arm from beneath his body and saw that his hand was clutched tightly around the receiver, thereby squelching all radio communications within the company. Beside the receiver lay a gooey gob of mucous slop the size of a fist. Gary went from disoriented to deranged. He looked back over at Sam who also lay face-down and noticed that his helmet was lying on the ground in front of him—both straps and the helmet liner were completely torn off. A large portion of Sam's brain was protruding from the back of his head. Gary started yelling for all he was worth, "Medic, medic! He's dead! The captain's been hurt bad! Medic!"

Joe Romagnoli had been watching the whole thing unfold in paralyzed disbelief. Then he felt something. The entire length of his leg was filled with a warm sensation and he crumpled to the ground. The next thing he knew, he was being dragged over to an area beneath some trees. He looked up through the perforated canopy of green. Way above he could see three command helicopters—hovering and circling—silhouetted against the blue sky.

Gary lifted his head once again from behind Sam's knee. A hail of bullets greeted him along with a fragment of Sam's ankle. Each time he moved, he provoked another raking burst and another piece of Sam's ankle would shatter in front of him.

Out of the corner of his eye, about 45 feet away to his right, Gary saw a soldier he recognized as one Ellis Parker, stand up with his M-60 machine gun. In an act of brazen defiance, he began cooking off rounds at the spider hole. There was a small ridge located about a yard in front of the spider hole which absorbed most of his fire, but it kept the occupants pinned down.

This gave one of the medics, easily identifiable by a shock of red hair, the opportunity to run to where Gary, Sam and John Bankowski lay. He took one look at Sam before saying, "There's nothing I can do for him," and took off running again. This reduced Gary to a state of screaming anger.

166

At this point the entire LZ was massive pandemonium, a theater from hell where the bizarre was turning into the ridiculous; the 1st Platoon leader stood up in an imitation of Ellis Parker, only he was shooting with his pistol.

Max Hanning, positioned about 30 feet to the south had seen everything. He saw that the bunker that had exacted such a devastating toll on HQ Platoon was still being pinned down by Ellis Parker. Hanning had already discharged his grenades, so he made the 30 meter dash over to Dave Bost, who provided him with two more. From there, he worked his way up the left side of the hedgerow toward the bunker. About three yards away, he pulled the pins on the grenades and launched himself at the bunker with a mighty running jump. Sailing over the top, he dropped the two grenades into the hole, landing on the other side as they exploded. When the smoke cleared, he went down inside. Seconds later, he emerged astride the bunker, holding aloft an AK-47 in one arm in yet another defiant gesture of bravura.

Meanwhile, Captain Paul F. Maxwell, piloting the last ship of the first lift, radioed to inform his flight commander that there were several wounded lying on the LZ. Then he broke away from the returning formation and headed back to where the battle was raging. In the midst of a terrifying barrage of fire raining in from all directions, he landed his ship in the center of the LZ.

Upon hearing the roar of rotor blades, Gary Davis looked to his right to see the skids of the helicopter setting down no more than five feet from Sam's head. Gary looked up. The look on the pilot's face said it all.

As the helicopter touched down, 1st Sergeant Dave Bost ran over to where Sam lay. Gazing down at his beloved commander, the full enormity of what had happened hit the proud old soldier with unmerciful force. In a voice trembling with emotion, he could summon only one solitary expletive, "Shit!"

The sergeant wrapped a giant arm around his captain and lifted him gently to his feet, with the help of Gary Davis who propped Sam up from the other side. Gary had his right arm under Sam's armpit and his left hand cupped against the huge area of open skull where brain tissue was protruding from the gaping wound on the right side of his head.

Once they had Sam aboard the helicopter, the 1st sergeant cradled his captain's head in his arms. Just as the chopper was about to lift off, the red-headed medic made a dash for the skids. The huge sergeant glowered at the young man who'd left Sam for dead. "You're staying here!" he roared and the helicopter took off for the 10 minute flight to the first aid facility at English.

By now, Dean Parker was in the air with the last lift from Bravo Company. He'd been listening to everything over the helicopter pilots' radios after Bankowski's death had suppressed the company net. The images generated over the air waves assumed visual reality as he approached the LZ. He saw complete and utter chaos—civilians, animals and children. It was the worst possible scenario.

The twenty-three-year-old lieutenant had just inherited the responsibility for rescuing what remained of his company from the clutches of disaster. And he had no radio communications with which to do it. To compound his problems, there were four tiers of commanders—the architects of the situation, presiding over the area from on high, all trying to talk to him at the same time, wanting to do everything at once. And Parker was trying to establish some sort of control over events at ground level. It was a sheer miracle that more people hadn't already been killed.

Once on the ground, Parker linked up with Joe Forgione, his commo chief, who wasn't yet aware of what had happened to Sam. Parker instructed Joe to locate and contact the platoon leaders by running hand-written notes between them to inform what he wanted done.

When he heard the news about Sam, Joe's frame of mind altered dramatically. He didn't care if he lived or died from that moment forward. The entire LZ was still a raging mass of fire as sorties from Charlie Company began to hit the ground. With the messages for each individual platoon leader clutched in one hand, Joe took off running. He saw that his new company commander was scared, but he also saw that he hadn't lost his cool. That was vital, if the lives of the remaining 110 men weren't going to be put in further jeopardy.

Once he had delivered the notes, he spotted John Bankowski, a bullet hole in the radio strapped to his back, lying face-down in the middle of the LZ. He scrambled over to the body and switched off the radio which had completely disrupted communications within the company. Slowly, a semblance of order was restored with the help of Charlie Company. A perimeter was established and any remaining elements of the enemy were cleared from the LZ. For his actions that day, Joe Forgione was awarded the Silver Star for Gallantry in Action.

From the medical facility at English, Sam, still alive, was transferred to a helicopter that took him to the 85th Evac. Hospital at Qui Nhon.

Back at the LZ, Max Hanning handed the AK-47 over to Dave Bost, who in turn gave it to Dean Parker.

Chaplain John E. Keplinger, a Seventh Day Adventist, was assigned to the 85th. He was present when they rushed Sam in for surgery. Looking down at the gaping hole in Sam's head, he didn't see how anyone could possibly survive such a wound.

Meanwhile, Gary Davis had been landed up the road at the 67th Evac., the sister hospital to the 85th. He was covered in blood, much of which was probably not his own, though he had sustained wounds to his arms and head. He stood inside the entrance of the brand new hospital in a trance-like state of shock and confusion. Learning that Sam had been taken to the other hospital, he wandered back out onto the dirt road before anyone had a chance to examine his wounds. Walking in the direction of the 85th, he made it about half a mile and was starting to stagger and lurch sideways when he was picked up by a two-and-a-half ton truck that dropped him off at the 85th. There he learned Sam was already in surgery and was prepared for surgery himself.

The morning after Sam was brought in, Chaplain Keplinger was visiting the sister hospital less than a mile away. Outside the emergency room he came upon a huge bear of a sergeant sitting on the floor beside the door. The sergeant's fatigues were covered

169

in blood and the chaplain asked him if he was hurt. The man replied, "No, its the blood of my captain." He went on to tell the chaplain that he'd been with his captain when he was wounded and had come to see how he was—whether he lived or died. The chaplain asked the sergeant his captain's name.

"Captain Samuel R. Bird," he replied.

The chaplain explained that Sam had been brought into the 85th and was indeed still alive.

"Thank God," replied the sergeant. "Can I see him? Where's the 85th?"

After pointing the sergeant in the right direction, the chaplain reflected for a moment on the amount of feeling this huge man seemed to have for his commander. The man was 1st Sergeant David Bost.

Gary Davis awoke the following day to find Sam in the bed next to his. They were in a quonset hut with Gary's bed beside the door and Sam next to him on his right. Sam's head was swathed in bandages and his left leg was up in traction. He was semi-conscious. "My men, my men; where are my men?" Sam repeated again and again. Repeatedly turning his head to one side and sobbing, he made countless futile attempts to get up. A variety of IV's were connected to him and each time he thrashed his arms trying to get up he caused himself to bleed more.

The following day, Lieutenant Colonel Hatch came to visit, accompanied by the battalion staff. On seeing Sam he caved in—distraught, devastated and crushed. It was as though it were his own son lying there.

★   ★   ★

It is doubtful whether the full reasoning behind the last-minute decision to divert the helicopters carrying Bravo Company's first three platoons can ever be ascertained.

We do know that the brigade commander, Colonel George Casey and his battalion commanders had been "restless" for some months because of the "routine nature of operations." They were "anxious for the opportunity to commence a big offensive." We

170

know they'd been frustrated just a week earlier following a similar scenario when the enemy did a quick disappearing act.

It's an open question whether this explains the order to land Bravo Company in the middle of an NVA battalion instead of following the standard operating procedure: dropping them at LZ Trout to establish contact with the enemy by walking toward them.

It should be pointed out on behalf of those who orchestrated the operation—although it was as much by sheer providence as good judgement—only three American soldiers were killed compared with 150 of the enemy battalion. By military standards, this made it a resoundingly successful operation.

Also, it's important to note that not once after he was wounded did Sam Bird point an accusatory finger at anyone involved in the operation. Not ever did he harbor one ounce of bitterness about what had happened to him. To Sam, it was the reality of war; it was part of the contract he had signed with his country six years earlier. As far as he was concerned, he just happened to be in the wrong place at the wrong time—period.

Sam's Grandparents

Samuel J. Houston

Dora Neaves Houston

Gertrude Hacker Bird

Richard Ely Bird, Sr.

Sam's Parents
Two years before Sam was born

Richard Ely Bird, Jr.

Pauline Frances Houston Bird

Sam's mysterious aunt

Helen N. Houston—1943

Paula and Sammy Bird at ages five and four—1944

Father and son—1950
Sam is a husky ten-year-old.

The Minneha School Band—May 1953
The enlarged images of Sam and Annette inset left and right
respectively with the "Heaven-sent" Miss Choate standing back
right.

Sam and Paula—Autumn 1953
Sam is in his Missouri Military Academy uniform.

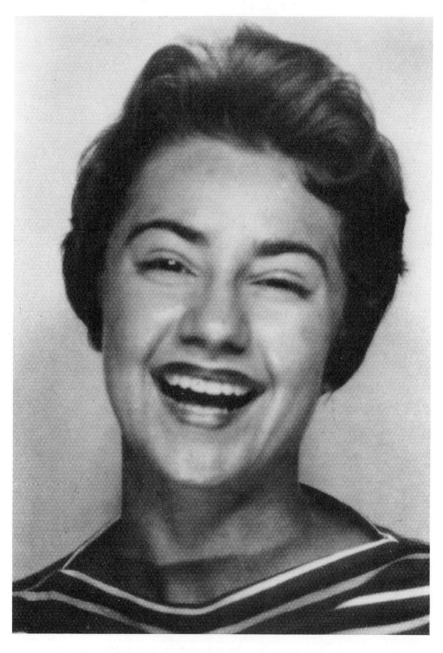

The irrepressible Paula Jo Anne Bird—1954
Fifteen years old.

Cadet Lt. Col. Sam Bird receives the Citadel's Distinguished Military Student award from General Clark.

October 1960

As president of The Citadel Post of the American Ordnance Association, Sam presents "The Boo" (Lt. Col. Thomas N. Courvoisie), with a post resolution.

Spring 1961

Pauline Houston Bird as she appeared in the 1961 *Sphinx*,
The Citadel yearbook.

"Straight Arrow"

181

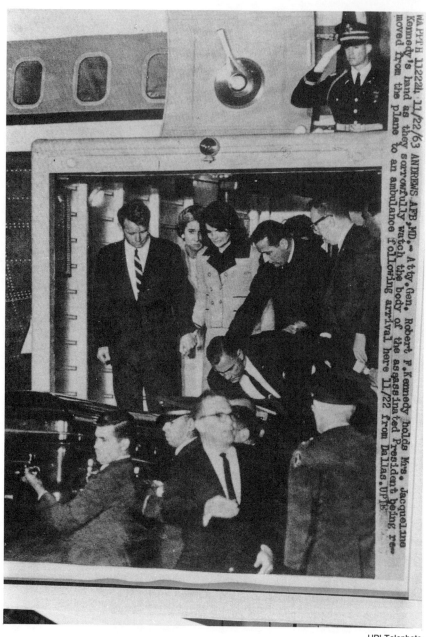

Lt. Sam Bird saluting—top right.
Shortly after 6:00 P.M. E.S.T. at Andrews Air Force Base, Maryland.
November 22, 1963

Leaving St. Matthew's Cathedral with the casket of President Kennedy.
November 25, 1963

Home of the 1st Cavalry Division at An Khe.
July 1966

Captain Samuel R. Bird (center) flanked by SP/4 "Beefsteak"
Harrison (right) and SP/4 Allen (left) in the lower reaches of the
Chu Pong Massif.

August 1966

Presentation of Combat Infantryman's Badges at An Khe.
Late August 1966

Home of "The Meanest Muthas" at An Khe.
September 1966

Definitive image of Sam Bird somewhere on Highway 19.
October 3, 1966

B.T. Collins and Sam Bird.
Bong Son
Approximately October/November 1966

Captain Sam Bird minutes before landing to the southeast of
LZ Trout (approximately 1345 HRS).
January 27, 1967

PART IV

*THROUGH HELL
AND HOME*

Chapter Ten

Hell

609 Rutland, Wichita, Kansas
January 28th, 1967
Around 8:30 A.M.

The chimes of the hall clock had barely struck the half-hour when the telephone rang. Dick rose slowly from the newspaper cocoon of his armchair, ambled over to the wrought iron stand near the hallway and picked up the receiver. He always answered the phone when he was in the house.

At the other end of the line, a desk sergeant read in a flat, measured tone, from the official telegram that lay before him. "The Secretary of the Army has asked me to express his deep regret that your son . . ." He took a moment to clear his throat, while Dick braced himself. ". . . Captain Samuel R. Bird, was placed on the very seriously ill list as a result of a gunshot wound to the head when hit by hostile weapons fire while with air assault to a landing zone. In the judgement of the attending physician, his condition is of such severity that there is cause for concern."

The sergeant went on to provide details of whom to contact for information. Dick jotted down every detail with a pencil on one of the note pads from Big Six, the last lumber yard to be sold.

"I'm very sorry sir," said the sergeant in closing. Dick thanked him and replaced the receiver.

To Addie, Dick had always appeared inscrutable, brooding, often sullen—"like an ol' bear!" This time he was no different, betraying little of what he had heard as he returned to his armchair.

"What's the matter Dick?" Pauline inquired urgently, having a keener appreciation for the nuances of her husband's emotional range than her long-time confidante and housekeeper.

"It's Sam. He's been hurt awful bad."

Her husband's words were like discordant bells. Pauline drew her willowy legs tight against the base of her armchair, her face dissolving into tears that streamed down both cheeks like so many petals from an aging flower. The sum of their hopes had been shattered in the realization of their worst fear.

The combined influence of a congressman and several generals helped insure that Dick and Pauline received daily bulletins on Sam's condition. The report on the 29th intensified their feelings of gloom and despondency.

"The patient's condition deteriorated and he became decerebrate (incapable of thought) and required re-exploration with the removal of more brain and bone fragments lodged within the brain. This procedure was carried out from the left side."

Unlike generally sterile bullet fragments, bone fragments were susceptible to contamination, transporting disease wherever they went. They carried an infection deep into Sam's brain. Unless every single one was removed, the infection would continue to fester and spread, resulting in a particularly horrifying death.

At about the time Sam was wounded, a small, bone china, Royal Worcester figurine in Dick and Pauline's living room was dropped and broken. Approximately six inches in height, it was a statuette of a young boy dressed in a white topcoat with a cranberry trim, hurling snowballs. Under a blond forelock, he had piercing, luminescent blue eyes and a mischievous grin. The figurine's head was shattered into tiny pieces, its right arm was broken off and the right leg was smashed away at the ankle.

The days of limbo following the initial notification brought little news. During that time, Dick set about trying to put the statuette back together again. He kept telling himself that if he could successfully glue the pieces back, Sam too could be put together again. One of the small china fragments from the top of the head was never recovered, so Dick filled the area, no more than a quarter of an inch in diameter, with glue. Despite the missing piece, the result was a superb reconstruction. Only close inspection could reveal the line across the right eye and the criss-cross cracks over the top of the head. The blemishes on the arm and the leg were barely visible.

On February 3rd, Dick and Pauline were notified that although still seriously ill, Sam was more aware of his surroundings. If he continued to show signs of improvement over the next few days, evacuation to a general hospital in Japan or Hawaii could be seriously considered.

It was the glimmer of hope Dick had been clinging to. Without further delay, he made an appointment to receive immunization shots for the Far East at the local health center.

The tone of the notifications continued to be more upbeat, although mention of anything alluding to Sam's complete recovery was conspicuously absent. On February 11th, word came that Sam had uttered the following sentence: "I have something to say and wish I could say it, but I can't think as I want to."

The following day at noon, Sam was flown out of Qui Nhon to the 106th General Hospital in Japan. Three days later, Dick and Pauline received word that they had both been invited to travel, at the government's expense, via military transport, from Travis Air Force Base to visit Sam at the 106th. Pauline didn't want to go. She was petrified at the thought of flying but she actually feared seeing her son so gravely wounded. Dick emphatically declared he was going whether she went with him or not. The thought of facing life alone for the next few weeks, perhaps months—coupled with several bottles of bourbon, redressed her balance. A few things were hurriedly packed and the two of them departed Wichita on the evening of February 15th at eight o'clock. They flew out of Travis the next morning.

★　　　★　　　★

On February 12th, Sam had been landed by helicopter on a large concrete pad that doubled as a parking lot in the center of the hospital unit. Modern-looking, gray buildings stood in orderly formation around the pad. The entire complex was surrounded by a barbed wire fence with guards strategically dotted around its perimeter. From a distance the place looked rather like a dingy hotel.

Sam was taken by ambulance from the helicopter to the neuro-surgery ward where a young captain named John Slater, the chief neurosurgeon at the hospital, saw him for the first time. "There were several things that were unique about this man," the young neurosurgeon recounted later. "When I first saw him, he was lying in the hospital bed at attention! He was so remarkably erect and proper, even though he was so gravely ill. It was uncanny. At that point in my career I had seen many patients, and even many soldier patients, but I have never seen this before or since. He was handsome. They told me he was such a perfect soldier. It still seems incredible to me that someone can have bandages on their head, literally brain sticking out of their skull underneath those bandages and to be lying in the hospital bed at attention. These things may have medical explanations, but from my point of view they were unique and special."

For two consecutive days after his arrival at the hospital, the swelling beneath Sam's bandages appeared to increase dramatically. When Dr. Slater unbandaged Sam's scalp and looked down, his eyes were greeted by the sight of Sam's infected brain bulging out of his skull through a large hole in his scalp—literally. Several areas of fungus, the size of large cauliflower florets, had developed on the brain's surface. Following the classical directions of World War II and Korean War medical texts, the doctor placed two sterile towels beneath Sam's head and began carefully slicing away the areas of dead and infected tissue. When he'd finished, the bandage was replaced. The procedure was repeated daily, cleaning off the surface of Sam's brain, removing a little more infected tissue each time, until the brain fit back inside the skull. In the meantime, massive doses of antibiotics were administered intravenously to try to stop the spread of infection.

Professor Henry Schwartz and General Hayes, two eminent neurosurgeons, had been visiting Vietnam when Sam was wounded. They were following the course of neurosurgical patients from the front lines through the hospitals. They saw Sam while he was at the 85th Evac. in Qui Nhon and became irate when they discovered no post-operative X-rays had been taken to reveal whether all infected bone fragments had been removed. The young neurosurgeon who operated on Sam there informed them it was impossible, pointing out that the X-ray equipment was in one tent and the operating room somewhere else. X-rays taken in Japan at the 106th revealed a bone fragment deep in the right hemisphere, almost at the center of Sam's brain.

When the eminent neurosurgeons arrived at the 106th and found Dr. Slater performing the so-called "classical treatments" on Sam, the general roared, "Debridement is no respecter of function! Debridement is no respecter of function!"

The general uttered the statement repeatedly and went on to tell the young doctor it was essential that all the bone fragments be removed. If they weren't, the bacteria would continue to live in the dead piece of bone and the infection would continue to fester until Sam died. Removing the bone fragments was imperative if Sam was to survive. The problem was, this would entail operating virtually in the brain stem itself and going through infected tracts, several inches into the right hemisphere.

Slater's was not an enviable choice. He could continue treating Sam as he was and watch him die a slow, agonizing death, or operate directly into the brain stem, which would probably kill him anyway. The following day, along with an assistant from the Navy, Slater performed the operation. The men were both brave and lucky. Every one of the fragments was removed and Sam was still alive. For weeks after the operation, Slater shuddered at the mere thought of what they had done.

Later in the week, the two young neurosurgeons stood in the receiving line at a party honoring the two eminent visitors to the hospital. As the general shook his hand, Slater presented him with the retrieved bone fragments. Both eminent surgeons were visibly surprised. Neither of them had thought much of Slater's chances for success.

On February 27th, Slater had to debride Sam's wound still further of infected tissue, removing most of the right rear portion of the brain (right temporal and occipital lobes).

★ ★ ★

On their arrival in Japan, Dick and Pauline were accommodated in military quarters close to the hospital. Their vigils were excruciatingly painful, for they could see no change in Sam's condition save for the frequent emergency visits late at night by Dr. Slater.

Lying in the bed next to Sam was a young black soldier from New York City whose father also had flown out to be with his son. Dick shared the man's helplessness as, one by one, each of his son's limbs was removed before he eventually died. The experience would haunt Dick for the rest of his life.

When it was discovered Sam had contracted gangrene in his right leg as a result of his wounds, the matter of amputation was raised by the doctors.

"No way in hell are you going to amputate Sam's leg!" Dick growled. "If my son dies, he's gonna be buried with all his body parts!"

During their second week in Japan, the Birds received a letter from Paula. It began by cautioning them to hold onto something before they read any further. Sonny had choked on a piece of steak while eating lunch and fallen face-down on the floor. Laura and Sam Brown had frantically slapped him on the back and tried to lift him up but he was too heavy for them. (The Heimlich maneuver was still unknown.) Neighbors had called an ambulance but he was dead on arrival at the hospital. He was forty-seven.

Sonny had adored Pauline, always asking to speak with "Potty" on his regular phone calls to 609 Rutland. The feeling was never reciprocated. Whenever Sonny had phoned, Pauline would implore Addie, "Tell him I'm not at home. I don't want to talk to him." To Pauline, Sonny was an unseemly irritant, an inconvenient blemish whose very existence seemed a black cloud on daily life. She had pestered Laura over the years until she finally agreed to "have the retarded *boy* put away." Sonny was placed in a mental institution in Oklahoma City for a year, much to Pauline's relief. At the end of the year, however, the home folded from a lack of financial support and Sonny returned home to Wichita.

Addie knew it wasn't her place to do so, but she wished she could ask Pauline how it felt now, to have a son who was in far worse shape than Sonny had ever been.

After two months at the 106th, the doctors reached a point where there was little more they could do to increase the prospects for Sam's recovery. They stabilized him enough that, in the opinion of Dr. Slater, there was at least a 75 percent chance he would survive the flight back to the United States. On the other hand, Slater wanted Dick and Pauline to be under no illusions about what the future might hold. He explained that if Sam were to regain some feeling on his right side and become able to think, plan and talk coherently, they should be very happy.

When Sam was flown out of Japan on March 23rd, there was a huge concave depression on the right side of his head. Despite its grotesque appearance, this was interpreted as a good sign since it indicated a lack of infection. The flight from Yokohama to Travis AFB was touch and go. Sam was strapped to a bunk in the rear of the aircraft. He was sick and nauseated for most of the journey, all but drowning in his own vomit on several occasions during the flight. The situation was compounded by his inability to communicate. He couldn't call for help and could only move his right index finger.

Dick and Pauline weren't permitted to accompany Sam on the military aircraft, so they took one that followed instead. When they landed in California, they were informed that although Sam's flight had been touch and go, he was still alive and was being flown on to Brooke Army Hospital in San Antonio, Texas. They followed on the next available flight.

Sam was conscious but completely disoriented when he arrived at Brooke Army Medical Center at around eleven o'clock that evening in late March. His once lithe and vital six foot, one inch frame was now an ashen emaciated 125 lbs. Removal of the head dressing revealed a pulsating hollow of skin and scar tissue the size of a cereal bowl on the right side of his head. Both his paralyzed lower legs were in casts, although only one was broken. He had developed sores and lesions over much of his body that were oozing as a result of lying in one place for such a long time. After taking a look at him, the doctors decided to wait and see if his condition was going to stabilize before even contemplating additional surgery.

Dick and Pauline arrived in San Antonio the following morning. They went straight to the hospital. Later in the day they made arrangements to rent a furnished apartment close by from where Dick, in particular, could maintain a near-constant vigil. The apparent futility and hopelessness of the situation was starting to take a toll on Pauline. All the stabilizing forces in her life appeared to be breaking apart. More than anything she craved to be back home again. Instead, Dick was the first to return to Wichita to pick up some nice china, silverware and a carpet sweeper, along with Michelle, their poodle, in an effort to make Pauline feel a little more at home. Addie closed up the house behind him when he returned to San Antonio and went to work at a local grocery store.

Although Dick, Pauline and Paula hadn't exactly enforced a news blackout as far as Sam was concerned, they had been extremely selective about whom they informed. As details of his condition began to trickle out, letters of condolence began to trickle in, mostly from Army comrades and Citadel classmates. In addition, a moving letter came for Paula from William Manchester, who had spent many hours interviewing Sam as part of the research for his upcoming book, *The Death of a President*.

28 III 67

Dear Mrs. Roberts,

I have just received your letter, and I am more distressed than I can say about your brother's wound. There is, quite literally, no way of expressing my anguish; as you will see in the book, I conceived a warm admiration for him. I thought of him—and think of him—as one of our best. His injuries sound grave; I pray they will mend.

As soon as my author's copies of the book [The Death of a President] *arrive, I shall send one to you for your brother, inscribed. Meantime give him my very warmest regards. The President would have been very proud of him, as indeed the country is grateful to him now.*

> *Faithfully,*
> *William Manchester*

With the onset of April and early May, Sam's condition finally began to stabilize. Most of the open wounds had healed, the casts were removed from his legs and he'd begun to put on weight. On April 28th, he was taken off the seriously ill list.

At the beginning of May, the doctors held a meeting to review Sam's condition and prognosis. They diagnosed him as having "Chronic Brain Syndrome; associated with Brain Trauma, manifested by difficulty in communicating and regressive behavior." In short, Sam was one step removed from a vegetative state. He was released from speech therapy because the doctors had come to the conclusion that his problems in talking came from memory loss rather than from any damage to the part of the brain controlling speech and language.

Everything pointed to the hopelessness of the situation as far as Pauline was concerned. She hated the gray hospital walls and the spartan room where Sam lay. The daily visits seemed vindictive and malicious indictments. Her senses swam in a sea of despair and bourbon; Sam had been the focal point of her life. He embodied all her aspirations—now, everything was a blurred emptiness. Long before the end of May, she returned home to Wichita.

Meanwhile letters continued to trickle in. One was from B.T. Collins, stationed in the Mekong Delta. He had returned to Vietnam with the Special Forces in the new year. Another was from Robert Kennedy.

United States Senate
WASHINGTON, D.C.

April 21, 1967

Dear Captain Bird:

I want to take this opportunity to tell you how sorry I was to learn you were seriously wounded while on duty in Vietnam. I know that with your usual determination and perseverance you will come through to a full recovery.

Mrs. Kennedy joins me in sending you our warm regards and best wishes for the future.

> *Sincerely,*
> *Robert F. Kennedy*

He went on to add the following post-script in his own hand:

Mrs. John Kennedy also asked to be remembered to you. I hope I shall have an opportunity of seeing you if you come back East.

> *Best Wishes*
> *Robert Kennedy*

On May 22nd, Sam's story was front page news in the *Washington Post*, accompanied by the headlines: "GUARDIAN OF KENNEDY CASKET WOUNDED IN VIETNAM." The story ran in all the major dailies across the country. The trickle of letters turned into a torrent.

On June 7th, Sam underwent an operation for an ulcer that had developed at the base of his spine. He came through the surgery with no apparent trauma. Indeed, there'd been little change in his mental state for some time except for a noticeable increase in irritability.

At the end of the month, Dick received a letter from Dean Parker informing him that B.T. Collins had been seriously wounded as a result of a grenade explosion in the Delta. He'd lost an arm and a leg along with much blood, yet somehow, had survived. Perhaps this had as much to do with his temperament as anything else. In his typically irascible style, he had screamed for the removal of the Catholic priest whom he thought had come to administer last rites and inquire whether he was sorry for his sins!

On the 6th of July, Sam was placed before a physical evaluation board which recommended that he be transferred to a Veterans' Administration Hospital for long-term custodial care.

Five days prior to leaving Brooke, Sam was presented with two Bronze Stars, the Air Medal and the Purple Heart by the hospital's commanding general. The presentation, which took place in his room with Dick in attendance, was carried on local television. The bars on the side of Sam's bed facing the camera were lowered to show him with the medals by his side. He lay limp and motionless with a faraway look in his eyes. With his head wound facing away from the camera, however, the lens captured a distant yet handsome profile.

★   ★   ★

Sam was transferred to Kennedy Veterans' Hospital in Memphis, Tennessee, on the 19th of July. Like so many veterans' hospitals, its trim exterior lines belied its inner decrepitude. Because a large, modern, fully-equipped hospital in Memphis was still a month away from completion, Sam had to be placed in a spartan room without air conditioning. And this was Memphis in July, which meant suffocating heat and humidity. Sam began to moan and groan almost incessantly. He was placed on high doses of Dilantin and Valium in an attempt to control his seizures and moderate his behavior. The biggest relief came after Dick, who had kept on at the staff about it, had Sam transferred to an air conditioned room. But now, in addition to frustrating the doctors and staff, Sam's condition was even beginning to wear Dick down. He had been at his son's bedside almost constantly for the past five months; lack of hope finally started to affect him too. Pauline lived in dread of having to visit Memphis, but now Dick was returning home more often since there appeared to be little he could do for his son.

The publication of William Manchester's *The Death of a President* and its attendant publicity at the end of July triggered another wave of mail from a grateful public. One letter seemed particularly eloquent.

> *I read about your injury in the New Britain Herald tonight. I have read accounts of the military from time to time who feel that folks at home couldn't care less about Vietnam and the agonies they must endure there. They are so wrong, but how can people let them know it—maybe by writing to you,* **one will know** *that we do care.*
>
> *I am a young mother, raising four small sons alone since their father deserted us five years ago. I've had to be on welfare since then, and things have been pretty tough at times. But no matter how rough times have been, we've had full tummies when we went to bed; we haven't had to crawl in the mud, roast under unmerciful sun, carry fear around in our hearts that each day might be our very last, and risk being bitten, blown up, or savaged by a tropical disease. Life at its worst here is heaven compared to the things you have endured for us. Because of your blood, sweat and tears, my little boys may someday be spared the horrors of war. But if the day comes when they too must fight and die, I hope they have your courage and gallantry. I thank you, Sam; I respect you; and I love you for the sacrifices you have made for me, my little boys, and for a grateful America.*
>
> *Mrs. Shirley Jaydosh*
> *New Britain, Connecticut*

The newspaper story that generated another wave of letters first appeared in the *Memphis Commercial Appeal* on Friday, July 28th. The article was kept for Sam by his father, to go with all the others, and included an extract from Manchester's book in addition to his own personalized inscription to Sam. Also included was a photograph of Sam in Vietnam and a characteristic picture of Dick holding open a copy of the book. Several parts of the article itself which made reference to Sam's physical condition were conspicuously scribbled over with a ball-point pen. In a classic case of denial, and also protective instinct, Dick crossed out the following lines from the article:

. . . leaving the career soldier with crippling brain damage.

. . . and there is still doubt about his complete recovery.

"With all the drive Sam's got, he'll make it out at a minimum," said the elder Mr. Bird, who arrived in Memphis early this week—immediately after his son, who was moved here from a San Antonio, Texas, military hospital.

. . . there still remains a lengthy, tedious recovery for the wounded hero . . .

More poignant, however, was Sam's inability to comprehend the sentiment and emotion expressed in the many hundreds of letters he received during those three months.

Article appearing in the *Memphis Commercial Appeal* on July 28, 1967. Dick's obliterations can be clearly seen.

Chapter Eleven

Memphis

After a week at home in Wichita, Dick returned to Memphis on Tuesday, August 8th. Pauline, in a radical departure from custom, set about cleaning the house herself. She cleaned the front hall, family room, kitchen and utility floors. Two days later she had all the carpets in the house cleaned. She moved lamps, clothes, every item of furniture in the dining room, the china cabinet and art treasures. She polished brass and copper until she collapsed into an armchair exhausted. When she came around, all she could think of was how God-awful it was not to have a single room in order.

Pauline rarely went out. Most of all, she dreaded the grocery store for fear of being recognized by someone who would surely ask about Sam.

Finally, on Friday she ventured out of the house to mail a letter to Dick and Sam and then plucked up the courage to go to Safeway. After returning home, struggling across the patio with a large bag of groceries, she was greeted enthusiastically at the door by Michelle the poodle, who had just left small "tokens" of her presence in three of the newly cleaned rooms. Lurching toward the kitchen counter between scattered pieces of dining room furniture, bags of groceries in both arms, she stumbled over Michelle and fell against the wrought iron chair next to the telephone. The side of her head caught a leg of the chair on the way down, causing a nasty gash on her ear. She picked herself up and rushed into the bathroom. In the mirror she saw blood streaming down the side of her face and burst into tears. She ran some warm water over a washcloth, pressed it against her ear, collapsed onto her bed and fell asleep. She awoke the following morning with the cloth sticking to the side of her face and an ear so sore she couldn't put her glasses on. Pauline felt completely and utterly helpless.

Paula, struggling with the "malediction" of parenthood, wrote Dick a letter that Sunday evening

> *Howdy Dood,*
>
> *Yesterday, we had one of our regular "character-building" Sundays, with the children [Bruce, Julie and Laurie] in "full force" all day long. I have just finished putting four bath rings in the tub and I'm not sure how long I can stay awake, but I thought you might like a first-hand report on Babe. The last day or two is the first time that I have noticed any improvement. Having all the furniture out of place really threw her, I think, but at last things are back where they belong and she seems at peace. It really seems to bother her when she thinks she must leave home. But it really bothers her, not knowing "what's in the future."*

Paula was well aware that her mother was helpless without her father—even though she preferred to stay in Wichita when Dick felt he had to be in Memphis. Paula suggested a compromise by which they could both live together, alternating between Wichita and Memphis.

> *I have felt her out on the idea and she seems agreeable, though I think her idea of a "compromise" might be three weeks here to one week there. Before she could mention it, I told her that I thought the only fair way was equal time in each city. I couldn't be certain, but in the end, I think she went for the idea. Now, I'm wondering if you might see some good in it.*

Paula told Dick she felt Sam was receiving better care in Memphis than he had in San Antonio, adding that he might get excited knowing the two of them were coming to visit together.

She was undoubtedly clutching at straws. Dick, however, was becoming visibly more despondent at Sam's lack of response to treatment. Sam might have an occasional semi-coherent day but the following day would always be heart-breaking as Dick would see his son revert to a near-vegetative state. The frustrating thing for the doctors was the lack of any discernible pattern to Sam's behavior. It was impossible to say he was improving gradually when after each relapse it appeared they were back to square one. In 1967 very little was known about the brain and even less about brain injuries.

The one phenomenon that really appeared to be eating away at Dick, on top of the false dawns, was the sight of Sam's brain palpitating beneath his scalp. Orderlies would find Dick sitting at Sam's bedside staring, transfixed, seemingly incapable of shifting his gaze.

In addition, Sam's behavior was even beginning to irritate both the nurses and the orderlies. Left alone for no more than five minutes, he would begin to groan and yell incoherently. The staff was becoming more and more frustrated and yet the doctors could tell Dick little, except they didn't think his son was in any pain. They had tried many different forms of therapy without invoking any response. There were just occasional days of semi-lucidity, which didn't appear to have any rhyme or reason. Any remaining optimism became centered on the move to the new hospital at the end of the month. By now, *everyone* was clutching at straws.

On the 29th of August, the patients at the Kennedy V.A. were transferred to the new 14 story, 23 million dollar hospital at Poplar Avenue and Pauline. The new hospital was located on the fringes of downtown Memphis, in a much less attractive area. In addition, the new hospital did not possess the same aesthetically appealing exterior as its predecessor. The main building of the new hospital was an imposing, generic, box-like structure with gray exterior walls. Its appearance mimicked the other general hospitals nearby. Yet, if the building itself wasn't particularly pleasing to the eye, the facilities inside more than compensated for its external shortcomings. With the Vietnam War at its height, government funding was in plentiful supply for the very best equipment. Inside, the wards were light, bright and spacious, meticulously designed to ensure patients' needs were optimally addressed. There were no staff shortages and the place had the reputation, before it even opened, of possessing one of the finest spinal-cord rehabilitation units in the country. Dick moved into an apartment across the road from the hospital at 1045 Jefferson.

The move generated a fresh wave of optimism in everyone. During the first week of September, Sam received numerous visitors. Even Pauline joined Dick at the apartment for Labor Day Weekend. Charlie Harrell, a good friend from Sam's tour in Korea, and his wife came from Fort Campbell, Kentucky, where he was stationed with the 101st Airborne, preparing to go to Vietnam. The initial impact of seeing Sam hit them both hard, although they did their best to put a brave face on it. At the end of their visit, they jotted down an expeditious message in Sam's diary. "Sam, it's wonderful to see you looking so well."

Sam's face registered nothing but a vacant expression.

The young couple had dinner with Dick and Pauline in the apartment that evening and returned to the hospital the following day. They were greeted by the same blank, expressionless face and resorted to the diary once again. "Sam, you look real good today, much better than yesterday!"

The following weekend, Dave Porreca and Bruce Wilson, Sam's counterpart with A Company, 2nd/12th, came to visit. Wilson was particularly distraught at the sight of his old friend. He recalled vividly how the two of them used to exchange stories over the "B/S" (Bruce/Sam) radio net while winding down during the evenings. Now, he could barely stand to look at him. Like countless others, Dave Porreca resorted to the diary, "You're looking great this time, Captain! Keep it up."

The visit took such a toll on Bruce Wilson he couldn't bring himself to return. Others, among them Citadel classmates, couldn't visit at all. Some called Dick to say they would, but never did.

Once the initial hope and anticipation of the change of hospitals had worn off, a cloud of pessimism established itself again. The doctors tried everything they knew, but nothing appeared to have an effect. Paula seemed to catch the prevailing mood in another letter to her father.

I have surely worried about Sam since this afternoon, but you've got to keep hoping, and not give in when things appear badly.

I can't believe that anyone could say that Sam has pro-gressed so "very little." It is so plain to us back here that he is making progress, but you forget easily because you see him often. I hope you'll be sure to drop me a line so I'll know if things are any better. I'm always thinking the worst until I hear from you. Then if I don't hear, I think that things are worse than worse!

Even Dick found himself engulfed by an air of resignation. There were no more brash pronouncements that Sam would "make it out at a minimum!" He'd been a stalwart, if somewhat broody and finicky presence beside his son for almost an entire six months. In the middle of September, he returned home to Wichita for a prolonged stay.

★   ★   ★

The Monday after Dick left Memphis, Sam received a visit from a thirty-two-year-old quadriplegic country singer and record-ing artist by the name of Bill Laundy. He had suffered irreparable spinal cord damage following a freak accident while diving into a river in Louisiana in 1956. The accident left him paralyzed from the chest down with limited use of his hands and arms.

Laundy, a charismatic figure with boyish good looks— complete with an all American smile—had experienced many dark days before regaining control of a severely impaired diaphragm and the ability to sing again. After cutting several successful records on the Zefco label and appearing on several live television shows in Memphis, he had become something of an inspiration to many of the paraplegics at the V.A. Laundy often visited the spinal rehabilitation unit in the hospital for treatment, during which time he would visit patients and sing for them. His singing, in particular one song, "The Impossible

Dream," (from *Man of La Mancha*) struck a positive chord with several of the patients and staff.

He had visited Sam on several occasions since they'd moved into the new hospital. Meeting Dick, Bill was struck by his meticulously co-ordinated apparel and preoccupied devotion to his son. Throughout the month of September, Sam had very few lucid moments. Yet whenever Bill stopped by, he appeared to be conscious of his presence. Unfortunately, the doctors, nurses, aides and orderlies were unable to elicit a similar reaction. Every one of Sam's incoherent ramblings and moanings had to be treated as though it was an emergency. The outbursts continued to dumbfound the doctors, who felt Sam shouldn't be in any physical pain.

Sam's predicament came to the attention of the nurse in charge of the two rehabilitation floors. A formidably tall woman of consummate dignity, with meticulously combed, thick, wavy hair, Major Tommye Davis commanded instant respect. Her countenance exuded both warmth and steel. One of seven children from an old southern family, she had never married. Tommye Davis supervised the Spinal Cord Injury Unit as though it were a garrison post, accepting no nonsense from anyone—aides, nurses or doctors. She strived continually to insure that patient welfare remained everybody's first priority. And she never showed favoritism, always taking time to visit each patient in turn. She was becoming increasingly concerned about Sam's lack of progress. Aware that fewer people were visiting him, she asked Bill Laundy to see what he could do.

Although Bill enjoyed some success in inducing positive reactions from Sam, the depressing fact remained that Sam would always revert to incoherence as soon as Bill left. His periods of lucidity were neither more frequent nor more prolonged.

At the end of September, Tommye Davis threw a party at her home in Bill Laundy's honor to celebrate his phenomenal achievement at re-establishing a singing career, also acknowledging the inspiration and encouragement he'd given to many patients at the hospital. Tommye invited all the staff from the two paraplegic floors: the doctors, nurses, aides and "gray lady" Red-Cross volunteers who visited patients, usually on a weekly basis.

One such gray lady was Doris McKibbin, an attractive, thirty-seven-year-old divorcee originally from Northern Ireland. Distinguished by thick auburn hair and a heart-shaped face, she had an infectious smile. Her engaging personality had been a tonic for many paraplegic patients at the V.A. during the past year.

Her puckish charm concealed the pain and bitterness that followed a disastrous marriage which ended in divorce. It was the first divorce in her Irish Protestant family and very difficult for her to bear. She felt she could never return home to her family in Ireland and turned inward, harboring a deep bitterness toward men. At the suggestion of her minister, she volunteered with the Red Cross in an effort to work through and exorcise these feelings as a form of therapy.

Her quick wit and sparkle earned her a reputation on the paraplegic ward for elevating spirits and restoring self-esteem with a simple, feel-good, mildly flirtatious style. In addition, she had the kind of Irish accent that always sounded like a song. Using a combination of gentle teasing and ego-stroking, she reaffirmed in many of the men their belief in their ability to be attractive to women. It was a delicate achievement, although the men were left in no doubt that Doris herself was off-limits. Nevertheless, she constantly encouraged the younger female volunteers to talk with the men and build relationships. "They're better men and more reliable than most of those 'walking cats,' " she would tell them.

Several volunteers married paraplegics. Many such marriages turned out very successfully. However, there were also stories of women suffocating their bridegrooms in the honeymoon bed in order to obtain their pensions.

At the party Tommye told Doris about Sam.

"Well I don't know, Tommye," Doris replied. "I've already got too many 'pets' as it is. I really haven't the time to take on any more."

"I tell you what Doris. Please just do me a favor and think about it."

Later Bill Laundy was wheeled over. Doris was quite taken with Bill. She had great admiration for what he had accomplished against such odds and she adored his singing.

"Doris, I want you to do something for me," he crooned.

"Sure Bill. What is it you want me to do?" she cooed back, "You know I'd do anything."

"I want you to see a friend of mine. His name's Captain Sam Bird. He needs help."

"Oh yeah? Sounds like a popular guy. What kind of help does he need?"

"I don't know, Doris. I've tried to get through to him, but it's very difficult. They've got him on the paraplegic floor because he's paralyzed except for his right hand, but he's not a spinal cord injury as such."

"Then why is he on the paraplegic floor?"

"He was shot in the head and lost a part of his brain," Bill said matter-of-factly.

"I see," replied Doris, inhaling deeply. Bill's words set off alarm bells. A fellow volunteer had recently been murdered by a patient she knew from the psych ward. While out on a pass, he had obtained her address, gone to her home and shot her. Therefore, the thought of visiting someone with brain damage produced an uneasy sensation with her.

"I'm gonna have to think about this one, Bill."

"Sure baby, I understand." Bill smiled and his aide wheeled him away to mingle with the other guests.

On the following Sunday afternoon, during her weekly visit to the hospital, she was met on the elevator by Dr. Huey, one of Sam's doctors. He wasted no time in coming to the point, "Hello there, Doris. Has Major Davis had a word with you about Captain Bird?"

"Yes she has, Dr. Huey—she, and it seems the entire hospital staff!"

"I see. Well, we really have reached the end of our tether. We don't know what to do next. He just doesn't seem to respond to anything we try. Not only that, he's starting to drive everybody crazy with his moaning and groaning. The thing is, he really shouldn't be in any pain.

"He moans as if the light is bothering him and then when that's taken care of, he still moans. We've tried everything, but nothing seems to work.

"I know it's a lot to ask, Doris, with all your other commitments—but you seem to have the knack of . . . well, you know what I mean—getting through to these . . . special patients." He paused, "Please, will you go and see him?"

Tight-lipped with her eyes closed, Doris took a deep breath and exhaled long and slow. "Sure, Dr. Huey."

His face lit up. "Don't pay any attention to the moaning and groaning," he said, walking away. "I don't think he's in any physical pain. He just might be trying to communicate."

Now she was less convinced than ever that this was a good idea. But how could she continue to ignore these requests?

She approached the nurses' station in the middle of the floor like a child who'd just been ordered to report to the principal's office. "I'm looking for Captain Bird's room," she inquired tentatively. "Dr. Huey asked me to see him."

The nurse pointed over toward the only closed door on the ward. "Best of luck!" she said, in a voice tinged with sarcasm.

Doris flashed her a hesitant glance.

"You sure are gonna need it, honey. There's nothin' anyone can do for him."

Doris crossed the hallway and halted outside the door. 'Well, here goes!' she said to herself in a half-whisper, and burst into the darkened room. All the blinds were rolled down.

Sam lay there emitting a noise resembling the whimpering of a sick puppy. He was wearing large, black oblong protectors around his eyes. For Doris, they evoked the blinders placed on spirited race horses in Ireland. A surge of adrenalin seemed to go straight to her mouth—"Whoops! I'm looking for Captain Eagle. Is there a Captain Eagle in here?"

For Doris, it was nothing more than simple word association with the name on the door—the first thing that came into her head. She had no idea that Eagle had been Sam's nickname at the Old Guard in Washington.

The whimpering ceased at once as the muscles in Sam's hollow, ashen cheeks tightened to form an exasperated grimace. The moment of silence took every nuance of life from the room. Then Sam let out a ghastly roar.

Recalling that Dr. Huey had counseled her to ignore such outbursts, Doris repeated the question, this time addressing her remarks directly to Sam. "Are you Captain Eagle?" she inquired, her voice rising an octave.

Once again Sam let out a furious roar, at which point one of the orderlies rushed in. Doris waved him back, motioning that she had things under control, while continuing to pursue the same line of questioning. "I'm looking for Captain Eagle," she announced somewhat pompously.

The aide was totally confused. "Well this here's Cap'n Bird," he replied, wrinkling his brow in a look of utter bewilderment.

He wasn't alone in his doubts. Doris was far from sure of herself, but she blathered on, playing the moment for all it was worth. "Are you sure?" she demanded, as though cross-examining the unfortunate man.

"Yes! Can't you see the name on the door?" His confusion gave way to irritation.

Doris flipped a quick glance at the door. "Oh my goodness, I am sorry!" she gushed. "Your name's Bird, not Eagle. Oh well, not to worry. I was close!" And with that, she breezed out.

By the time she had reached the hallway she felt giddy. 'You've really gone and done it this time, girl,' she admonished herself openly. 'What have you done? You've flipped!' She hurried into the elevator and left the hospital.

The following Sunday, Doris went to Sam's room as soon as she checked in. This time she opted for a more cautious entrance and saw that the window blinds were halfway up and the protectors had been removed from Sam's eyes. Before going any further, she addressed him in her soft, lilting voice, "Captain Bird, I've come to apologize to you." Coating every word in a velvety, Irish brogue, she continued, "I'm sorry for calling you

214

'Eagle' but I was so tired the other day, and I'd heard so much about you, and I wanted to talk to you, and . . . I'm sorry." The apology rippled melodiously across to where Sam was lying.

When she finished speaking she noticed he had trained his gaze on her.

"Do you want me to sit down for a while?" she asked softly, motioning to the chair beside his bed. Sam looked at Doris intently, appearing to nod his head ever so slightly. She sat down beside him. "You probably don't understand what I'm saying because I'm from Ireland," she continued, laying the accent on thicker than ever. She talked non-stop about herself and Ireland for about half an hour. All the time Sam lay motionless, with his gaze fixed on her. Eventually she rose from her chair and bid Sam, "Good night and God bless," giving him one more lingering glance before leaving the room.

Her first feeling upon reaching the hallway was one of relief. She had successfully put to rest any residual guilt feelings from the previous Sunday's "performance." But then a surge of uncertainty overcame her about what she should do next. 'How can I possibly help him?' she thought to herself. 'And besides, what about my other pets? No, there's no way. I can't possibly go back to see him again and that's the end of it. Now, pull yourself together, Doris!' She crossed the ward to visit her other patients.

A week later, one of the nurses on Sam's floor stopped Doris and pleaded with her to go back and visit him. She told Doris that Sam had spent his most peaceful night of all following her visit the previous week; not to mention the fact everyone had been given a much-needed break. Indeed, a group of orderlies had been lobbying the nurse all week to get her to return. So Doris walked deliberately over toward Sam's door.

★   ★   ★

"I know you can blink your eye, Sam. If you understand what I am saying, blink once." It was a quality that only women seem to possess—the ability to coax the little boy out of the man at will. Sam's right eyelid closed and opened emphatically.

Before long, Doris was coming in every evening after her secretarial job. If she missed an evening, the orderlies would pay for it that night. They were supposed to feed Sam his meals in the evening, but he always refused to eat unless Doris came to feed him. After she fed him his evening meal, Sam would indicate to Doris that he wanted his teeth brushed, a procedure that could take anywhere from 15 minutes to half an hour. One such evening, following a particularly trying day at her job, Sam looked over at his electric toothbrush meaningfully.

"Just for once Sam, please don't make this take forever," Doris pleaded. Ten minutes later, the electric toothbrush was still buzzing. She looked at Sam helplessly while he motioned her to continue, his eyes full of mischief. Doris became more and more agitated. Finally, reduced to a state of utter exasperation, she demanded, "Well, are you going to rinse?"

He signalled that he wasn't through yet and wanted her to keep brushing. At this, Doris yanked the brush out of his mouth. "Sam, you're making me lose my temper!"

A large grin spread across his face and he took some water to rinse. When he'd finished, he looked up at her. Still smiling, he said, clearly and slowly, "Your temper Doris, you're going to have to work on your temper." It was the first time Sam had spoken since February 11th, some eight months ago. The previous rigors of that difficult day melted away before Doris's eyes.

It certainly appears now that much of Sam's moaning and groaning could be associated with the frustration he was feeling about his inability to express clearly what was on his mind. We can trace this back to that February 11th statement at the 85th Evac. Hospital—"I have something to say and I wish I could say it, but I can't think as I want to." This was before Dr. Slater had been forced to debride big chunks from Sam's brain in Japan. It seems only logical that as more brain tissue was removed, Sam's cognitive processes became more confused, not less.

Sam was living in a world of scrambled communication. It was as though he'd awakened one morning to find the world had gone topsy-turvy. People couldn't understand what he was trying

216

to say. In this sense, Sam may have been experiencing the symptoms of aphasia, the technical term for interference with the comprehension and use of language.

Today, treatment of aphasia involves recovering, as far as possible, the use of language the person possessed before: Sam hadn't lost his language, but his ability to remember it sometimes. So, recovery didn't mean re-learning English from the beginning like a child, but recalling what had already been learned.

Certainly, Sam exhibited some symptoms of aphasia, but that really doesn't explain his condition sufficiently since he would have good days and bad days. Because Doris didn't treat him like a child, she had a very significant effect.

Sam's lack of memory, particularly short-term memory, was certainly pivotal. This was combined with a series of cognitive deficits, described by his doctors in San Antonio and Memphis as follows: disorientation to time and place, distraction—the inability to maintain attention over a period of time, concentration deficits—difficulty recalling and storing recent information and inability to plan—difficulty in understanding abstract concepts. All these symptoms would seem to plague Sam for the rest of his life.

★   ★   ★

Doris knew little of Sam's background, although she had been aware of some talk on the ward referring to his role in the Kennedy funeral. She thought this would be a good way to stimulate his memory.

Up till then, Doris had done most of the talking. Once she raised the subject of President Kennedy, however, Sam had plenty to say. In the beginning, he would repeat again and again how much respect he had for the late president. He expounded at length on the deplorable condition of the first casket and how it had to be replaced. But Doris was more interested in what he had to say about Jacqueline Kennedy, having delighted in much of the tabloid gossip written about her. "Well, what kinda' person was Mrs. Kennedy, Sam?"

Each time, he would answer without hesitation, "A great lady—dignity—that's what she displayed that day." Night after night, Sam would speak of little else during those first few weeks.

As the strength began to return slowly to his right arm, Sam could use his right hand to feed himself. In addition, he could operate the electric toothbrush! Sam began to say grace before every meal and this left a deep impression on Doris.

Doris noticed Sam's fingernails were starting to look like talons. He refused to let any of the orderlies near him with a pair of nail clippers. No one could understand why he didn't want them cut, especially since he was so particular about the rest of his appearance.

One evening Doris arrived with her manicure set. "No!" Sam exclaimed, before she had a chance to lay it out on the bedside table. She looked up, taken aback by his reaction. "Now Sam, I think you're more than ready to join the others in the rec room, but I sure as heck am not going to take you looking like a sissy!"

Sam reached across to a plastic cup on his bedside table, clasped it in his right hand, crumpled it and flung it to the ground. His eyes were filled with anger. "Get out!" he cried. Doris quickly packed up her manicure set, stuffed it in her bag and rushed out of the room.

'I am not a sissy,' he said to himself quietly.

Once Doris reached the hallway, a feeling of unease began to set in. She felt she'd gone too far, but dared not go back to apologize.

She stayed away from the ward for a couple of days, not returning until the following Sunday afternoon. She'd barely stepped off the elevator when a note was thrust into her hand; Dr. Huey wanted to see her at once. He told her that since the other evening, Sam had been acting up more than usual. The aides could do nothing with him so would she please go back and see him.

On her way to Sam's room she was stopped by one of the aides who had grown particularly fond of Sam. "Doris. Go in and see him, but please don't upset him again. The other night after

218

you left, we had a hell of a time. We couldn't get him calmed down, let alone off to sleep. The last couple of days have been hell. Please, can you go in there and try to calm him down?"

Sam was lying in bed wide awake, as she entered the room.

"Oh, Sam," she twittered like a country singer, "I'm sorry if I upset you but I've been so sad and lonesome for you. I've been cryin' every night since then. Can't we be friends again? I didn't mean to call you a sissy 'cause of those nails."

Sam replied in a gruff, authoritarian voice, "You're forgiven. Maybe one hand. But just a little."

"No, it doesn't matter," she replied. "We'll keep your nails as they are. I'll still take you down to the recreation room."

"I told you to cut my nails," he retorted gruffly. "Do it!"

Doris smiled, sat down and took out her manicure set. After finishing Sam's left hand, she started to pack up her things. But Sam summoned her back, once again in military fashion. "Now you can cut the other hand," he said with a good deal of conde-scension.

"I'm sorry, Sam, but it's late and I really have to get home."

"Doris, I want you to cut the nails on the other hand . . . tonight!"

"Oh, Sam, the orderly will do it for you," she simpered nonchalantly.

"No! You do it. Right now!"

"Yes, BOSS!" she replied in a deep southern drawl. This time Doris had mischief in her eye. She claimed to an aide afterwards that she had planned it that way all along. She left Sam's room that evening having manicured both hands. Almost before she reached the hallway, his eyes were closed and he was fast asleep, snoring loudly.

The following Sunday Sam asked Doris if she would wheel him down to the hospital chapel. This would also provide a means of introducing him to the other patients who could help him by visiting during the day.

During the service, the minister asked Sam for his favorite hymn. He replied without hesitation, "God of Our Fathers."

Doris had never heard the hymn before, yet Sam would request it each Sunday without fail from then on.

★   ★   ★

Sam continued to improve over the next few weeks while Doris coaxed him into telling her more about his past. In some areas his progress was painstakingly slow, as was the case with writing—Sam struggled with the simplest of words like "dad." He repeatedly confused a "d" with a "b". At the same time, he could confound and amaze Doris with his command of the English language as they openly discussed politics, religion, music and philosophy—notably Socrates. But the day after was always the same. He would have forgotten everything they'd discussed the evening before. He could recall many inconsequential incidents from way back in his childhood, yet he couldn't remember what he'd had for breakfast that morning. There was more to it than that, however. Often he knew what he wanted to say but was unable to say it. It was as though a vital link in his thought process was missing. On other occasions his thought process appeared completely intact. Everything seemed to revolve around memory. Doris could see Sam's frustration. At every opportunity she tried to absorb or deflect it with a joke or a wisecrack, accentuating the Irish brogue that appeared to captivate Sam.

★   ★   ★

Dick and Pauline returned to Memphis on the 14th of October, a Saturday. Dick dropped Pauline off at the apartment before lunch and drove out to the airport to pick up Jack Morgan, Sam's roommate and "illustrious" bagpiper from The Citadel. Jack was living in Chicago and was en route to a business trip in Miami. He had scheduled his flights to allow a three-hour layover in Memphis. Jack had been in touch with Dick earlier in the week to finalize plans. Dick had taken the opportunity to warn him he should think twice about the visit because Sam might not be able to remember him. Jack, however, was insistent. "In any case, Mr. Bird," he said, "I've already booked my tickets."

During the drive to the hospital, Dick elaborated on the severity of Sam's wounds. He was trying to make the point that Sam wouldn't know Jack, but to try not to let that upset him. Jack really didn't know what to think; he felt himself becoming numb and started to wonder whether the whole thing had been a terrible mistake.

When they left the elevator on the sixth floor of the hospital, Dick told Jack to stay at the nurses' station while he went into Sam's room first to try to prepare him for the visit. For some reason, Jack found himself ignoring Dick's request and followed a couple of yards behind him.

The sight of Sam lying in bed, pale and much thinner than he remembered—with a gaping depression on the side of his head—shocked Jack. The image before him was the antithesis of the proud, vital individual he had known at The Citadel, and he wished for a moment he had taken Dick's advice.

While Dick moved over to the bedside, Sam opened his eyes and saw Jack standing in the doorway. In the soft yet unmistakable tones of a voice Jack remembered so well, Sam called out from the bed, "Hey Tweetie, let's have a couple of 'Mickies' and talk it over."

The tears tumbled down Dick's cheeks; he couldn't believe it.

The two roommates spent a couple of hours talking about old times while Dick looked on incredulously. After eight and a half months of darkness, there was light. All the way back to the airport Dick probably smiled more than he had in his entire life. After that day, Jack always felt in his heart that at least once in his life he had done a very good deed.

Now that Dick and Pauline began to witness improvement in Sam's condition, they began to visit more often and stay longer. If they were at their home in Wichita and knew Doris was on duty, they would call and she'd roll the portable telephone over to Sam.

The first time Doris met Sam's parents she could see the depth of feeling Dick had for his son. She also noticed that he seemed bewitched by the palpitating depression on the side of Sam's head. During Dick's six weeks at home, he had sought the opinion of several specialists about having Sam fitted with a plate in his head so he would look more "normal." Doris saw that for Dick, everything hinged on the normality of Sam's appearance. If his head looked normal, then somehow everything else would be normal too. Meanwhile, the doctors at the V.A. in Memphis were adamant that under no circumstances should plating surgery be considered for another couple of years. In their opinion, Sam was still very vulnerable and the wound needed more time to heal.

When Doris heard that Dick and Pauline were coming to visit Sam in Memphis that weekend, she decided to stay away from the hospital until her usual visiting hours on Sunday. That afternoon she was greeted by Dick and Pauline on their way to Sam's room. After thanking Doris generously for everything she had done on Sam's behalf, Pauline drew her to one side as all three of them entered the room. "We had such big plans for him, and now look at him," she lamented.

Doris could tell Pauline had been drinking and she was much relieved when Pauline moved over to Sam's bedside. She watched as Pauline talked about what was going on at home, almost as though she were talking to herself, flitting from subject to subject without any reference to Sam. The expression on Sam's face was blank; he obviously didn't understand what she was talking about but Pauline wasn't paying any attention to that.

During the week following their visit, Doris asked Sam to tell her more about his parents and quickly wished she hadn't. "I wish my mother wouldn't drink," he retorted.

Doris could see this was something that really upset him. "Well, Sam, maybe she can't face what you've gone through," she said, searching in vain for the right words. "Maybe she's trying to get her life back together."

"Why don't you talk to her about it, Doris? I don't like alcohol. And I don't like women who drink!"

"Oh, Sam, she's not drinking that much and she loves you so much—she's so proud of you," Doris replied lamely, having been caught completely off-guard by his follow-up request.

"*You* don't have to kiss her!" he exclaimed. "I kissed her and I know she's drinking!"

Doris never broached the matter with Pauline.

★   ★   ★

On the last weekend in October, Doris wheeled Sam down to the hospital entrance to meet his father. He wheeled Sam across the road to the apartment for the first time. At first Sam didn't want to go, displaying confusion and bewilderment at what was happening to him. Once Doris was able to reassure him, however, a small but discernible wave of euphoria appeared to ripple over him.

During this time, Dick and Pauline called Doris at home, asking her questions about where she came from, her past history and marriage and other personal questions. When they continued to pry on subsequent occasions, Doris put a stop to their curiosity. She thought it rude.

Wednesday, November 1st, was a momentous day for Sam. It was lunch over at the apartment again, but this time he was going to wear his uniform—for the first time since he'd been wounded. As Doris helped get him ready, she could see the thrill in his eyes, how proud he was of himself and his country. It made her stop and think for a moment. After spending almost two months with him, not once could she recall him complaining about what had happened—there was no resentment, no bitterness. She thought how different this was from so many others on the ward.

After she had finished straightening his brass, Doris took a step back to express approval in her own inimitable way, "Uhmmm, You really do look sexy."

"Don't say that, Doris!" Sam reproved her sharply. "It sounds so undignified."

"OK, Sam," she giggled. "How about, 'Uhmmm! You really do look handsome'?"

"Yes," he smirked, "I'm one handsome officer with a hole in my head." They both chuckled.

223

Once she had dropped Sam off at the apartment, Doris returned to the ward and went over to a group of her other patients.

"How's the captain doing today?" asked one of them, with a mildly caustic note of irony detected by everyone but Doris.

"Well, he seems to be doing pretty good. He's real happy to be in his uniform," she chirped.

"Yeah. He sure is one straight arrow," said another. Several heads nodded in agreement.

Doris looked at them quizzically. "What do you mean by that?" she asked. But before the man had a chance to answer, another interjected, "He means, Doris, that you're becoming too attached to Bird. Don't do it. He's brain damaged. Ease up. You're getting too involved with him. He's brain damaged and nothing can come of it."

Doris was going to let the remarks go until the last admonition, which sparked an indignant response: "Nothing is going to *come* of this! We're good friends, that's all!"

"Of course you are, Doris, and I'm the man in the moon," chimed in one of the younger ones.

"Hey! Shut up, man! Leave her alone. You're just jealous, that's all," retorted another.

The general feeling amongst the older men on the ward was that Sam must have been a pretty darned good officer. As for most of the younger ones, they were just thankful to be in better shape than he was, although no one ever made fun of him. But, everybody who came in contact with Sam was struck almost immediately by his tremendous faith in God.

★   ★   ★

Now that Sam was showing signs of real progress, Doris pressed to have him moved into a room with other patients for company. The doctors agreed and he was moved in with a World War I veteran and a younger man. As soon as Doris went into the new room that night, she sensed something wrong. Her cheery fusillade of wisecracks didn't draw the usual sharp response. Instead, Sam lay there as though he were in a trance.

"What's the matter, Sam?" she asked, changing the tone of her voice instantly. He stared at her a long time before replying, "I want you to tell me the truth."

"Sure, Sam."

"I want the truth, Doris." His tone became more insistent.

"Yes, Sam, I'll tell you the truth," she asserted softly. "No matter how hard it hurts, I'll tell it to you."

"This is the psychiatric ward I'm on, isn't it?"

Doris burst out laughing, "Heavens no, Sam!"

"It's nothing to laugh about, Doris," he rebuked her sternly. "I want the truth! Which ward am I on?"

"You're on the paraplegic ward, Sam," she maintained somewhat diffidently, plainly taken aback by the fervor with which he was pursuing the matter.

"No, I'm not!" Sam stormed, detecting the uncertainty in her voice. "I'm on the psych ward, aren't I?"

"No, Sam!" she exclaimed with far greater assurance. "Listen, to put your mind at rest, I'll swear on the *Bible* beside your bed. In any case, I can't do duty on the psych ward."

"You can't?" he replied apprehensively.

"No," she asserted, "I refused to do it. What on earth made you think you were on the psych ward, anyway?"

"It's that man over there," he said, pointing to the younger man with his right hand. "He asked me if you were my mother. And when I said no, he asked me if you were my grandmother. He sure acts crazy . . . so I got to thinkin' I must be on the psych ward."

"Or, you look so young that you look like my grandson!"

Sam cracked half a smile, but Doris could see he remained unsure. When she rose to leave that evening, he asked her once again, "Doris, are you sure I'm not on the psych ward?"

"Well there's one quick way of finding out, Sam."

"What's that?" he replied eagerly.

"Spell psychiatric!"

Letters on the tip of his tongue were going in opposite directions. Sam began to tense up, exasperation building on his face. He could articulate complex words and feelings but cognitively he couldn't identify their point of origin, let alone spell them. Therein lay the source of his frustration and anxiety. Doris saw it and knew she had to think quickly. "You know what, Sam? I can't spell it either!"

Visible relief came over his face as he retorted in more characteristic style, "Yeah, but *you* don't have a hole in your head!" They both dissolved in laughter.

While Sam continued to improve, Doris witnessed Dick's continued obsession with the shape of his son's head. She overheard him one day as he spoke to Sam about it, "Sam, we've got to do something about your head. You're getting along so good, we're going to have to do something about your head."

Sam looked at his father with an expression of utter bewilderment. When Dick left, Sam asked Doris, "Do you think I ought to have a plate put in my head?"

"Sam, I would go by what the doctors say and nobody else." This was always her firm reply but she could see he remained uncertain.

The doctors at Memphis were adamant. Under no circumstances was Sam ready for a plating operation of any kind. The divergence of opinion merely served to compound Sam's confusion. On one side were the doctors who did not want to insert any plate—least of all a metal one. On the other side were Dick and Pauline who felt it was a necessity because of the increase in requests from various groups and organizations to see Sam in public. In his search for allies, Dick wrote twice to Dr. John P. Slater, the neurosurgeon who had operated on Sam in Japan. He had since left the Army and now had a private practice in California. The doctor wrote back on November 25th.

> *The plating operation is not very difficult. It will be a big and tedious job, but shouldn't be at all the touch and go serious business that Sam has already been through. Of course I'd be glad to do it, if this was convenient for you, but in as much as Sam will need periodical care, indefinitely, it might be wiser to stick with the Army 100%.*

Sam, meanwhile, was starting to ask more questions of Doris. "Does my head look bad, Doris?"

"Well, I just don't notice it very much," she would reply breezily. "But now that you call my attention to it, it kind of looks like one big beauty spot."

"But the first time you looked at me, what did you think?"

"Well, I didn't look at your head. All I could see were the blinders on you! You know, everyone is handicapped in some way or other. The only difference between you and me is that my shortcomings are covered."

Dick and Pauline flew back home on the 29th of November. The doctors had granted permission for Sam to be flown home for the Christmas holiday, so they returned to prepare for the homecoming.

As the winter evenings began to draw in, Doris borrowed from Robert Frost for her nightly farewells. A pattern developed each time she got up to leave. Sam would say, "See you tomorrow, Doris." Then there would be a pause before he'd ask, "Oh, by the way, isn't there something you're going to say?" And Doris would say, "Sure, Sam.

> The woods are lovely, dark and deep,
> but I have promises to keep
> and miles to go before I sleep
> and miles to go before I sleep."

"Good night, God bless."
"God bless," Sam would reply.

★   ★   ★

Sam was flown into McConnell Air Force Base on the evening of December 19th. There to greet him at the foot of the steps to the aircraft were many family members and a reporter and photographer from the local newspaper; Paula had seen to that. This was his first time back in Wichita since he had left for Vietnam 18 months earlier. He was glad to be home.

At Dick's suggestion, a photograph was taken of Sam in his dress blues and made into a Christmas card which was mailed to numerous friends and acquaintances. For some it was a wonderful Christmas present; others were shocked at the sight of Sam in a uniform that no longer fit a pale, thin body. The image was a grim parody of someone they didn't know anymore. They found it painful to look at.

Dr. Slater visited 609 Rutland on January 3rd. He could barely believe it when he saw Sam sitting up in his wheelchair, albeit with the support of a leather strap. He looked down at the immaculately polished shoes on Sam's feet and cracked a wry smile. 'His father must have done that for him,' he thought to himself. 'What a wonderful thing.'

In fact Sam had polished the shoes himself with his one good hand. Dick had secured them on a table in front of him.

Later that day, Sam was flown back to Memphis.

★   ★   ★

Sam continued to improve gradually, and on January 27th, 1968, one year after receiving the near-fatal wounds, he celebrated his twenty-eighth birthday at the apartment with his parents and Paula.

Doris continued to spend more and more time with Sam. Now that all her free time was spent with him, she had not been dating for some months.

On February 26th, thanks to the efforts and influence of several generals and colonels on his behalf, Sam was promoted to Major. The promotion would have far-reaching financial consequences; the new pension and compensation entitlement far outstripped those of a captain. With one stroke of the pen, Sam's financial future had been secured.

On March 1st, Dick drove Sam to Fort Campbell, Kentucky to carry out a special observance of Army tradition. At the main gate, a military policeman named Larry Etheridge was completely taken by surprise when Sam handed over a dollar for rendering him his first salute as a major.

Later in the month, B.T. Collins, who had just been fitted with his new prosthesis, arrived with Dean Parker for a visit. Everyone, including Sam, stayed at the Memphis Holiday Inn for the weekend. Parker brought the red and white 2nd/12th guidon, embroidered with Sam's name in feathered black stitching across its bottom half. He also brought the rifle Max Hanning had recovered from the bunker on January 27th, 1967. With everyone gathered in Sam's room, Dean presented the rifle to Dick and Pauline, saying he felt reasonably confident it was the rifle that had been used to wound Sam. It's a tradition in the Army to recover the weapon responsible for wounding a fallen leader. As soon as he presented the rifle and saw the look in Pauline's eye, Dean realized he had made a terrible mistake. The effect on Pauline was shattering; she broke down completely and withdrew for the remainder of the weekend.

The following weekend, Doris returned from a holiday spent visiting her family in Ireland. She brought back a shillelagh (a club) for Sam and gave it to him on the condition that he never use it on her! Sam promised he never would. Instead, he said he would use it as his secret weapon to bash the calories if he ever put on too much weight as a result of his lack of mobility. That weekend, which happened to be Saint Patrick's Day, Sam stayed awake for the hitherto record time of seven-and-a-half hours.

At last it really seemed as though Sam was making genuine progress. But other matters were coming to a head. Dick was unshakable in his determination to have Sam fitted with a plate in his head and the doctors at Memphis were equally adamant in their refusal to oblige. Dick had therefore contacted the V.A. Hospital in Oklahoma City, the closest to Wichita. They agreed to perform the operation in May. In the meantime, it was decided to have Sam transferred from Memphis to the Wichita V.A.

Doris was informed of what was happening by Major Tommye Davis. Doris knew she could speak frankly with the major. "What do you think about it, Tommye?"

Tommye was equally frank with Doris. "I think he should stay here in Memphis, and that's that! We've got him in such good condition now, compared to when he arrived. He's comfortable here. The other patients have accepted him the way he is and he can be himself without having to worry about covering anything up.

"But the thing that worries me most is—what if he doesn't get the right kind of care afterwards? I mean, the regular turning to stop the bed sores, taking care to watch his catheter and what if they don't give enemas? It could be a real disaster. That's what worries me, but I guess it's his father's decision."

Sam's last night in the hospital at Memphis was Friday, April 5th. For Doris it began like any other evening. First she checked in on her other pets to see if any of them needed wheeling down to the recreation room for a movie. Finishing that, she headed over to visit Sam. Dick and Pauline were spending the last evening getting things ready to move from the apartment.

When Doris entered the room, she found Sam in a state of utter consternation. Several of the orderlies had already spoken with him about how much they didn't want to see him go, which left him looking lost and confused.

"What's the matter, Sam?" Doris began.

"I don't think I want to leave. I have my routine and I know everybody here," he uttered haltingly.

Doris really didn't know what to say. "Oh, you're gonna be fine," she said, but without much conviction. "And just think; you're gonna go home and meet all your old friends." Now she sounded like a mother with a young child. She had never spoken to Sam that way before and he knew it.

"But, will I be able to remember them?"

"Sure you will, when you see them," she insisted. "You'll remember me when you see me; won't you?" she said, sounding more like her old self now.

"I'll never forget you, Doris."

From that moment, they both tried to pretend this was like any other night. When Doris finally got up to go and collect her other pets from the recreation room, she leaned forward, put her arms around Sam's chest and hugged him tight. It was an involuntary gesture she never made to any other patient. Then she rose slowly and kissed him on the cheek. All at once, she felt herself crumbling inside. Beseeching herself not to break down in front of him, she stood up in order to regain her composure.

"Aren't you forgetting something?" he said with a smile.

"Yes Sam, 'The woods are lovely, dark and deep.' " Before she could continue, he broke in, " 'But we've got promises to keep.' " There was a short pause before Doris picked it up again, " 'And miles to go before I sleep.' " Her voice was starting to quaver while her eyes filled. Sam finished it off, " 'And miles to go before we sleep.' "

This was too much for Doris. She turned and fled from the room, heading across the hallway, past startled patients, nurses and orderlies, straight to the staircase. Her eyes were red now as tears streamed down her cheeks. She ran down six flights of stairs without stopping and burst out of the east door of the hospital into the parking lot. She continued running without looking back, until she reached her car. She fumbled in her purse for the keys before hurriedly opening the door and collapsing into the driver's seat where she cried hard and loud until she had no tears left and the salt had dried onto her face. After composing herself, she prayed out loud, "Dear Lord, why does this have to happen to such a person? What's going to happen to him when he leaves this hospital? Please, please God; take care of Sam Bird—he loves you so much."

When she had finished, a heavy sensation gripped the pit of her stomach. She had felt this sensation before on several occasions. It was a feeling that she would never see that person again. This time the feeling was very strong.

Chapter Twelve

Home

Before traveling to the V.A. Hospital in Oklahoma City for the plating operation in May, 1968, Sam spent six weeks at the Wichita V.A. Many of the fears expressed by Tommye Davis and her colleagues in Memphis were never realized and Sam settled into a daily routine at the new hospital with little apparent difficulty.

On Monday, May 13th, Sam was taken to Oklahoma City by ambulance for the plating operation. He arrived at the hospital at four o'clock that afternoon and surgery was scheduled for the following Monday.

In fact, the nine-hour operation did turn out to be every bit "the touch and go serious business" Sam had already been through in Japan. For two weeks following the operation, Sam's life hung in the balance as he drifted in and out of consciousness with regular bouts of hallucination. During these periods of apparent delirium, he continually insisted he could see an angel dressed in white. "God has sent an angel to take care of me," he uttered repeatedly, rambling on in a barely coherent garble. "On our wedding day, she will be dressed all in white," said Sam. Dick's heart sank. His son's condition appeared worse now than when he first saw him in Japan.

After this precarious fortnight, Sam's vital signs stabilized. Fully regaining consciousness, he became coherent once more. On June 14th, Dick's birthday, Sam returned home to 609

233

Rutland where his totally revamped bed-sitting room had now been completed.

The bedroom had been extended. Three imposing rectangular windows extending from floor to ceiling had been fitted on the room's north side. A bathroom and two closets had been added, along with a couch and two built-in desks—one of them antique— situated on either side of the room. On top of a cabinet beside Sam's bed lay a fingertip control for activating the TV, radio, lights and curtains. Dick and Pauline had created a self-contained luxury annex for their son on the north side of the house.

A full-time aide was hired to administer to Sam's needs during the day. He would arrive in the morning, wash and dress Sam, take him over to the V.A. for physical and occupational therapy, and after that they often went on an outing somewhere in town. He always seemed to be laughing and joking and invariably addressed Sam as "Major." Sam liked that and especially looked forward to the outings in town. Then one afternoon, for no apparent reason, Pauline fired him.

According to Addie, "She'd been drinkin' and just started cussin' him out." Her drinking had not decreased. As a matter of fact, during their visit in March, Dean Parker and B.T. Collins witnessed Pauline polish off two bottles of bourbon. This amazed even Dean and B.T., who were partial to the odd drop of brown whiskey themselves.

When the aide didn't appear the following day, Pauline asked where he was. Dick told her he'd quit. She telephoned him and said she was sorry, could he please reconsider.

"Ma'am, you can kiss my grits!" came the reply. "I don't have to take that kinda' talk from no one. And he put down the phone. A new aide was hired but he wasn't the same.

Pauline remained on the outer edges of Sam's world. As much as she loved her son, and she dearly loved him, she couldn't bring herself to be close to him, to take care of him hands on. It broke her heart to see Sam the way he was but she found herself incapable of being maternal.

When the aide left every afternoon at 3:30, it was Dick who took care of Sam's basic needs, with occasional help from Addie, whom Pauline had coaxed back into service. It was Dick who cleaned up the diarrhea, Dick who lifted Sam in and out of bed, dressed and undressed him, washed him and slept beside him when he couldn't sleep.

As in Memphis, Sam would have good days and bad days. On good days he was noticeably alert and lucid for long periods. Something Addie particularly noticed about him on such days was his sense of humor. This was not the same serious guy she remembered.

The Memphis doctors' fears that the plating operation would have a deleterious effect seemed to have been justified, however, when during bad days Sam would appear detached and listless, often appearing to black out for short periods. He complained of hearing music when there was none, and voices in his head. He could develop a fever and break into a sweat. He could become nervous and irritable. Such symptoms would often be accompanied by bouts of confusion when he could be heard to repeat questions over and over. Sometimes he would insist he was to be married that day or planning a picnic with cousins who didn't exist. Such days pushed Dick to the brink of despair; for as in Memphis, there didn't seem to be any discernible pattern to his son's behavior.

After the initial deluge of welcome home social calls from family, friends and Army comrades, visits became fewer and less frequent. Bill, the half-brother who had been virtually inseparable from Sam every time he was home on leave, could no longer— except on very rare occasions—bring himself to stop by even for a little while. Paula too, was going through problems. A crumbling marriage coupled with the dawning realization that she was not, nor ever would be, cut out to be a homemaker, resulted in her return to the work place. Also dawning was the realization that she never was going to connect with her father, no matter how hard she tried. All this resulted in fewer and fewer visits to 609 Rutland. One Army comrade who did make more than just one courtesy visit to Sam was B.T. Collins. Between 1968 and 1971, he made more than half a dozen trips to Wichita from California.

In early May of 1968, before traveling to Oklahoma City, Sam had spoken to Doris on the telephone from the V.A. in Wichita. She promised to come and visit him at home after the operation. Pauline took matters a stage further and made her a lucrative offer to become Sam's full-time, live-in aide. Doris recoiled from the idea. In fact, she never came to visit Sam in Wichita.

However, the two of them continued to correspond, sending each other Christmas and birthday cards. Sam would normally ask his aide to write the card after he'd told him what he wanted to say to her. For Saint Patrick's Day in 1969 though, Doris received a hand-written card from Sam. The writing had the uneven appearance of a young child's, tapering diagonally down the page. The message, however, was unmistakable. It read simply, *"I love you. I love you. I love you."*

Doris was somewhat taken aback by the card and began to feel increasingly confused about how to respond to it.

In the end, she mailed Sam a card which said, "We at the V.A. Hospital in Memphis thank you for your kind thoughts and we hope your recovery continues to progress well."

Subtlety had never been one of Doris's strong suits, although the clumsy note sounded a lot worse than she intended and didn't come close to reflecting the range of emotions she was feeling at the time. But Sam's note had made her feel uncomfortable.

The days began to merge into months and years at 609 Rutland. The composite image, despite a surface veneer, is one of three unconnected lives, each spending the days in their own way—drifting, aimless, hopeless.

Chapter Thirteen

Paula

At first Paula's marriage to Rich Roberts had seemed happy enough. She had three children over a period of five years. Then, as Paula told it later in a magazine interview:

"There was a problem. My children were growing fine, but there was a tomato garden disaster year after year. Finally, after all the summers of mowed-down, drowned-out, sun-dried, disease-ridden tomatoes, we had a crop that bloomed and bore fruit. Lovely, huge, round, green tomatoes that promised to ripen to the perfection we had strived for for so long. It wasn't to be. One morning, I looked out of the window and saw my one-, three-, and five-year-olds [Bruce, Julie and Laurie] using the beautiful fruit to pitch into traffic going by the house. This was the end of my total gardening and home-making career."

Letters written to her parents between September and November 1967 when Sam was in Memphis further indicate that Paula and parenthood didn't mix:

September 27th:

I had just returned from 609 and hedge trimming. The children were so much trouble that I got them away from there as soon as possible. They are driving me crazy—as usual. Late yesterday afternoon they got into some old purple indelible lipstick (left over from garage sale) and smeared it all over themselves. What really made me mad was that Bruce and Julie begged me to wear their brand-new school clothes which of course were ruined. I was so

237

mad that I sent them to bed with no dinner or anything. They got several good belt-lashings (which you probably figure we've never been strict enough to give!) and off they went—that was about 4:30 P.M. At around 8 P.M. they both woke up, crying for food—which I knew they would; since they had run off with [their friends] Jim and Tracy, leaving almost all of their breakfast and lunch. By that time, I was beginning to feel sorry for them but I kept my word about no food. I did promise them I'd fix them a big breakfast, which I did (Bacon, eggs, pancakes, toast, honey, etc.). Julie was ready to eat but Bruce refused! I forced him to eat (which is something I never do—hoping to avoid the 'restaurantitis' I had) which caused him to throw up all over the carpet and kitchen floor. Ah, and my day has not picked up since! I did try once again, however. They begged me for lunch at 11 A.M. and I was glad at last to have them both agreeably hungry. I had no more placed it on the kitchen table when Jim and Tracy's mom 'honked' for them to go swimming, so off they tore!! Do parents ever win??

It is 103 degrees outside and rains are threatening. Julie just brought me a good size piece of the back door and Laurie just wet on the chair cushion to the library table.

September 29th:

Only had a chance to mention the art course that I am taking at the art museum. It starts Monday and will meet every week on that night for two hours. I am so excited about it that I can hardly wait. It will last until Xmas. I am excited about getting some help soon. Nothing as fancy as Addie but I'd settle for anything. A client of Rich's (very nice girl my age) has told him about something better than school girls. It sounds funny but they are 'unwed mothers' waiting for their babies to come! They live in and work and baby sit around the clock! They do hard things like floors, cleaning bathrooms, tubs and everything—of course, the turnover is frequent, as they leave right before their baby

238

comes. They would be so handy, I think. They are not allowed to date, or run around, like school girls, and I think Rich's client said they are really nice and polite. You interview them, rather than taking what the home sends. The more I think about it, the more excited I get! If I had one I could trust with the children, why, I could walk out of the house any time I wanted. Go to the store, get my hair fixed—maybe even get to Memphis. Rich has a big out of town deal hanging in the balance. If it pans out, he said he'd try to get me some help. It could never come about, but just 'dreaming' that someone might help me is enough to keep me pushing the toilet brush, etc.

Since I began this letter, Laurie has wrecked the entire house. All the clothes from the upstairs dresser are heaped in the middle of every downstairs room—and that's the least of the messes she's made! Wish I had an unwed mother for her to play with.

October 6th:

Yesterday, there was a good movie shown at the university about President Kennedy and his funeral. Because I couldn't get a sitter, I took the children. They were so bad, I bawled all the way home. Whenever Sam came on the screen, they got loud or had to go to the bathroom, etc. So I would have to leave the auditorium. By the time I had them momentarily settled down and we could go back in, Sam was gone. After so much of that, there was nothing to do but leave.

When I finally got home, there was only enough booze left for one 'good' drink. I had only had about a third of it when I reached for it again—and found that Laurie had polished it all off! I bawled some more. She, who was feeling fine, was soon feeling great—and I was worse off than before!

When I was as low as could be, Rich came home and told me that his big Tulsa deal had fallen through.

I am still hoping that we can work something out to get an unmarried mother to help me. Speaking of unwed mothers, Lucy Carter's talking big about being Sam's girlfriend these days. [Sam had been really fond of her, according to Addie. They would date when he was home on leave, although that wasn't very often. When Sam was in Vietnam, Lucy dated other guys regularly and amazed Addie by informing Paula about it. Of course, Paula wrote Sam immediately and "that was the end of that."

After Sam was wounded and was being praised from all quarters as a hero, Lucy started making rumblings that she was Sam's girlfriend again.] *I set a group of girls straight the other night by saying he didn't even know who she was.*

October 24th:

Mrs. Roberts [Paula's mother-in-law] *stayed from 1:00 P.M. Saturday until evening, then came again and stayed all Sunday. It was sure nice of her, but she gave the kids so many toys and such awful haircuts that I sure felt bad. I had picked up a twenty-cent book for each child at the Memphis airport and carried them all the way home (no sack) then found all those stuffed animals, books, crayons, etc.—so I just didn't give them anything. Bruce cried and I felt bad because I had told him I'd try to bring him something. Santa Claus will be glad to have them though!*

Today, I filled out the necessary papers for an unwed mother from the Kansas Children's Service League. There are no girls available at the moment, but the lady said there are usually many who apply in November, so I am hopeful. She did suggest that we furnish her room as soon as possible.

November 1st:

I am having trouble ending Halloween. The kids are still wearing their costumes around the house and I am trying to think of some way to throw their candy over my shoulder into the trash. Can chocolate be sent to Vietnam? Still no help at this end, but things are under control—well, as much as they ever are!

★   ★   ★

Paula and Rich were divorced in 1970. She never managed to land an unwed mother. But now she'd have to work full-time anyway.

Paula's first job (in 1968—part-time) was as a copywriter and layout artist for a local department store. After three years there, she joined the art department of the local newspaper, *The Wichita Eagle and Beacon.* "When they found out I couldn't draw or spell, they put me in ad sales," she chuckled. In fact, someone recognized her talent and drive and pushed her into accepting a position as an account executive. She was the first female to hold such a position at *The Eagle.* "I started out with a 'dog-bone' list," she said. "Then one day the man handling all the financial accounts fell over in a drunken stupor and I inherited his list." One of those accounts, Transamerican Investment Properties, lured her away, hiring her as a leasing agent for a proposed specialty shopping center. Within six months, Paula had leased 75 percent of the center. Then the operation confessed they had no financing and she was dismissed without notice.

In a later interview with another local media magazine, Paula said the following:

"The hardest part of growing up for me was finding out that life wasn't all lilacs and roses—that good guys don't always finish first. I was twenty-eight years old before I ever finally gave up thinking things would somehow be perfect."

The events of January 27th, 1967, took place 16 days before Paula's twenty-eighth birthday.

PART V

CLASS REUNION

Chapter Fourteen

Coming Home

In September of 1970, Paula enrolled her eight-and-a-half-year-old son, Bruce, in the East Heights Cub Scouts. The pack met on Tuesday evenings at the Methodist Church, which was located in a picturesque spot on the corner of Douglas and Crestway Avenues. This was less than a mile from Paula's modest three-bedroom home at 156 North Ridgewood Drive where she lived with her three children.

Often during monthly pack meetings, which parents were expected to attend, Paula found her gaze drawn toward a slim, bespectacled woman with short brown, hair who appeared to be in charge of the group of cub scouts sitting to the left of Bruce's. The woman's face had the kind of ordinary familiarity that proved too elusive for Paula to place, yet not provocative enough to pique her curiosity further. At the final monthly pack meeting of the school year, Paula looked over to her left and she noticed the woman was no longer sitting in her usual place. Scanning the hall, she caught sight of her sitting in the position of Den Leader Coach beside three male scout leaders who were there to oversee the meetings.

One evening the following September, the week before pack meetings were scheduled to begin for the 1971 school year, Paula received a telephone call.

"Hello Mrs. Roberts," the voice said softly, "This is Annette Blazier from the East Heights Cub Scouts. I'm just calling to let you know that I have assigned Bruce to Den Number Four for the coming year."

"I've noticed you at monthly pack meetings," Paula replied engagingly. "Did you by any chance grow up in Wichita?"

"Yes."

"Did you go to Minneha School?"

"Yes."

"I'm Paula Bird Roberts; Sam Bird's sister."

"Really?" Annette sounded enthusiastic. "I remember Sam in my class. What's he doing now?"

"Ohh Kid!" Paula exclaimed with typical dramatic flourish, "A lot has happened." She paused for a moment. "Sam was severely wounded in Vietnam. He's paralyzed and now lives at home with the folks." She paused again. "Hey, you ought'a go by and see him."

"Do you think he'd remember me?" Annette replied somewhat tentatively, recalling an occasion two years earlier in the Ozark's when a friend had mentioned reading a newspaper article about Sam's return to Wichita with devastating wounds. "Gee, that's too bad," she'd said to her friend lamely, allowing previous memories to float by. But this was different. For one thing, Paula wasn't going to let her off the hook that easily.

"Oh Kid, yeah! He has a memory problem—he has trouble remembering what he's had for breakfast, but he can remember what happened 20 years ago as clear as day. Why don't you give Mom a call and make arrangements to stop by and visit?"

"Okay," replied Annette. As soon as she hung up, Annette telephoned 609 Rutland. Addie answered the phone. Annette asked if she could speak to Sam's mother. "Hello, Mrs. Bird, this is Annette Blazier speaking. I went to school with Sam."

"Annette! How wonderful!"

"I just got off the phone with Paula, who told me about Sam's recovery. I wondered if it would be possible to visit him?"

"But of course!" Pauline was effusive. "Sam would just be so thrilled to meet someone from grade school. Why don't you come over on Saturday at one o'clock?"

No sooner had Annette replaced the receiver than her thoughts were flooded with recollections of that special childhood friendship. With chagrin, she remembered the profound teenage embarrassment that had been solely responsible for the inglorious demise of their relationship in the spring of 1953. Since then, her life had followed a markedly different course from her childhood sweetheart's.

★   ★   ★

When school was out for the summer at the end of May 1953, fourteen-year-old Annette left Wichita for Denver to spend the entire vacation with her grandmother.

Mabel Black was moderately forbidding to those who didn't know her well. Always appearing prim and proper, she was a petite woman with a sympathetic oval-shaped face. Widowed in 1942, she never wore any colors but gray or dark blue and never left the house without a pillbox hat and a clean set of underwear—in case she was involved in an accident. Mrs. Black had arranged an extensive program of trombone and violin lessons for her granddaughter. Though a proficient trombonist, Annette had never played the violin before and was eagerly looking forward to both kinds of lessons. To be able to spend an uninterrupted summer with her favorite person in the whole world, engaging in her favorite pastime, was a dream come true. Mrs. Black loved her granddaughter without reservation and took a great interest in her life. Annette had never felt closer to anyone.

Both music teachers had come with high recommendations; both were married men in their mid-forties, both were renowned as pillars of the community. Mabel Black would accept no less for her granddaughter. The tutors each lived only a short distance from the house, granting Annette the additional boon of a pastoral morning stroll to and from lessons.

Annette took to both men with alacrity. The trombone teacher was voluble in his praise for his new pupil who completed every assignment with consummate zeal. The reaction of the violin teacher mirrored that of his counterpart, though it was expressed with slightly less exuberance. The two good friends were in agreement; Annette was the best pupil they'd ever had. As a special treat, the violin teacher took her to the Red Rocks Amphitheater to see the Denver Symphony. Annette had never been happier. She feasted on undiluted attention from both teachers and her grandmother. It was like being an only child for the summer and she was loving every minute of it. The time passed much too quickly. As the last week of August drew to a close, she wished that summer would never end.

Her final music lesson came three days before she was due to return to Wichita. That morning as she strolled nonchalantly to the trombone teacher's house, she was both happy and sad—bubbling over with bittersweet feelings.

About halfway through the final lesson, the trombone teacher looked across at his young protegee fondly. "Before I forget, I've got a special mouthpiece to show you," he said. "Come with me."

Annette rose swiftly from her seat and eagerly followed him into the bedroom. She adored surprises.

Before she was fully aware of what was happening, a pair of hands had reached up and grabbed her by the shoulders, forcing her onto the bed.

It was all over very quickly.

"You'd better not tell anyone about this," he warned her. "They wouldn't believe you anyway."

Numb and bewildered, Annette got up from the bed, packed her trombone in its case and hurriedly left the house. The walk back to her grandmother's was a blur. Dazed and confused, she felt as though she were in a dark dream world. Had it really happened? What had happened?

Mrs. Black sensed a mood of despondency in her granddaughter. "You don't look very happy, Annette," she said sympathetically. "I know summer is coming to an end, but there's always next year."

Annette couldn't bring herself to tell her grandmother what had happened. 'Anyway,' she thought to herself, 'What could I tell her?'

Back home in Wichita Annette wrestled with her emotions, struggling to make some sense out of the experience, waiting for the right opportunity to approach her mother. They attended a wedding at church where a girl was getting married because she had become pregnant. Annette saw her chance.

"How does that happen, Mother?" she inquired tentatively.

"Well, it's because girls ask for it nowadays," Lois Blazier declared resoundingly. "In the way they dress, the way they act, the way they flirt."

"Oh."

Annette had been given her answer. She was guilty. The verdict was reinforced by Sunday sermons berating the "fallen woman" who was the worst kind of sinner—the woman who succumbed to temptation. The man? Well, "Boys will be boys."

Finding little comfort in church doctrine, Annette sought solace from the *Bible*, where she found partial consolation in Jesus' compassion for the woman at the well. However, she felt powerless to shrug off the lingering cloak of guilt that settled around her.

The following summer, now having turned fifteen, Annette returned to Denver. Mabel Black had once again made arrangements for music lessons. However, both lessons were rescheduled at a studio in the center of town. Annette never returned to the trombone teacher's home. At the studio, he acted as if the incident had never occurred. She was still his "best" pupil. As for Annette, she too acted as if nothing untoward had ever taken place.

In August, Mabel Black suffered a major heart attack. The doctors decreed she could no longer live at home alone; either someone must live with her or she would have to go to a nursing home. Annette pleaded with her parents to allow her to stay with her grandmother. At first they were reluctant to condone the idea. However, after successive weeks of lobbying on her granddaughter's behalf from Mabel Black and the ultimate realization that there was no practical alternative, Ed and Lois Blazier reluctantly gave their consent, if not their blessing, to the arrangement.

Thus Annette started high school in Denver that September. At school Annette avoided contact with the opposite sex whenever possible, electing to play the part of wallflower. She wore scant traces of make-up, prohibitively conservative—not to say austere—dresses and refusing all dates with boys. Lois Blazier attributed her daughter's behavior to the fact she'd been spending so much time with her grandmother. In the end, for the senior prom, Mabel Black arranged a date for her granddaughter. The evening turned out to be an unmitigated disaster, as the two hapless wretches spent the entire time not knowing where to look or what to say to each other.

Annette graduated from high school in May of 1957 and began training as an X-ray technician at Denver's Saint Luke's Hospital the following month.

During her final year of high school, Annette became acquainted with Gene, a young airman, and his wife. They met at church. Annette really enjoyed Sundays with her grandmother and was always in a good mood when they arrived at church. Each Sunday without fail, she would smile to herself as her grandmother executed her customary body-swerve to the outer edge of the sidewalk when they passed the entrance to the nearby Charismatic Christian Church. Mrs. Black had little time for the "antics" of these "Holy Rollers."

Gene, the young airman, completed his military service at the same time Annette graduated from high school. He and his pregnant wife moved to California. Annette maintained contact with the young couple by letter and as the tone of the correspondence began to change, she began to sense their marriage was running into problems.

In January of 1958, Mabel Black died of congestive heart failure. It came as a crushing blow to Annette because she had lost more than her grandmother; she had lost her best friend. Reluctantly she agreed to return home to Wichita. She was able to rent her grandmother's home to a good friend who had recently married.

Life back home in Wichita with her parents was irksome for Annette. She felt a strong sense of not belonging. She barely knew her brother and two sisters; she hadn't seen Hal, Dona and Carol for a long time and they seemed very young. Her mother was always bustling to and fro, while her father had become a complete stranger. After five months of not trying very hard to make the situation work, Annette moved back to Colorado, taking a job as X-ray technician in Colorado Springs. Her sister, Dona, four years younger than Annette, came out from Wichita to live with her. But without her grandmother, Annette felt abandoned. She didn't know what she wanted from life; she was confused, muddled and still grieving.

Ever since Mabel Black's death in January, the letters from the now ex-airman, Gene, had taken on a more romantic tone and Annette was drawn to them. In June, he wrote to say that he and his wife were separating and the unions at the steel plant where he worked were about to call a strike. If they did, he would like to come to Colorado Springs and stay for a while.

"That'll be fine," Annette replied. "Dona's here too." However, Dona was beginning to miss her friends in Wichita, so she decided to return home. The week following Dona's departure, Gene arrived in Colorado Springs. He stayed with Annette for a week and then returned to California.

Six weeks later, in the middle of August, Annette discovered she was pregnant. The first person she called was Dona in Wichita. "Please can you tell Mother?" she beseeched, "Because I just can't." Annette was in shock. Feeling alone and isolated, she wondered, 'Why *me*?'

Lois Blazier tearfully implored her eldest child to return home to Wichita to have the baby, which was due in March. Meanwhile, Annette's father said nothing. Later in the week, Annette received a letter from Gene stating he truly wanted to marry her and was obtaining a divorce from his wife.

For two months Annette stewed over the matter while she put her grandmother's house in Denver up for sale. She was by no means sure she loved Gene but was only too aware in 1959 of the ramifications of an empty space on a birth certificate where the father's name should be. In addition, at nineteen years of age, Annette Blazier was wilful and stubborn.

Following the sale of her grandmother's house in November, despite repeated tearful pleas from her mother, Annette resolved to marry Gene and move to California. She received one last call from her mother on the eve of her departure. "Please, Annette!" Lois cried, "For heaven's sake, think what you're doing. Please, please come home!"

"Mother, I've made up my mind," she said unequivocally. "I am going to make this work, no matter what!" Annette's primary feeling was shame. She was too ashamed to go home to her parents. This led her to marry Gene as a way of "righting a wrong" and thereby receiving a kind of absolution.

The next morning, Annette gathered herself and her belongings and loaded them onto a train bound for Riverside, California. She arrived the following day at noon. Gene greeted her by saying they would drive to Tijuana to get married that evening. He reassured her they would have a formal ceremony in the United States once everything had settled down.

A year to the day after her grandmother's death, Annette went into labor. The baby, a boy weighing only two pounds, was born that same day, in Kaiser Hospital. Immediately following the birth, the child was rushed away to an incubator. Five hours later, at four o'clock in the morning, the doctor returned to Annette's bedside.

"I'm sorry, your baby died," he said with quiet calm. "It just wasn't strong enough." Then he turned away and walked out the door.

The black void of desolation was like nothing Annette had felt before—a searing emptiness intensified by the fact she'd been unable to hold her baby.

On the death of her baby, she felt more isolated than ever. But more than that—her "righting a wrong" means of trying to find redemption for herself in the eyes of God and others didn't appear to have worked. She had done everything "right" but now there appeared to be no justice in the final outcome. She felt utterly betrayed. Residual feelings of guilt and responsibility didn't take hold until later.

★　　★　　★

One afternoon, about a month after losing the baby, the couple were together in their living room shortly before Gene was due to leave for his evening shift at the steel plant. He was sitting at the table, engrossed in a paperback novel, as usual.

"Why have you practically ignored me for the last few weeks?" Annette demanded.

Her husband continued reading without offering a reply.

"What's the problem?" she went on insistently.

"No problem," he replied in a tone suggesting he would rather she dropped the subject. It had been gnawing at her though, and she could no longer restrain herself.

"Am I the problem?" she cried. "Because if so, you can have a divorce if you want!"

Gene raised his eyes from the book. "OK, we'll get a divorce." And with that, he got up, left the room and went to work.

As soon as Gene left, Annette went into their bedroom. Her head was swimming as she carefully removed the .22 revolver from the drawer beside the bed. Gripped by a sudden urge to be reunited with her grandmother, she clasped the gun shakily with both hands, pointed the barrel toward her chest and pulled the trigger. Clearing the top of her left lung, the bullet embedded itself close to her armpit. Shock at the discharge knocked her to the floor. Seconds later her senses cleared and she felt a powerful rush of relief. 'Grandmother would have killed me!' she thought to herself.

She rose to her feet gingerly, still feeling a little woozy, walked across the living room and out the front door to where a neighbor was standing in his garden.

"Did you hear that?" he exclaimed.

"Yes," she replied limply. "I just shot a .22."

"Are you all right?" he asked with visible concern.

"I think so," she mumbled.

"I think we'd better get you to the hospital." He rushed her to the emergency room. She was released a couple of hours later. The doctor told her that since the bullet was sterile and doing no harm, it was better to leave it where it was. Which is where it remains to this day, without even a twinge of complaint.

Meanwhile, the police had contacted Gene at work to inform him of what had happened. He arrived at the hospital in a state of shock.

"We will never talk about this again," he asserted as they walked through the front door of the house.

In July, Annette found she was pregnant again. On February 25th, 1961, she gave birth to a son, Eric. But now their marriage was in complete disarray. Annette and Gene were total strangers. Finally admitting defeat two years after Eric was born, Annette filed for divorce, only to be told that marriage papers had never been filed in the United States. A lawyer told her that it didn't matter, since they had been together for more than three years, they were considered common law man and wife. She reclaimed the Blazier name for herself while omitting to change Eric's surname because of the stigma attached to a child with his mother's maiden name.

Since the divorce wasn't contested by either party, it was swift and straightforward, with Annette retaining custody of her son. The aftermath was another matter. She hadn't reckoned with the guilt feelings that came with single parenthood. In an attempt to assuage these feelings, she established a small day-care center in her home for a handful of children from other one-parent families. Disproportionate pangs of guilt and shame had once again led her to try to correct a perceived "wrong" with an unrelated "right." The result was ever-deepening depression. The more she did to try to offset the way she felt, the worse she became.

Eventually, the depression began to manifest itself in physical distress as the tension within her built up. Headaches became frequent and intensified until they eventually brought her to a halt. She could no longer function. Utterly debilitated, she was admitted to the hospital.

For three days she tried to fight the headache. Deep inside she felt like a dismal failure. From within, she heard herself crying out, 'Help!—I can't do it any more.' And then she saw the image of a loving God. At that point, she consciously let go—releasing everything inside her. Then she fell asleep. She awoke to find herself completely at peace, as though a soothing oil had coated her body. Her head was clear.

Two days after her discharge from the hospital, Lois Blazier telephoned her daughter from Wichita. "Annette, we've just sold the house and bought a place on the outskirts of town with an adjoining apartment," she said. "Would you at least consider coming back to Wichita?"

"Yes, Mother," she replied assertively. "I'm coming home."

Annette left Riverside with her son in the summer of 1965, never to return. Her opinion of men was even lower now than it had been in Denver. The next six years were punctuated by few meaningful encounters with the opposite sex. She focused all of her attention on the task of raising a son, with much soul searching in the process.

The prospect of returning to Wichita, specifically to the walls of her parents' home echoing to the refrain of "I told you so" did not enthrall her, especially when she thought of her father. He had always seemed aloof and distant to her—unapproachable. She'd always felt invisible around his stolid stubbornness. But they were more alike than either of them wanted to believe. The real problem lay in the fact that neither of them knew how to make the first move.

Most of Annette's fears proved unfounded. To Lois Blazier's everlasting relief, her daughter and grandson had returned home from California. Above all, she was eagerly looking forward to having a grandson to spoil full time. Because of her difficult relationship with her father, Annette had always taken him to be uncomfortable around children. Yet, whereas Annette was continually waiting for her father to make the first move, Eric didn't wait for an invitation.

"Granddaddy, Granddaddy, listen to me!" was the cry whenever Eric felt he wasn't receiving his grandfather's undivided attention. Undaunted by Ed Blazier's lengthy periods of silence during fishing expeditions, Eric was well up to providing his own non-stop commentary.

Whether the affection for his little companion was gained through sufferance, or whether it was merely a quality that had previously lain dormant, it was apparent to everyone that Ed Blazier derived considerable pleasure from the presence of his newly acquired appendage.

When Annette took a job with Beech Aircraft, this produced an unlooked for problem. Eric began to associate his grandfather with the father figure he'd never had and he viewed Lois Blazier as his mother. Annette found herself being relegated to the role of big sister. Perhaps it should not have come as a surprise since Annette always referred to her parents as "Mother" and "Daddy" in Eric's presence. And they in turn normally called her "Annette" and not "Mommy." Although the experience was both unpleasant and disconcerting, the fact Eric now had a male figure to anchor his life was not lost on her either.

In 1968, after three years of living with her parents, Annette moved to the small town of Winfield, located 45 miles south of Wichita. She accepted a job as an X-ray technician at the local hospital and hoped the move would regenerate a mother-son relationship with Eric. Despite her misgivings about Eric's role-association with his grandparents, she was generally pleased with the way he was growing up. She often found herself biting her lip, however, when she witnessed the emergence of traits that reminded her of Gene.

One weekend during their first year together in Winfield, Annette was leaving the hospital with Eric at the end of her shift when she was summoned back inside. Seeing the look of dejection unfurl across her seven-year-old's face (he'd already spent the last hour in the waiting room), she told him, "You can start walking home and I'll catch up."

Ten minutes later Annette returned to her car in the parking lot and set out for home, taking the usual route. After driving for a short while, she started to become concerned since there was no sign of Eric. She reached home to find that her son wasn't there. Just as she was really beginning to panic, Annette looked up and saw Eric walking nonchalantly down the road toward the house. He had simply taken a different route from the one they normally took in the car.

"What do you think you were doing, Eric?" she called out reprovingly. "You really had me worried about you."

"It's my life and I'm gonna live it my way!" he yelled back. "You can't tell me what to do!"

Annette and Eric spent nearly three years in Winfield until the erratic nature of her job finally proved too difficult to juggle with Eric's needs. The earnest mother and her increasingly recalcitrant son returned to Wichita toward the latter part of 1970, once again moving in with her parents while Annette went to work at a local doctor's office.

Whenever she allowed her thoughts to meander through the 10 years since Eric was born, Annette found herself reflecting on the ebb and flow of joy and frustration. The peaks of joy came from such rewards as a son who came up to her every now and then, flung his arms around her and said, "Don't worry, everything's gonna be all right." In this capacity, as with many others, Eric was trying to fill a husband's shoes. This may well have contributed to the shift in his conduct from dependence to self-reliance.

The worst of times for Annette during those years were rooted in her feelings of isolation and solitude—when the burden of having to make all the decisions for two people weighed heavily. She recalled times of sitting and watching despairingly at parks and playgrounds as other children played enthusiastically with both parents. She was painfully aware that she alone was incapable of providing that benefit for her son.

However, Annette could cast her mind back over Eric's formative years and evoke several joyous reminiscences. Their early forays together as would-be anglers produced some of her fondest memories. Annette tapped her work colleagues for a few fishing basics, producing slightly indifferent results in terms of the number of fish actually caught. "I don't think we ever caught anything," she recalls wistfully. "Yet, sitting beneath the shade of a tree on the riverbank, discussing teachers and classmates, hatching plans for the future, looking into each other's eyes; the fish were totally superfluous."

Another wistful thought carried her back to one particular winter's evening in Winfield. The mantlepiece clock was edging toward 10:00. Mother and son were getting ready for bed when Annette drew back a curtain, peered out the window and saw snowflakes the size of small saucers falling. After bundling up in some warm clothes, the two of them ventured out of the house onto the deserted street. Not a tire track or footprint was to be seen; the snow lay 10 inches deep in places. The glow from the street lights evoked a fairy-tale atmosphere and suddenly the two of them began to run, laughing and kicking up the snow.

"Look at me, Eric!" Annette called out as she fell back with her arms outstretched. After landing on the soft blanket of snow, she began to move her arms up and down like windshield wipers. Lifting herself carefully out of the snow, she looked down with satisfaction at the angel imprint she'd made. For a fleeting moment, the child within had returned. For the next hour, daily routine and inhibition were cast aside like so much outgrown clothing as mother and son came together with one another and their surroundings.

The return to Wichita helped relieve much of the stress that had built up between them. Annette felt especially good about enrolling Eric with the Cub Scouts, looking on in sheer delight as he mixed happily with the other boys. She couldn't have imagined the eventual consequence of her son's enrollment.

★　　★　　★

Now in September 1971 after talking to Pauline Bird, Annette thought she should call her back and cancel. What if seeing Sam in his present condition was too painful? At the same time, she recalled their hours together in the music room at Minneha—the feeling of being co-conspirators, the hours on the telephone, the compact and the valentines. She felt compelled to make contact and didn't call to cancel.

Chapter 15

Sunrise, but It's Cold Outside

By early autumn of 1971, Annette had purchased a double duplex of small, neat apartments at 231 and 232 South Belmont Avenue. In the mid-twenties, this had been an exclusive residential district with huge, ornate, iron entrance gates located no more than a hundred yards to the north of her new home. Even though the area was no longer looked upon with quite the same reverence, it remained a singularly pleasant neighborhood in which to live. Annette had taken Eric and moved from her parents' house into the top apartment at 231, while renting out the three other units.

The move provided a foothold toward securing their future, but there was another reason for this change. Annette had sensed a recurrence of Eric's confused perception of his mother. He had started playing Lois against her daughter once again. Annette decided to move out before the situation became completely unmanageable.

At thirty-three, Annette was slender and attractive. Her fashionable horn-rimmed glasses conferred an added prominence to the delicate features of a gently elliptical face. Her smile, though tentative on occasion, was warm and sincere. In slight contrast, the depth of her green eyes evoked composure and self-assurance—perhaps even a suggestion of mild defiance. Annette was always eager to please and often appeared excessively earnest; but this didn't prevent an occasional out-and-out belly laugh.

In the years following her divorce, her contact with men had been rare, yet it would be wrong to think she no longer wanted a relationship. Much of her time had been taken up with the demands of a full-time job and proving she could raise a child alone; all this was in an era when women in her situation were treated like second-class citizens. Over time, she relegated the desire for a relationship behind all her other priorities.

★   ★   ★

Early autumn in Kansas is typically balmy, although the weather can be unpredictable. The Saturday of Annette's visit to the Bird's was no exception—everything was bathed in warm sunshine.

While she was getting ready, Annette asked Eric to wash her turquoise Comet. He covered the car in suds and then rendered his opinion of his mother's outing by rolling all the windows down before turning on the hose to rinse it off. Wearing a prim, navy blue dress with a lace collar of white daisies, Annette made her way out to the car, oblivious to the machinations of her ten-year-old's mind. She delicately slid into the driver's seat while being extra careful not to scuff her shoes on the door trim. It was only a matter of seconds before she felt the dampness seeping through the back of her dress. Despite her misgivings about the visit, a minor disaster of this kind, which might have presented a perfectly good reason to cancel a date for the senior prom, somehow mattered not at all.

Although not possessing the imperious facade of 18 Lakeside where Annette's never-forgotten first dinner with the Birds had transpired, 609 Rutland was nonetheless an imposing ranch-style brick home. Once again she felt like "Alice through the looking glass," on the threshold of another world, as she unlatched the iron gate and slipped into the courtyard. Once inside, her gaze was drawn immediately to the ramp that led to the doorway. For a moment she pondered the changes wrought upon this family.

After crossing the courtyard, she paused long enough to be sure the wet spot on her dress didn't show, took a deep breath and rang the doorbell.

The door was opened wide by Sam's father. He proceeded to greet Annette in the grandiosely open-hearted manner of a southern gentleman. Annette was taken aback by the fervor of his welcome and wasn't sure how to react. Her confusion was further heightened when Pauline threw her arms around her like a long-lost friend. For someone unaccustomed to such things, the "socialite's embrace" had a disconcerting emptiness to it.

Positioned directly behind his father, sporting a light blue, turtle-neck sweater that accentuated his sparkling blue eyes, Sam sat in his wheelchair wearing a smile that stretched from ear to ear. Any misgivings or apprehension she might have had evaporated in that instant. She moved toward him as though drawn by an invisible force, leaned forward and stretched out her hand. "So good to see you," she said softly.

Sam clasped her hand firmly with his good right hand, losing his balance in the process and keeling sharply over to the right. Annette recoiled, withdrawing her hand as Dick moved swiftly over beside the wheelchair, grabbed Sam and sat him up. "It's OK," said Dick.

'Oh dear, what have I done?' she thought to herself. Sam responded with an easy smile.

On seeing his reaction, Annette felt a great surge of reassurance and 18 years seemed as nothing. Her desire to get to know him was stronger than ever.

An hour and a half passed in what seemed like seconds. If Sam had been nervous at the prospect of meeting Annette again for the first time in 18 years, he never let it show. She was particularly struck by the lucidity with which he recalled their time at Minneha together. Dick and Pauline remained in the room at first, thinking they might be called upon to carry the conversation. But they became almost embarrassingly superfluous, so they left. The eager chatter ranged across the entire 18 years. They swapped stories, with no single event deemed to warrant special emphasis.

When Annette rose to leave she took Sam by the hand and pressed it gently before bidding everyone goodbye. As she walked down the ramp and back out through the courtyard, she savored her feeling for a moment. The sun had dawned again.

The next day Sam telephoned. This time, Annette didn't slam down the phone; instead, they giggled, kidded and laughed for about an hour—just like old times.

Later the following week, Dick called Annette and invited her over to dinner. Once again, it was like that time 18 years ago. She was captivated by the splendor of the property, the presence of the maid and the sumptuous interior decked out with fine paintings, artifacts and sculptures. The place felt like a museum, with all the attendant comforts of home thrown in as an after-thought.

The elegant dining room was the setting for a formal dinner. The food was in dishes with heat covers at Dick's end of the table ready to serve. Before the meal began, Annette watched as Addie came out of the kitchen carrying the plates with a large, white, terry cloth bib on top of them. She set the plates down beside Dick, then went over to Sam with the bib. Annette watched in disbelief as Addie fastened the large, white bib around Sam, tying it at the back of his neck. 'He's not a delinquent three-year-old,' she thought to herself. 'Why not just use a large napkin?' The bib seemed grotesquely inappropriate.

When Dick and Pauline finished eating, they both auto-matically lit cigarettes. Sam was still eating and it was clear that the smoke bothered him. He let out a barrage of suppressed coughs which were ignored by his parents.

After dinner, the two classmates retired to his bed-sitting room and picked up where they'd left off on the phone.

Two weeks after their first meeting, Annette telephoned Sam to ask if he would like to accompany her to an organ recital at the Eastminister Presbyterian Church. He accepted without hesitation. However, after putting the phone down, she was again overcome by a host of misgivings and doubts. 'Gee, what have I done? How do I react if people stare?'

Once again panic was beginning to overtake reason when the thought came to her that the only way she could resolve such feelings was to approach Sam directly with them.

On their way across the courtyard of 609 Rutland she asked, "Sam, how do you react when other people stare at you?"

He didn't hesitate, "I fought for my country and the wounds were the consequences. That's the price for being able to ride around in a free land. I'm proud to be a part of the freedoms that we enjoy."

Annette found herself looking at Sam in awe. If he could react that way, then she could too. The matter never resurfaced in her mind.

Dick drove them to the church in the specially modified, startlingly uncomfortable, garish-looking, red van resembling the "Creepy Coop" which had appeared in an early 70s children's TV cartoon show. They both enjoyed the recital, though it was little more than a backdrop to rekindling a friendship.

Upon their return to 609 Rutland, Dick drew Annette aside. He'd obviously been stewing over something all evening. He told Annette he felt the strain of going out in the evening was too much for Sam's body to take and it would be in Sam's best interests if they didn't make any further plans like this.

Concealing any apparent feelings of disappointment or disagreement, she nodded. After all, it wasn't her place to upset the apple cart, especially since she had no plans to pursue a relationship at that time—did she?

★　　★　　★

Dick's relatively emphatic statement of Sam's limitations came across to Annette as more of a put-down than an honest plea for his son's well-being. However, it was merely indicative of an overall cooling in Dick's attitude toward her. During the weeks that followed, Annette reflected with amusement on how, during the first few visits to 609 Rutland, one ring on the bell had been sufficient for Dick to spring out of his seat and hurry to the door and greet her. As her visits increased, her wait at the door became longer and longer until it took three rings to elicit a response. When he eventually did come to the door, his smile was replaced by an expression of mild irritation. In the end, it was left to Addie to answer the door.

Meanwhile, a similar phenomenon was beginning to show in her own father's reactions. Ed Blazier made the point on several occasions that his oldest daughter ought to be concentrating her efforts on looking for a suitable father for Eric, instead of wasting her time and energy on a relationship that had no future.

★　　★　　★

Despite the harsh darkening of hair that was once fine blond bristle, the shimmering blue incandescence of Sam's eyes had not dimmed. Annette found herself drawn more and more to their magic.

Their second outing was initiated by Sam, who paved the way with an insistence that pre-empted any objection by Dick. It was Thanksgiving Day and *West Side Story* was being re-run at the Crown Uptown Theater on Douglas Avenue. Sam had invited Eric too, after he'd cycled across with his mother to visit for the first time the preceding Sunday. He had been very quiet for the whole afternoon, answering Sam's stilted questions with a simple yes or no. He declined the movie invitation by saying he disliked musicals, yet it was evident this wasn't the only reason.

Dick drove them to the theater and told Annette to stand back while he positioned the hoist and lowered Sam into his wheelchair. Dick wheeled Sam into the theater while Annette followed. Before he purchased the tickets, Dick demanded to see the manager about arranging for Sam to be allowed to sit in the aisle. It was a reasonable request that Dick elevated to epic proportions. The manager smiled compliantly while Dick berated him. When Dick had finished his tirade, the manager said he would be glad to oblige—flashing Annette a knowing look in the process. After he parked Sam in the aisle, Dick ordered Annette to stay put in the aisle seat next to him until after the movie was over, when he would return for them.

Even with the hand brake applied to the wheelchair, the gently sloping aisle made the top half of Sam's body tend to pitch forward, so he had to compensate by pulling back with his shoulders. However, nothing was going to be allowed to interfere with his obvious delight at being out on a date that afternoon.

264

About 15 minutes into the movie, in the time-honored tradition of boys young and old, Sam reached over to his right and clasped Annette by the hand. Memories of their childhood courtship came flooding back and Annette squeezed Sam's hand ever so slightly. At that point, the movie could have gone on for ever.

On screen some characters appeared on a brownstone rooftop and began to sing, "I like to be in America . . ." Sam suddenly let go of Annette's hand and began to exercise his paralyzed left hand with his right to the rhythm of the music. When the song and dance finished, he let go to give his arm a rest. Then he reached over for Annette's hand, only he picked up his own left hand which was lying limp beneath his right elbow, and began to caress it!

'Gee, this is different!' Annette thought to herself.

After several minutes, Sam glanced down at his lap, gazed across at Annette's hand resting on the arm of her chair and looked down at his own hand again. A sheepish grin crept across his face and broadened into a smile as he let go of his left hand, reached over and retrieved hers. Leaning toward her tentatively, he whispered, "I suppose you think I'm a little peculiar." They both chuckled.

When the movie finished, everyone else left the cinema and Dick still hadn't arrived. Annette looked across at Sam and asked, "Sam, do you want to try it?"

"Are you brave enough to try it with me?" he replied with a mischievous smile.

"Sure," she declared.

Annette grasped the chair firmly and braced the back while Sam released the brake with his right hand. She then proceeded to pull the chair back up the aisle the five feet beyond the seats, turned it around and pushed Sam out into the lobby. When Dick pulled up outside the theater, Annette and Sam were on the sidewalk waiting. He got out of the van and didn't say a word, although it was clear he was fuming inside.

★   ★   ★

265

Whenever she was with Sam, Annette felt the deep emptiness within her disappear. Stern warnings from both fathers echoed all around, but she blocked them out. Maybe Sam wasn't what she'd been looking for but he provided everything she'd always wanted. Around him she felt like a complete woman, not from romantic outpourings of words, but through his genuinely unaffected caring manner. It was like putting on a new shoe and feeling it mold snugly to the contours of your foot. For the first time in many years, she was genuinely happy.

Eric's feelings were the faithful antithesis of his mother's. His disapproval of the developing relationship was readily apparent, manifesting itself in a refusal to carry out chores that had been second-nature for years—like making his own bed, tidying up the house and starting dinner when his mother was at work. He no longer expressed any desire to do things that involved the two of them, thus heralding a lasting period of alienation between mother and son.

The relationship between Annette and Pauline took on a similar complexion. From the mildly unsettling ardor of their first embrace, Pauline drifted far away. During Annette's early visits she would join the two of them in Sam's sitting room, pulling up a chair to chat for 10 or 15 minutes. The duration of her stay diminished gradually to where she would simply pop her head around the door long enough to say "Hi." Soon she disappeared from view altogether. "I don't know what it was," says Addie, "But Mrs. Bird just never did like Annette."

Meanwhile Dick said less and less, expressing his own disapproval with cold shoulders and disdainful looks.

As far as Annette was concerned, there was a significant benefit to all this: She had Sam all to herself. As she put it, "It was really kind'a nice that they weren't around."

As a matter of fact, one night Dick and Pauline went out for the evening. Apparently, during the function, Pauline felt that Dick's eyes had begun to wander in the direction of other women so she reacted by getting drunker than usual.

When they returned home, she passed out in the doorway. Dick had to carry her to her bedroom carefully so Annette wouldn't notice. According to Addie, "He put her over his shoulder and drug her through the hall like an ol' whipped cat."

The first verbal skirmish with Sam's father didn't occur at 609 Rutland, but on a Sunday afternoon at 231 South Belmont, after Dick called earlier that morning to say he was coming over to see her.

The meeting lasted no more than a quarter of an hour. Dick informed Annette that he was well aware her relationship with his son was becoming more serious and he didn't want to see anyone get hurt. "But," he growled, holding up a withering finger and looking her directly in the eye, "If you ever hurt my son, you'll be sorry!" With that, he made his excuses and left.

Annette, who remained sitting at her kitchen table for several minutes after he had gone, was numb. By now, her love for Sam had anesthetized her senses and she received the world through a misty haze.

★　　★　　★

On January 29th, 1972—Kansas Day—three months after their reunion, Annette was visiting Sam in his bed-sitting room. Before her arrival that evening, he had switched his radio to one of the stations that played classical music and dimmed the lights. He had a solemn expression on his face when she came in and began by saying he had something he wanted to talk about.

"Fine," she said, not sure what to make of his seriousness.

Sam continued formally, "I planned my military career in such a way that I could get my overseas duty out of the way before entering a serious relationship with anyone."

(While they were at Fort Myer with the Old Guard, a friend named Cy Shearer had expressed his personal preference for the timing of marriage as, "Some time after the Pope gets married." Sam had said he would get married right after Cy.)

"In my life," Sam continued, "God comes first, my country comes second and if you so desire, Annette, you may be third."

This unorthodox proposal took Annette completely by surprise. "Uh-huh," was all she could manage at first, before the full implication of Sam's monologue began to sink in. After a short pause, he had his answer.

"Yes," she said softly.

They both sat in silence for a moment before Annette leaned over and kissed her childhood sweetheart on the lips.

Sam considered this the perfect time to invite both Annette's parents and Pinky and Lucille, his godparents, over so they could tell everyone the good news together. Fear of her father's initial reaction caused Annette to suggest that she phone her parents first, giving them time to digest the news. Sam agreed.

Ed Blazier answered the phone.

"Dad, I'm over at Sam's. He proposed tonight and I accepted."

"Oh no," were the only words she heard. In the background, Lois Blazier intuitively sensed the content of the call without having to be told and burst into tears.

After Annette got off the phone, Sam called his godparents and asked if they could come over immediately. Five minutes later, Pinky and Lucille entered the sitting room, accompanied by Dick and Pauline.

"I want you to be the first to know," Sam declared, "that I have proposed to Annette Blazier, and she has accepted!"

Pinky guffawed his approval while Lucille smiled extravagantly. They both offered whatever support they could give. In stark contrast, Dick and Pauline seemed extremely subdued.

Pauline Houston Bird had an obsession with money—both in how it could be made, and lost. It had been her long-considered opinion that Annette's motive for staying around Sam was founded upon her desire to acquire his wealth. In fairness to Pauline, she was not alone in this idea. When Annette prepared to leave that evening, Pauline drew her to one side.

"Don't be surprised, my dear, if Sam has no recollection whatsoever, tomorrow morning, of what he has said to you and everyone else this evening. I didn't want to see you get hurt, my dear," she drawled, "but I thought it was something you should be aware of. Good night."

Instead of driving home on air, Annette felt as though she had been set adrift. It would have helped had she known that not only did Sam not forget but he kept his father awake half the night making plans.

Dick's subdued reaction to the betrothal could be explained by Sam's taking his father to one side in the kitchen the preceding day and excitedly informing him of his intentions. Before Sam had a chance to finish what he was saying, Dick launched into a lecture about how preposterous the idea was. He said it was foolish to even think about marriage in Sam's condition; it would be best for everyone if he banished the thought from his mind entirely.

All his life Sam had deeply respected, even revered his father. Yet on hearing Dick's words, he erupted into a furious rage. With the sudden surge of energy, he somehow spun the chair around and pushed himself vigorously with his right hand toward the open patio door and over the threshold. On the other side, the wheelchair hurtled down the ramp on its own momentum. When the two small front wheels hit the level floor of the patio, Sam pitched forward and was catapulted head-first onto the concrete surface. Panic-stricken, Dick rushed onto the patio where Sam was lying unconscious. After a couple of seconds he came to, and with the help of Addie and Tom Webber, Sam's long-time aide, Dick was able to get his son safely back in his wheelchair. Never again did Richard Bird question the wisdom of the marriage in front of his son.

Annette had precious little time to bathe in the reflected glow of the wedding announcement before having to co-ordinate the arrangements for the two sets of parents to meet. An evening after dinner the following week was selected for the momentous occasion. Meanwhile, both mothers preoccupied themselves with selecting the suitable "look" for the evening. Pauline had her hair done twice while Lois fretted with her daughter about what she should wear, how she should act around Dick and Pauline and how they would react to her. Ed Blazier did little to conceal his lack of enthusiasm for the occasion; doubtless he would rather have gone fishing, especially since his wife insisted he wear a suit and tie that evening.

After the formal round of introductions, Dick offered Ed and Lois a couple of stiff highballs. Though the two of them rarely drank, they accepted. Lois barely managed to suppress a tremor on seeing the potency of the concoctions. The two sets of parents sat down facing each other on opposite sides of the living room. Sam and Annette sat next to each other to one side, between them. At first, both sets of parents eyed each other warily. After 60 polite, if somewhat strained minutes, Ed and Lois rose to leave. After saying goodbye to Dick and Pauline, Ed walked over to Sam, firmly shook him by the hand and looked him straight in the eye. "I would be pleased and proud to have you as a son-in-law," he affirmed.

Such words, coming from a man for whom the expression of sentiment did not come easily, made a profound impression on his daughter; she knew the words came straight from the heart. In the light of forthcoming events, the gesture of acceptance from her father would assume an enduring significance in the life of his daughter.

The announcement of the engagement triggered an all-out rebellion in Eric. He'd already expressed his abject disapproval of the relationship in both direct and indirect gestures. He kept his distance from Sam and aimed most of his venom directly at his mother. Now, Eric's conduct around the house was distinguished by indifference, reluctance and a surly reticence.

Annette had encouraged her son to believe in his ability to accept and assume the role of the man of the family, thrusting burdens and responsibilities onto him that would normally be inappropriate for a child his age. Throughout the time she had looked to her son for support, he had relished the challenge, much to her delight and surprise. He had grown into a protective, albeit opinionated, eleven-year-old. Now he was confronted by a demotion in his role—or, as he saw it, he had been unceremoniously dumped for a mental cripple in a wheelchair.

★   ★   ★

270

Ed Blazier had been preparing to retire that April and move with Lois to Beaver Lake, in the heart of the Ozarks, and put the finishing touches to their retirement home there. For Eric, this would create an unwelcome distance between him and his grandparents. Ever since moving to Wichita from California with his mother, he'd been very close to them. He had also learned very early on that he could rely on his grandmother to be around whenever there was a conflict of interest with his mother. Now, she would no longer be there.

Despite envisaging a problem period of adjustment, Annette hoped that in time Eric would come to identify with Sam's inherent qualities in the same way she had and latch onto him as a role model. Things didn't turn out that way.

Adding to the mounting tension, Annette received another impromptu visit from Sam's father. This time, he brought with him the urinary apparatus which Sam used during the daytime. The odd-looking contraption, or Davall Bag as it was called, consisted of a tight-fitting, rubber hose-piece that was attached to the penis with a tube leading down into a leg bag strapped on below the knee. At best, it could be uncomfortable—at worst, excruciating.

"Do you think you can handle that?" Dick snarled as he flung the apparatus down on the table in front of her.

Annette had never seen a Davall bag before, and yet, like all the other threats and innuendos going on around her, Dick's words went in one ear and out the other. He continued to vent his fears about Sam's future welfare and urged her to seek the advice of Sam's doctors. This, she did. One neurosurgeon advised her over the phone, in the strongest possible terms, not to marry Sam. He cited the severe nerve damage which had taken place around the area of brain that remained. His conclusion was that it could take up to five years for Sam to make the adjustment to married life and it was doubtful he would live half that long. Annette thanked him politely and replaced the receiver.

In order to give her a representative picture of what life with a disabled person was like, Dick suggested she visit a friend of his whose husband was confined to a wheelchair with multiple sclerosis. "My dear, turn around and run as fast as you can in the opposite direction, away from Sam Bird," this woman beseeched Annette. "And never stop to look back!"

All Annette saw before her was a desperately unhappy woman railing bitterly against the injustice of the predicament she'd landed in. 'I'm where I am by choice,' Annette thought to herself.

Then there were the girls at work. The rumor circulating in the doctor's office was that the only reason for the marriage was to provide Sam with a full-time maid. For Annette, it was something like a lottery win with a few unpleasant strings attached. At first she felt crushed, but that was shortly followed by a welling up of rebellious pride. 'I'll show them a thing or two. They'll be sorry!' And then she became confused. In the end, she made up her mind what to do. That evening Annette went over to 609 Rutland and announced to Sam that they couldn't get married.

"Do you mind telling me why?" he replied calmly. She told him what she had heard at the office that day.

"Well, is it true?" he probed gently.

"No! You know it's not true!" she exclaimed.

"Then don't pay any attention to it."

The calm and simple rebuttal restored her notion that when you know in your heart what is right, you set your course and don't allow yourself to be swayed from it, least of all as a result of innuendo from those who have no involvement in the situation. She felt another overwhelming surge of strength and resolve.

*　　*　　*

In April 1972, five months before Sam and Annette were due to get married, Paula married Jim Oliver. At some time during that intervening period, Paula approached Dick with a "surefire strategy" that would solve her own domestic and financial problems as well as allay her father's concerns about Annette. She told her father that she'd picked out a house about four miles east of town that would house Sam, Annette and Eric on the bottom floor and Jim, Paula and her three kids on the top. During the day, Annette could take care of the housework and look after the kids. And Paula could unleash the full force of her creative talents to bring money into the house to help support both families. The "added bonus" would be that she could keep an eye on Sam to make sure Annette was treating him properly. Needless to say, Dick squashed the idea. It wasn't until years later that Annette learned of Paula's "scheme"—from Paula.

★　　★　　★

Annette continued to wrestle with her own hopes and fears. She so wanted to be the fully complimentary partner, the perfect foil for Sam, so the enormous potential of his earlier years in the Army might be fulfilled as a reflection of their married life together. Her fervent desire was to be wife and mother in a home where peace and security prevailed—where Sam would feel protected but not constrained in his rehabilitation. She indulged herself with the vague hope that Eric might come to love and respect Sam, recognizing his place in their lives. She hoped he would seize the opportunity to do all the things a child his age would normally enjoy, and above all, that he would no longer feel so strongly the responsibility for the guardianship of his mother's virtue.

Every now and then, she would panic at the thought of losing Sam before she had him. Annette knew from the various doctors' reports that his life expectancy could never be long-term. Would the enormity of marriage overwhelm Sam, causing him to feel the need to withdraw into a world of his own? She questioned whether her own physical capabilities would prove to be limitations, realizing full well that her arms and legs would have to act as Sam's arms and legs. And what if she dropped him?

And then there was sex—the frustrations, feelings of inadequacy, expectations and limitations. Before the wedding, they talked at length about it. They touched, they sensed, and they were patient—although not always. While waiting at a stop-light, Annette looked across at Sam sitting next to her in the front seat of the car she was driving and said, "If you ever feel the urge to, well . . . you know. Just let me know."

He looked at her with mischief in his eye. "How about now?" he said.

Chapter 16

. . . And They All Lived Happily Ever After

Ed and Lois Blazier had moved to Wichita from Lawton, Oklahoma, in 1942. Ed had obtained a job with Beech Aircraft Corporation. The company was then undergoing a vast and rapid expansion as a result of the outbreak of war with Japan. He remained with them for the rest of his working life, retiring as the company's safety director at the age of sixty-five on April 25th, 1972.

Three years earlier he had begun work on a cabin overlooking Beaver Lake in northwestern Arkansas—the heart of the Ozarks. The remote, two-story, wooden hideaway perched serenely above the lake shore in a thicket of green trees and overgrown vegetation. Its only means of access was a winding, two-mile dirt road, cleared through the trees to a narrow gravel pathway leading up from the boat dock below.

No sooner had the applause from the speeches at his retirement celebration died down than Ed and Lois Blazier set off for the unsullied tranquility of Beaver Lake. A few, small, finishing touches remained to be completed on the property, though it was more than habitable. Above all, Ed Blazier was now free to pursue his favorite pastime without unnecessary interruption.

On Thursday, June 8th, Ed spent most of the day fishing with a couple of friends from Beech Aircraft. At around nine o'clock, just before sunset, he put his two companions ashore at their cabin, about three quarters of a mile from his own boat dock.

"How about a beer, Ed?" one of them inquired.

"Not tonight guys," he apologized, "I really ought'a be getting back so Lois doesn't worry about me."

At a quarter past nine, or thereabouts, a woman on the lake shore caught sight of an unmanned craft going around and around in the water on the other side of the lake. At ten o'clock, Lois, frantic with worry by now, telephoned the police to say her husband had not returned home. Just before eleven, Ed's 15 foot aluminum fishing boat was found washed up on the south shore of the lake. His hat was floating upside down in the water alongside his cork-handled fishing rod, about 10 yards from the boat. Firemen had begun dredging the deep, murky, brush-laden waters by 11:30. They were assisted in their task by a curious-looking man in a boat with his own self-styled divining rods. The search was abandoned at noon the following day without a body having been recovered.

Lois remained at the cabin for the next four weeks, accompanied by Eric. At first she called the police every day for news and would rush to the phone each time it rang.

"They've found the body," was her usual assertion before picking up the receiver. Each time, her face reflected the same look of hapless dejection; the call was never what she hoped. In the end, the waiting became unbearable and she and Eric returned to Wichita.

A memorial service was held in hopes it might provide some resolution. Lois, however, merely pushed her feelings deeper down and put on a surface display of coping by launching herself into a hectic round of meetings and church functions. She moved into the duplex next to Annette's at 232 South Belmont. In particular, she wanted to be close to Eric. Ed Blazier had been a monumental part of his grandson's life for the past six years.

Eric withdrew still further from his mother and became very quiet. He had regularly accompanied his grandfather on fishing trips with another of Ed's friend's from Beech, Lawrence Peachin. Two weeks before that Thursday, Lawrence Peachin collapsed at the cabin from a heart attack and died two days later. In the aftermath of his grandfather's disappearance, Eric could be heard recounting repeatedly, "Three friends went out in a boat. One came back and two didn't."

Lois and her grandson turned to each other for solace and Eric turned his protective instincts, previously assigned to his mother, over to his grandmother. An already close bond became still closer. Lois went out and bought a sheltie pup—supposedly for herself. Eric named him Yogi.

In addition to its inherent trauma and uncertainty, the failure to recover Ed Blazier's body caused other problems. Arkansas Law stated that a period of seven years had to elapse before someone missing and presumed dead could be so pronounced. And so began a nightmare of legal wrangling for Lois and her family that added to their lingering, unresolved feelings of grief. The situation wasn't finally cleared up until Ed Blazier's perfectly preserved body surfaced 18 months later and was discovered by fishermen. Alas, too late for his wife to ever know about with any certainty. It was not a suspicious death. Annette later suspected he'd had a heart attack.

The news of her father's apparent drowning was another body blow to add to those raining in on Annette from several directions. But there was always Sam to turn to. In the months that followed he was always there to hold and he invariably said all the right things. Even Dick and Pauline temporarily dropped their air of icy indifference, giving her a glimpse of some compassion. It was a conciliatory period that turned out to be all too brief.

Before the drowning, September 9th had been set for the wedding date. Annette felt strongly the wedding should be postponed until after her father's body had been recovered. Lois disagreed, saying this would mean turmoil and consternation for Sam. She said unequivocally, "Life must be allowed to go on."

It was Dick's view that the wedding day itself should be kept low-key, restricting the guest list to close friends and family. It was proposed that the reception be held at 609 Rutland, so if Sam tired, he could be transferred from wheelchair to bed with a minimum of fuss. Those friends and acquaintances who weren't invited received a formal announcement of the wedding two days

277

after the Saturday ceremony. Doris received hers on Monday and took it as a clear statement to "keep away."

In discussing the color scheme for the wedding, Annette suggested fall colors, since it was September.

"There are only three colors," retorted Sam. "Red, white and blue!" The theme for the wedding had been decided! Uppermost in Sam's thoughts was the notion that Annette wear white. She argued that this would be hypocritical. Dick told her of the times when Sam had been close to death and had spoken repeatedly of his wedding day, when God sent him an "angel" dressed in white. Annette tried her best to make the point to Sam that she was certainly no angel! But she was never able to shake this image from his mind. The vision had been clear to him, despite sounding like hallucination to everyone else. His bride was wearing white. She contested the issue no further.

During their pre-nuptial counseling, the minister did everything short of refusing to marry them. He pointed out forcefully to Annette that she should be fully aware there would come a time in Sam's life when circumstances and pain would combine to put him under such intense pressure he would lash out in anger and frustration. She should prepare herself for the likelihood it would be directed straight at her. The minister's words were treated with the same patient reserve as those she had heard before.

They selected slender gold bands of the same carat gold as Sam's Citadel ring. He wore the two on the same finger. While they were at the jeweler's, Sam decided he would like a special inscription engraved inside the two gold bands. Annette suddenly felt a fillip of anticipation. "Maybe he's thinking of something simple like 'I Love You,' " she mused. "Or perhaps, 'Yours Forever, Eternally.' "

She was mildly taken aback therefore, when Sam announced he wanted the words, "In God We Trust," engraved inside each ring. Yet in the years to come, these words would foster a deep resonance. When life was at its bleakest and accompanied by great uncertainty about the future, as if to remind them what was written across their hearts, it was written in gold around their fingers.

Four weeks before the wedding, B.T. Collins paid an impromptu visit to 609 Rutland. Annette was summoned for an audience. Like most everybody else, B.T. found it impossible to understand why this marriage was taking place. "This woman, whoever she was, just had to be after Sam for his money. What earthly reason, other than this, could she have for marrying Sam Bird?"

A few days before arriving in Wichita, he'd raised his concerns over the telephone with Dean Parker.

"Just look at Sam's eyes when she walks into the room," Parker said. "All your questions will be answered."

They were.

★   ★   ★

The wedding took place at Saint Stephen's Episcopal Church in Wichita. Sam, looking rather plump from Addie's cooking, wore a navy blue suit and tie with a white shirt and a smile that lit up the entire church. Annette was dressed in white. Dick, who had been his son's devoted protector for the past five years, was best man. Paula and Annette's sister, Dona, were bridesmaid and matron of honor respectively. Both wore long blue dresses trimmed with white lace and carried bouquets of red carnations. Lois Blazier was serene. Her face radiated a warmth and compassion that embodied a lifetime of caring. Not once did she allow herself to betray the suffering she was still enduring since the disappearance of her husband. Eric sat through the entire ceremony with his arms crossed and a look of detachment on his face.

After the service, everyone returned to 609 Rutland for the reception. Pulling back the curtain from one of the living room windows that looked out onto the patio and garden, Dick captured a special moment with his camera. Sam was in his wheelchair looking down into the eyes of his bride who was seated in an armchair. His right hand, cradled beneath his limp, left arm, clasped his new bride's right hand. The look of love between them was enough to render an observer motionless; it transcended everything and everyone around them.

Annette harbored three regrets in particular after the wedding. She wished that Eric had been allowed to play a more active part in the wedding, instead of standing on the outside looking in. The ceremony served merely to drive home Eric's perception of a demotion in roles and she regretted desperately that she hadn't asked him to give her away. It just hadn't seemed natural at the time.

She regretted too not having elected to have a chair brought up during the ceremony for her to sit in so Sam didn't have to constantly look up toward her in order to gaze into her eyes.

And she had lasting misgivings about not demanding a honeymoon away from mothers, Dick, Eric and the aide, Tom Webber. Instead, at the insistence of Sam's father, they spent the three days after the wedding at 609 Rutland.

The night after the wedding, Sam and Annette went out for their first dinner alone together as a married couple. Upon their return to 609 Rutland, they were greeted by Dick and Pauline sitting on the back patio. When Annette closed the wrought iron gate behind them and wheeled Sam toward his parents, Dick rose somewhat shakily to his feet. Visibly dejected, he spoke with a distinctive slur, in a voice quivering with emotion. He proclaimed softly that his life might as well be over, since it no longer served any useful purpose. Sam chided his father for such thoughts, making the point that he and Pauline now had the opportunity to do all the things they'd been unable to do when Sam had been their sole responsibility. Pauline nodded in agreement with her son, while Annette wondered for a moment, 'What on earth have I done to this family?'

After the three-day "honeymoon," Sam and Annette moved into her duplex on South Belmont while awaiting construction of a new bungalow about three miles away. The situation called upon Sam to cope with some major adjustments immediately. As doctors and others had predicted, it did not come easily to him. The carpets were padded, which prevented him from moving freely about the rooms. The apartment was so small he found it impossible to maneuver his wheelchair into the bathroom or kitchen. And the process of getting herself and Sam to bed each night presented Annette with a conundrum of major proportions. First she would have to use the hoya lift to lay Sam down in his special hospital bed. (This was a chrome-plated hydraulic pump mounted on a center post, with a U-shaped base that could be adjusted around Sam in the wheelchair. Above that base was an arm with an attached V-shaped bar. At the end of this bar was a chain that could be attached to the sling underneath Sam.) Only after getting Sam into bed with this Rube Goldberg device could she begin to move all the sundry equipment out—first the lift, then the wheelchair commode and finally the wheelchair itself. When all this was moved into the living room, she could pull the roll-away bed out of the closet and set it up beside Sam's bed. If all the romance hadn't been extracted from the situation already by the maneuvering of commodes, there was always the six inch difference in height between the two beds. Even without Sam's disability, it would have required considerable ingenuity for them to get amorous. But at least they were able to hold hands!

★　　★　　★

A couple of weeks after the wedding, concluding that her hair was in dire need of rejuvenation, Annette paid a visit to a local beauty salon.

"Say, Annette, what did you say your new married name was again?" inquired the beautician meaningfully, while putting rollers on her client's languid tresses.

"Bird, why?" Annette replied.

The hairdresser thought for a moment. "Oh, nothing," she said. "I was just thinking; I went out with a 'Bird' once. It was a blind date. Some friends of mine told me they had this great-looking guy for me to meet, who was just great fun to be around; and on top of everything, he had just helped bury President Kennedy. Well, I tell you, honey, they might as well have buried him too! I mean, this guy was so square! All he could talk about was the Army. He never paid much attention to me!"

Annette smiled, but said nothing.

★　　★　　★

281

By now Annette knew without doubt that Sam's love affair with the Army had begun in earnest the day he passed through the gates of the Missouri Military Academy at the age of thirteen-and-a-half and that it would last the rest of his life.

Four months after he was wounded, the Army had placed Sam on what was known as its Temporary Disabled List. Once it became apparent that he was never going to be able to return to active duty, the Army initiated moves to phase Sam off the list into retirement. Thereupon, Dick engaged in a battle of wills that he knew from the outset he could never win. Regulations stated that personnel were entitled to no more than five years on the list before being transferred back to active duty or being retired. Meanwhile, every time moves were initiated by the Army, Dick would lodge a vociferous objection. By October 1972, however, the day of reckoning was at hand. Only too aware of the inevitable, Dick had long since set plans in motion for the day in question.

The Army could provide for two forms of acknowledgment of retirement. One arrangement dispensed with any formality and Sam would be served notice of his retirement through the mail. Alternatively, he could choose a formal retirement ceremony with all the attendant fanfare befitting his rank. Dick chose the latter of course, with Fort Riley, Kansas, the closest major Army establishment to Wichita and home of the 1st Infantry Division, selected as the venue.

Annette's first inkling of what was happening came when she and Sam were summoned to 609 Rutland for a meeting with two officers from Fort Riley. It was one week before the ceremony was scheduled to take place, on October 26th, 1972, at King's Field House. Since the officers had already been briefed as to Sam's requirements, the occasion served merely to confirm what had already been decided.

It was agreed Sam and Annette would travel to Junction City the evening before the ceremony in his parents' car. Dick and Pauline would follow in the battered, red Creepy Coop. It was just after four o'clock in the afternoon when they arrived at the

Holiday Inn in Junction City, where they were joined by Pinky and Lucille.

Annette wheeled Sam into their room, only to discover that Dick and Pauline had taken the adjoining unit with a connecting door. Much to her disquiet, all night long, every hour without fail, Dick would stick his head around the door to check that everything was all right. Dick was clearly incapable at that point of relinquishing responsibility for his son's welfare. It had been his sole preserve for five-and-a-half years. At the same time, Annette felt uncomfortable about, not to say incapable of, asserting herself with respect to Dick just a month into married life—especially since he still retained legal guardianship of Sam's affairs.

However, of far greater concern to Annette was Sam's reaction to his impending retirement, the severing of the umbilical cord to the only career he had ever known. She had no idea whether the full ramifications of the occasion had sunk in. What if he went into an irreversible decline when the realization finally took hold?

Sam awoke the following morning at six o'clock in a cheerful mood. Once again, Annette was a little unsure of how to interpret his behavior. She decided not to try. Instead, she asked her husband if he felt like setting down some of his feelings on a tape recorder. Sam thought that a great idea and picked up the microphone with his right hand. The deep, booming resonance was no longer there. His voice was softer now, occasionally slipping up an octave, though the same laconic delivery was still in evidence, accompanied by the occasional sprinkling of typical Sam Bird humor.

"I have just noticed it is 0600 HRS and I am trying to get my eyeballs opened and bounce out of bed! And say hello to the cold, cruel world here in the Fort Riley area.

"Then I will say goodbye to the United States Army as an official member of it. However, I will still be on the Army team watching from the civilian sidelines.

"I feel remorse and sad that I wasn't able to do more, but I am grateful to be here and to be alive today. And maybe I can help in other ways, other than in a military capacity.

"I feel very happy and lucky that I can be here with my lovely wife, Annette, and family, friends and loved ones . . ."

The soliloquy was cut short by Dick, who entered the room and commandeered the tape recorder in order to set down some of his own observations.

Throughout the morning before the ceremony, Sam remained calm, in stark contrast to his parents who appeared to be in a state of perpetual animation. Pauline was pre-occupied to distraction about which outfit to wear and went into a tailspin when she couldn't find the matching belt.

Annette, on the other hand, was subdued, almost detached, from everything. Nagging qualms of uncertainty and apprehension over Sam's reaction to the day's events weighed on her. But in time, better instincts impelled her to follow Sam's lead.

Sam's family was well represented at the ceremonies but it was Dean Parker's presence that gave him special joy. Eric made the trip with his grandmother. Annette hoped that gaining insight into Sam's past might engender a desire to get to know Sam better. Eric enjoyed the day, primarily because he was given the job of helping push Sam around in his wheelchair; he was included in something at last. However, the day did not produce the long-term results Annette hoped for.

In the early afternoon, King's Field House resounded to the loud, stirring sounds of the Army Band. The Retirement Order was read by the post's commanding general and telegram tributes from friends around the country were read. Sam sat through it all impassively. His solemn expression refused to give way to even a flicker of emotion.

At the conclusion of the formal ceremony, Sam was presented with a shadow box displaying his medals and given a brief tour of the post. The occasion was rounded out with a luncheon at the Officer's Mess. Dick suggested the rest of the family disperse and get acquainted with the other officers while he seated himself between Sam and the general. Annette found herself shunted off to an outside table with her mother and Eric. In the end, they were seated with a group of ex-Citadel graduates. The atmosphere around the table was strained. Everyone was afraid to talk about the future and uneasy talking about the past. The officers in particular, groped for words; the Guidon (Citadel rule book) did not contain a section for times such as these.

The end of the meal signaled the conclusion of the proceedings. For Annette, it couldn't have come soon enough. As for Sam, he was still giving nothing away.

★   ★   ★

Dick ordered Annette and Pauline to stand back while he rigged up the travel lift on the passenger side of the car. He then wheeled Sam below the lift, thrust the sling-support beneath his seat and hoisted him out of the chair. When he tried to move Sam in above the passenger seat the runners on the lift became stuck. Instead of propelling Sam inward, the pressure on the lift handle caused Sam to begin swinging above the wheelchair. Dick became increasingly irritated, muttering and cussing under his breath, and began jostling and shoving Sam to try to force him bodily into the car. Annette felt her anger building rapidly but said nothing. Pauline, Pinky and Lucille shuffled uncomfortably while trying to find somewhere else to look. Mercifully the runner freed itself and Dick was able to slide Sam into the car and lower him onto the passenger seat. Throughout the ordeal Sam remained totally passive, without so much as the meekest look of reproach toward his father.

It was agreed that everyone would rendezvous at 609 Rutland in time for the six o'clock news, where televised highlights of the ceremony were to be shown. After returning to Wichita at breakneck speed to catch the broadcast, it turned out the highlights would be shown on the ten o'clock edition instead. Sam was loaded into the Creepy Coop and Annette drove them back to their apartment.

Turning onto South Belmont, Annette could see that part of the street near the apartment had been cordoned off and blacktopped. The new asphalt surface was still damp and tacky, quite unsuitable for wheelchair traffic. In addition, the huge vehicle used to disgorge the black top was parked right in front of the pathway to the house. To get home, Annette would have to push Sam around a block to the east and then back across a couple of lawns. She felt a surge of panic—not because she doubted her ability to negotiate this obstacle course, but at the thought that this might be the trigger for Sam's emotions to finally burst their banks. As she wheeled him back toward the apartment, she braced herself for her husband's sudden outpouring of disappointment. Instead, he came out with a series of wisecracks.

When one of its front wheels plunged into a hole, the wheelchair lurched to one side as Annette briefly lost control. She let out a squeal as Sam pitched forward, then held her breath.

"Don't worry, Sweetie-Pie. When the tough things are difficult, the impossible takes a little longer, that's all," he replied.

PART VI

IN GOD WE TRUST

Chapter 17

Beginnings and Endings

That winter at South Belmont was as severe as any Annette could remember. It was as though everything froze at Halloween and didn't thaw until Easter.

Early in the new year of 1973, Sam, Annette and Eric paid a visit to their new home for the first time. The foundations had been laid and a wooden framework had been constructed. Eric dragged out a couple of planks from a pile of wood and constructed a ramp path to the front doorway. Annette wheeled Sam up the improvised drawbridge. Eric then took a broom to clear the debris from the floor while Yogi scuttled hither and thither.

Sam criss-crossed the floor in his wheelchair surveying every inch of every proposed room and hallway. Sam and Eric sized up the dimensions and collaborated to visualize what the final product might look like. It was a precious moment of unity—one of the few they all shared during those early years of marriage.

At first Sam tried constantly to build a rapport with Eric. However, the problem was that he would always begin each conversation with a question. It was the only means at Sam's disposal for establishing contact. He didn't know how else to begin with Eric and he thought if he could somehow get a sense of where Eric was coming from, he might know where to go from there. Another problem was that he would use a tone of voice that had survived from his days of addressing privates and sergeants. So, what was intended to be the precursor of a conversation started off sounding like a military interrogation. Not surprisingly, Eric took exception to this approach.

Compounding it all, one of the most unforgiving by-products of Sam's brain damage was his propensity to repeat himself. He'd been raised in a house where the question, "Did you wash your hands before coming to the table?" was always posed before meals. For Sam to pose the question once was enough to make Eric indignant. When he repeated the question several times, Eric became hostile. This left Sam completely at a loss. The painful fact was that although Sam meant well, the result of his endeavors was often disaster and heralded the beginning of a period of alienation when Eric would refer to his mother and Sam as "Her" and "Him." It is doubtful that anything could have effectively turned Eric toward either of them in those days.

The new home was completed in February of 1973. Bearing a strong resemblance, on a smaller scale, to Sam's first home at 18 Lakeside, 8230 Brookhollow, or "Fort Bird," as Sam called it, was a pleasant sight. The red brick contrasted perfectly with its white trim, presenting a neat, compact vision of uncluttered coziness. A flagpole stood proudly in front of the house, the centerpiece of its exterior.

Inside, Dick's fastidiousness for the smallest detail (although often outraging the embattled building contractor) had paid off handsomely. Everything was on one level and catered to Sam's needs: the width of the doorways, the size of the rooms, every single detail down to the smallest stipulation. Sam could move throughout the house at will, wheeling from room to room, soaking up the fact that he was master of his own home.

Ever since the wedding, the domestic situation with Tom, Sam's aide for two years, had become increasingly difficult. Annette and Tom rarely saw eye to eye over anything, whether it was how Sam's hair should be washed or Tom's strained communication. One day during lunch, Sam told Tom he felt as though he needed to be placed on the commode. Tom replied that he didn't, since it wasn't his scheduled day. As a result, Sam had an accident and Tom belittled him for lacking the self-control to prevent it. Sam's paralysis meant it was impossible for him to ever control his bowel movements. This was the last straw for Annette, who stormed over to 609 Rutland and demanded Tom be fired.

For the first six months of their marriage, Dick had retained all financial and legal control of Sam's affairs. He refused Annette's demand point-blank, saying it was not practical to fire Tom until the two of them had settled into their new home. Annette was furious but there was nothing she could do about it. Four months later, Tom beat her to the punch and handed in his own resignation. Thereafter, Annette assumed responsibility for every aspect of Sam's welfare. This entailed a drastic rearrangement of the daily routine, the main consequence of which was that she now had even less time to devote to her son's needs.

Their first year of marriage was to have many milestones and turning points; this was only the beginning. Yet no matter what problems presented themselves during the day, Annette always had the consolation of being able to crawl into bed alongside Sam at night. It was worth the hard work just to have him put his arm around her and tell her everything was going to be OK. It meant so much to be able to do that. Every night the bond between them grew even though tumultuous times lay ahead.

★ ★ ★

Their home had been built using the proceeds from Sam and Annette's savings and the compensation he'd received for his injuries. The couple lived on Sam's pension and disability check which came to $1200 per month. It was not an inconsiderable amount in 1973, although a significant portion of it would go to cover the aide's monthly salary. Even so, the marriage was never under threat of financial pressure. Sam's promotion to the rank of major saw to that.

The furnishings inside the house consisted of an amalgam of Sam and Annette's accumulations over the years, supplemented by a small donation of castoffs from 609 Rutland. The prerequisite for any furniture was that it had to be functional; all the rooms needed to remain uncluttered to allow Sam unhindered passage. Once established, the interior of the house would have to retain the same character in order to prevent Sam from lapsing into any temporary confusion. There was a mild controversy, however, over how the rooms should be decorated. The conventional wisdom, as espoused by doctors and staff at the V.A. in Wichita, was that a clean break should be made with the past. In their opinion, nothing that might serve to remind Sam of his past should be placed on display in the house for fear of the traumatizing effect they might have. After listening to Sam, Annette disagreed with this, thinking instead that by decorating the interior of the house with an array of military memorabilia and pictures pertaining to Sam's past accomplishments, the decor could serve as a positive stimulus to his memory and a catalyst for redeveloping his thought processes.

Innumerable times after decorating the house her way, Annette would catch Sam out of the corner of her eye, wheeling up and down the hallway, stopping by each picture and artifact. She saw the gleam in his eye as he surveyed a photograph of The Citadel and watched as he savored the experience for a short while before wheeling on. The memorabilia also served as a springboard for conversation with visitors.

If the climate had permitted, Sam would have taken up residence in the back yard the year round. During that first spring at Brookhollow, piles of dirt, rubble and sand scattered about a desolate wasteland of flattened, barren soil was all that passed for the back garden. When they took lunch on the cement patio, Sam would lapse regularly into a lyrical descant about a white picket fence set against lush, green grass and roses in full bloom. Each time this occurred, Annette found herself staring at her husband with a look of perplexed incredulity. "All I see is work out there!" she would exclaim.

"Through the eyes of faith, I see a gorgeous garden," would be his immutable response.

Through the employment of several different contractors, (not to mention the uncomplaining efforts of his wife!) Sam's vision was realized in every detail.

Despite being without peripheral vision and having a left eye that barely functioned, Sam continually amazed Annette with an uncanny knack for noticing every cardinal that landed on top of the white wooden fence. In the same way, when they were out driving he would occasionally catch her trying to run the yellow caution lights.

During the countless hours Sam spent basking in the presence of nature in the back garden, numerous tankers would take off from McConnell Air Force Base and shatter the serenity of their home. One day while sitting in Sam's favorite room outdoors, Annette cringed as one of the tankers roared overhead.

"How on earth are we ever going to get used to living with that?" she wailed.

There was a short pause, while the aircraft flew out of earshot, before Sam delivered his reply. "They're ours," he declared softly.

From that moment forward, the sound of the planes never bothered Annette Blazier Bird.

★   ★   ★

While the newly put together family unit was moving in and adjusting to life at 8230 Brookhollow during February of 1973, Lois Blazier had embarked on an extended vacation. She was visiting her son and two other daughters in Colorado and Washington State. She figured this would allow Sam, Annette and Eric the freedom to find their bearings as a family in their new home.

As a child, Lois Blazier had been delicate and tender-hearted; these traits remained with her throughout her life. She came from a close-knit Denver family, graduating from Colorado State University as a dietician.

Lois left Colorado just before the outbreak of World War II, accepting a post as a dietary advisor to the government at Fort Sill, Oklahoma. It was there she met and married Ed Blazier. They had originally planned to settle in Lawton, Oklahoma, but the opportunity for Ed to work at Beech Aircraft in Wichita was too good to pass up. They plunged all their savings into the

293

deposit for a two-story wooden home and adjoining gas station with four acres of land located on the opposite side of Central Avenue, across from the aircraft plant.

Ed had been a working man of his day. His great passions were fishing, skeet-shooting and fiddling around with car engines. He tended to prefer his own company and that of a few well-chosen friends. Lois was the opposite of her husband. She was never happier than when she could give a big dinner party with her finest china on display. But community service was her passion.

During the middle of one night when her children were little, a tornado took the roof off a house two blocks away. Before daybreak, Lois had organized a group of neighbors to help the family get back on their feet again in the quickest possible time. Meanwhile, she had fixed a breakfast and had it on their doorstep by eight o'clock that morning.

If Sam Bird was the ideal of American Youth, the kind who doesn't seem to exist any more, then Lois Blazier was the unsung woman of a bygone era.

Lois seemed to be a member of every conceivable local organization. She was president of the PTA, the Farm Bureau and her church group, while at the same time acting as bookkeeper for the family gas station and chauffeur to her four children.

Sunday mornings offered a sight to behold, as various waifs and strays from the neighborhood were rounded up, crammed in the back of the Blazier station wagon and carted off to Sunday School. The faint hope that some form of spiritual enlightenment might be induced came second in most of the grateful parents' minds to their much-needed respite from the thundering herds. For the children, Lois Blazier was the type of woman they all wished at one time or other was their own mother.

★　　★　　★

On her return to Wichita, Lois decided to move into an apartment. The complex of mock Tudor dwellings was located about half a mile southwest of Brookhollow. It was the same place where she and Ed had stayed before moving to Beaver

Lake. Here she could remain close to her daughter, yet unobtrusive in her presence; if Eric was in need of refuge, he merely had to hop across the creek.

When Lois arrived back in Wichita at the end of March 1973, her grandson was on hand to help her move into the new apartment.

The next day around noon, Annette received a telephone call from her mother. "Don't worry," said Lois; the tone of her voice causing her daughter to do exactly that, "I've got some pains in my chest and running down my left arm. I think it's the flu, but the doctor has told me to come in for a check-up. Would you mind dropping me over at Saint Joseph's?"

Annette, accompanied by Sam and Eric, picked her mother up at the apartment, took her to the hospital and sat down in the waiting room. As the minutes turned to hours, she became increasingly concerned. Finally, the doctor emerged to inform Annette that her mother was in the Cardiac Care Unit; she had suffered a major heart-attack.

From that moment on, day-to-day life acquired a surreal quality. Annette's brother, Hal, and sister, Dona, traveled out from Colorado that weekend. Lois's mind was still in turmoil over her husband's disappearance. Hal and Dona went to Beaver Lake to close the family checking account and put the house up for rent to allay some of their mother's worries.

Eric was in a state of limbo. After Ed's disappearance, Lois and her grandson had given much comfort to each other. The hospital, however, forbade visits from children under the age of fourteen. Eric was twelve. When the doctors eventually made the decision to perform bypass surgery, Annette felt that somehow she had to get Eric in to visit his grandmother. That evening she took him by the hand and led him up the back staircase to the third floor, where her mother's room was located. On their way up, they were met by a young intern. "Are you fourteen?" he demanded with haughty self-importance, looking directly at Eric.

"No," Eric replied meekly, looking down at his feet.

"You can't come up here. It's against the rules."

Annette stood there mouth agape as the intern trotted off down the stairs. She looked at her son unhappily. "If you go out into the parking lot, Grandma will come to the window and wave at you," she said, knowing her words offered little consolation.

Eric dropped his head once again and walked slowly back downstairs. Lois was wheeled over to the window where she looked out at her grandson, standing forlorn and alone in the middle of the parking lot. She tapped on the window and waved. Eric looked up and waved back. They smiled at each other sadly.

The following afternoon, Lois was granted permission to come down to the hospital lobby in a wheelchair to spend some time with her youngest daughter, Carol, and her one-year-old son. Eric was in school at the time.

The day before surgery, Lois told Annette not to worry. "If the surgery goes well, then I will be able to live to see my grand-children grow up, and be with my children," she said calmly. "If it doesn't go so well, then I will be with Ed and the Lord. Either way will be fine." She looked at her daughter with reassuring eyes.

Lois was taken into the operating room the following morning at six o'clock. Annette decided to stay home that day to be with Sam and look after her sisters' children. Lois came out of surgery at five o'clock that afternoon. The doctors told Dona and Carol, who'd been at the hospital since early morning, to go home and get a good night's rest; they had some concerns about Lois, but her condition was stable.

It was 3:30 in the morning when the phone rang at Brook-hollow. The hospital called to say Lois had taken a turn for the worse and the family should return to her bedside as soon as possible. Annette was very uneasy at the thought of leaving Sam and Eric alone in the house. At a loss, she telephoned Dick and Pauline who agreed to come over and stay while she was at the hospital. When they arrived on the doorstep at four A.M., Annette felt a strong sense of relief; she no longer had to worry about Sam becoming confused without her.

When Annette arrived at St. Joseph's Hospital, her mother's doctor explained that Lois wasn't responding to treatment, her heart wasn't picking up the pressure as it should and there was very little that could be done. Annette went into her mother's room with her two sisters. Lois was conscious and could see them but was unable to speak because of the tubes attached to her nose and mouth. Despite its partial concealment by tubes, her face bore the same expression of warm serenity that had been so evident on Sam and Annette's wedding day.

First Dona went over to the bedside, looked down lovingly at her mother and said, slowly and affirmatively, "Mother, I love you." Carol followed, saying the same thing—more quietly but with the same insistence. Finally, Annette went over to where her mother lay. She wanted so badly to be able to say what her sisters had just said, but found herself saying instead, without the same emphasis as her two sisters, "Mother, we love you."

As the three women left the room, Lois closed her eyes.

When she returned to Brookhollow at about six A.M., Annette found to her dismay that Sam's door had been closed for the entire time she'd been away. Dick and Pauline hadn't been in to see him at all and promptly left upon her arrival.

Annette opened the bedroom door to find Sam in a state of utter consternation. He had been awake for the whole two hours, working himself up into greater and greater paroxysms of exasperation. She sat down on the bed, took his hand and slowly began to explain what had happened. After about five minutes of Annette's story, a look of calm returned to his face. As she came to the end of her explanation, the phone rang. It was the hospital again—Lois had just passed away in her sleep. Annette climbed onto the bed and clung to her husband as she had never clung to him before.

After a short time to collect her thoughts, Annette made her way slowly down the hallway to Eric's room. The early morning light was filtering in through his bedroom window as she opened the door. She went over to her son's bed and sat down beside him as Yogi scuttled in behind her and hopped up on the bed. "The hospital just called," she said softly. "Grandmother died this morning."

Eric lay there with his eyes wide open. "Everything I like dies," he said, his gaze focused beyond his mother.

After saying a few more things that failed to elicit a response, Annette heard her husband call out from their bedroom, "Honey, I need you!"

Eric hugged Yogi closer to him as his mother turned to leave.

On the day of the funeral, as the house filled with people and flowers, Eric gathered Yogi in his arms, took him back to his bedroom and closed the door. This was his only place of refuge now, from a family he perceived as hostile. Meanwhile, Annette was busy welcoming her sisters, their husbands and children. She had neither time nor words for her son.

Chapter Eighteen

Trials and Tribulations

Following the plating operation at the V.A. Hospital in Oklahoma City in May of 1968, Sam had been dogged by epileptic seizures. It wasn't until after they were married, however, that Annette became fully aware of their impact. The seizures were attributed to a chemical imbalance caused by the interaction between the remaining portion of brain and a massive residue of scar tissue.

Annette would usually receive warning of an impending seizure from Sam, himself.

"I feel like something strange is going to happen," he would say, as the pallor of his skin would turn chalky white. His eyes would glaze over and lose their capacity to see. They remained open but registered only an eerie blankness. His jaws would begin to move as though he were chewing gum and his right hand would tighten up—clenching into a fist as the upper part of his body became rigid. The seizure would normally last anywhere from 45 seconds to a minute, after which Sam would slump into a languorous stupor.

The doctor told Annette to think of it as an old-fashioned telephone switchboard whose plugs had been ripped out at once. In order to make it fully operational again, each plug had to be fitted back into its respective hole, one at a time. Complete recovery could take as long as several hours.

Sam's seizures gradually became more frequent until one day in August 1973, he experienced seven of them—one after the other.

Annette first became aware that Sam was sustaining some serious internal damage that day when she noticed the change in color of his urine bag; it was bright pink. Sam was sitting in a languid, dream-like state—the seizures themselves merely provided transitory jolts from his stupor.

In the past, a drug called Dilantin had been used to control the chemical imbalance. (While he was taking it, Sam befriended a neighborhood dog who was on the same medication for the same disorder whose name was also Sam.) Now it appeared that the use of the drug alone was insufficient. By three o'clock that afternoon, Annette noticed the "jolts" were coming closer together. She telephoned the V.A., who informed her she could bring her husband to the hospital, though not as an emergency patient; he would have to wait his turn to see a doctor. Past experience told her that waiting for a doctor at the V.A. could take anywhere from one to six hours. Sam was far too weak for that so she called a civilian specialist who advised her to check Sam into one of the local hospitals immediately.

Annette recalled that Dick had told her about Sam's tendency toward confusion and hallucination when he found himself in unfamiliar surroundings. She thought that if Sam had a familiar person with him for most of the few days at the local hospital, this problem could be eliminated.

Annette thought of Dick right away but unfortunately she hadn't foreseen that he had made plans to leave town for a few days. Her call to set up a schedule for visits was met by less than enthusiasm but, nonetheless, Dick agreed to spend a couple of hours in the early afternoon with Sam. Annette made arrangements with an aide to stay in the morning and she would take over at three o'clock and stay until visiting time ended.

Everything went smoothly the first day. The following evening, Annette returned home late, having stayed at the hospital a little longer than the previous night. When she pulled up the drive, it dawned on her that the freshly laid turf at the front and back of the house had gone without water for the whole day. After putting the car in the garage, Annette turned on the sprinkler in the back and then went out to the front of the house

300

to water the turf by hand, staying outside until past midnight. When she came indoors for the night, she heard the phone ringing and picked up the receiver, sitting down in the armchair beside the phone. "Hello?"

"You God-awful whore! Just exactly who the hell do you think you are?" The words were slurred together.

"Pauline?"

"Out on the town carrying on when my son is lying in his hospital bed."

"But, Pauline . . ."

"Don't 'but' me, you cheap slut! I knew we should never have let you marry our Sam. And another thing, I know it was that cretin of a son of yours who sent him into hospital in the first place!"

Before Pauline had a chance to continue with the frenzied verbal assault, Annette interjected, "Pauline, I realize you are speaking under the influence of alcohol." She spoke in a soft but measured voice, "And I would rather not listen to any more." Then Annette hung up the receiver.

Less than a minute later, the phone rang again. This time it was Dick. "No one ever hangs up on Mrs. Bird!" he stormed, and slammed down the phone.

Annette felt the pit of her stomach knot up. She slid down onto the floor from her armchair, clutching a cushion to her chest. She felt utterly devastated and alone. Her only thought was to rush back to the hospital, wrap Sam up in a blanket and bring him home, locking the doors behind her and never coming out again.

Fortunately Eric was spending the summer with his father in Grand Junction, Colorado. For that at least, she was grateful.

The following day as Annette was visiting the hospital, she met Dick and Pauline emerging from Sam's room. Annette hesitated briefly, then walked toward them. Pauline smiled at her as though nothing had happened and walked by. Dick followed his wife as Annette went into Sam's room.

When Annette came out of the room about an hour later, she saw Dick sitting on one of the chairs on the opposite side of the ward with a bag in his lap. She walked over to him. He stood up and took a large Indian Squash necklace out of the bag.

"This is from Pauline," he said, offering it to her. "It's her way of saying she's sorry. She never apologizes in person."

"Thanks," replied Annette.

His job done, Dick turned and walked to the elevator.

As a result of several tests, Sam was given a combination of Dilantin and Mycelin which had a stabilizing effect and combined greatly to reduce the incidence of seizures. Sam was released from the hospital after a week.

As far as other items of jewelry were concerned, specifically Helen's diamond earrings, which had been willed to Sam's bride, Pauline made several trips to the bank vault as a result of prodding from Addie. Each time, several days later, she would return them. They were never given to their rightful owner.

★   ★   ★

As summer became autumn, Sam began to exhibit more signs of frustration with his condition. These manifested in sporadic bouts of irritation and outbursts of temper. The success of his marriage had reawakened his desire for a complete recovery—an eagerness that had slowly receded during his years at 609 Rutland.

One evening in October, while a fierce thunderstorm was raging overhead, Sam decided he wanted to go out in the garden.

"Sam, it's too dangerous out there," Annette pleaded, fearing that lightning might strike either the wheelchair or the metal plate in his head.

Sam said nothing, but reared up in his chair, the burst of energy causing his face to flush as he forced his way out through the door onto the patio and wheeled himself down into the garden. After sitting alone there for several minutes, he asked his wife to wheel him back inside the house.

It is almost impossible for an able-bodied person to have an accurate perception of a disabled person's physical limitations and frustrations, especially at crucial moments. When able-bodied people become frustrated, they simply diffuse tension throughout the entire body. The effect is an almost instantaneous retrieval of composure. For Sam, the very means that most people use to release their frustrations *was* his frustration. In addition, muscle relaxants had been prescribed to help negate the impact of seizures, if and when they did occur. Their unwanted side-effect limited Sam's physical capabilities as well, but this was not diagnosed until a year later.

When Sam erupted like this, Annette was unable to communicate with him. He'd never been one to verbalize his frustrations, especially to her, although she often wished he would. Because the outbursts came and went so quickly, Annette, who had a particularly slow-burning fuse herself, found she didn't have time to feel rejected since she was so engrossed in trying to alleviate the situation at hand.

★   ★   ★

One constant of their lives which drew Sam and Annette closer than any other was religion; their deeply held convictions had been evident as far back as their near-simultaneous confirmation, 20 years earlier.

Sam's initial push toward Christianity, through the Episcopal Church, probably came from his father. Dick was born a Methodist and became an Episcopalian while studying at Washburn Law School. He was drawn to the formality and structure of the Episcopalian services. Pauline was a Christian Scientist like her mother. It is doubtful this had any great impact on Sam's religious development.

As Sam grew up, both parents relinquished any discernible commitment to either church and it was left to the Grandfield godparents, notably Lucille, to actively encourage his continued attendance. By the time he was confirmed at the age of twelve, however, it was clear that Sam was setting his own course. Eleven years later, in 1963, Saint Stephen's Episcopal Church was founded barely a block or two from 609 Rutland and Sam became one of the original members of its congregation.

Annette was born a Presbyterian, though her father, like Dick, had been born a Methodist and had long since watered down his church attendance. Annette's Presbyterianism came directly from her mother and grandmother, both of whom were devout churchgoers. Ed's reluctance to attend church probably stemmed as much from his aversion to suits and ties as anything else. Lois, following her mother's footsteps, made certain all four children, along with half of those in the neighborhood, received a generous exposure to church. When Annette went to Denver to look after her grandmother, the religious beliefs that were an integral part of her life were consolidated and reinforced.

After they were married, Annette's first inclination was to accept Sam's specific Episcopalian preference without discussion, not wanting to provoke the traumatic mental upheaval several "learned" minds had predicted. She decided to put Episcopalian beliefs into practice for herself. After all, like the Presbyterian Church, it was but another sect of the Protestant faith.

After six months of trying to adapt, Annette found herself retaining a strong sense of detachment from the new church. She kept telling herself it was the church's rigid adherence to ritual and dogma in its services that formed a straitjacket through which she could not release her love of God. But the real cause for her discontent lay elsewhere. Throughout that whole six-month period, Annette was very much aware that only three members of the congregation came over to extend any form of warmth or friendship toward Sam. The rest skirted around the wheelchair, refusing to acknowledge his presence, as though he represented some unfortunate distraction from the tastefulness of their landscape.

Trying to suppress her feelings of resentment, Annette resolved to give the matter of adjustment more time. Throughout the next 18 months of listening to sermons almost exclusively directed to the question of whether women priests should be ordained, Annette felt a spiritual void. In the end she started praying under her breath each time she wheeled Sam into the sanctuary, "Lord, if you are here, please let me feel your presence. Please give me some indication."

In February of 1974, Sam and Annette were introduced to a nondenominational *Bible* study group which emphasized "spiritual values" and reliance upon biblical scripture over church doctrine. As significant as their philosophy, however, was the way they received new participants. The home that played host to the study had a set of forbidding steps leading to the front door, yet whenever Sam and Annette arrived, they were greeted by men from the group who promptly lifted Sam and the wheelchair up into the house. These people weren't going out of their way to avoid them—instead, their unspoken message was clear, "Welcome, we accept you."

In addition to providing Annette in particular with a fertile domain to channel her pent-up faith, this was the first significant social contact following their marriage that proved wholly positive. Coffee and dessert were served at the end of each session, which enabled Annette and Sam to mix socially. Tentatively at first, then as they gained confidence, they developed the ability to communicate within the group as a couple. This experience, more than anything else, encouraged Annette to venture beyond the confines of Brookhollow, instead of retreating behind the protection of its walls.

In the spring of that year, the leader of the group extended a blanket invitation to attend a "revival" at his church. Annette looked at Sam quizzically. Neither of them had attended a revival before; however, they had both been so encouraged by their experience in the group that they decided to give it a try. The week-long revival, which was designed to infuse new life into a person's relationship with God, was held each night at a church called "Faith Chapel," located about three miles southwest of Brookhollow. The little, red brick, Full Gospel church, perched on a rise of ground with its white wooden steeple and cross, would undoubtedly have fallen into Mabel Black's category of Holy Rollers.

When Sam and Annette arrived at the church entrance on the first night, the ramp for wheelchair access beckoned like a neon welcome sign. It was a little steep but there was always someone on hand to help them in. As she wheeled Sam into the church sanctuary, Annette felt something happen to that spiritual void within her soul. The two-hour service flashed by in what seemed like minutes. On their way out, Sam recounted a similar experience and suggested they return to Faith Chapel the following Sunday for their regular church services. Annette recalled, however, that they had agreed to teach Sunday School at Saint Stephen's through the month of May. She also felt Sam's suggestion might well have slipped his memory by Sunday, so she decided they would remain at Saint Stephen's until the end of the month. In the meantime, they paid regular midweek visits to Faith Chapel to find out more about the church. Annette wanted desperately to leave Saint Stephen's, though she was completely unprepared for the fallout from their departure.

On the first Sunday in June when they left Brookhollow for Faith Chapel, turning left at the end of the road, instead of right to go to Saint Stephen's, Sam demanded to know what was happening. Annette reminded him they had chosen to go to Faith Chapel, something she had discussed with him just five minutes earlier while they were getting ready to leave the house.

"Why aren't we going to Saint Stephen's?" Sam repeated insistently.

"But Sam, we just talked about it and it was you who suggested it some time ago," Annette replied.

"I don't remember that."

Once again, Annette would explain and again Sam would ask why. When they reached Faith Chapel and the service began, Sam was reassured. Each Sunday, for the next six weeks, the same thing happened. As soon as they turned left instead of right, Sam would ask what they were doing. After six weeks of the same questions and answers, Annette began to have real doubts about whether she had done the right thing. Had she moved too swiftly? Maybe Sam wasn't ready yet. Would he ever be ready?

The following Sunday they started down the street as usual, only this time Annette turned right at the bottom. About a mile from the house, close to the turnoff to Saint Stephen's, Sam announced suddenly that he wanted to go to Faith Chapel.

Annette sighed with relief, but it had been a valuable learning experience for her. She realized it was essential to lay extensive groundwork and preparation for every change made, for Sam no longer possessed the capacity to make the mental adjustments on his own—he needed help.

It was a significant departure for both of them in that they had uprooted the beliefs they had been taught as children, replanting them in a form of worship they had chosen for themselves.

Sam took especially well to the new minister's booming, no-nonsense delivery. Pastor Pruitt spoke in such a way that, when he wanted to make a point, he would pause and repeat it in order to emphasize the message behind his oratory. The effect on Sam's comprehension was noticeable. On Sunday afternoons following the morning service, Sam could retrieve the thoughts of the sermon without any cajoling from Annette. This was a major breakthrough. Up until that point, Sam's cognitive thought process had appeared redundant.

At first the reaction to their departure from Saint Stephen's seemed somewhat muted; there were no calls, no letters, no visits. Then, at an open house thrown by Paula and attended by several members of Saint Stephen's congregation, the minister came over to Sam when he saw Annette had left his side for a moment. When Annette returned, the minister changed the subject. After he left, Annette could see that her husband was confused.

"What's the matter, Sam?" she asked.

"He told me that I was letting the church down by not fulfilling my obligations," Sam replied.

Annette was incensed but fought to suppress any display of anger in front of her husband. Sam was such an easy target. 'But what use would a confrontation with a clergyman be?' she wondered.

Lucille's reaction, on the other hand, was far from muted. She considered herself to have been deeply affronted and directed the full force of her anger at Annette. "You should be ashamed of what you have done!" she railed. "If an Episcopalian member dies and is not buried in an Episcopalian church, he doesn't go to Heaven."

"Could you provide to me the chapter and verse from the *Bible* which states that?" Annette inquired calmly. "Because if it's there, we will gladly return to Saint Stephen's."

Lucille huffed, muttered something unintelligible under her breath and stormed off. She took it so personally because she had brought Sam to the church in the first place. Also, she snobbishly thought Annette lower middle-class.

Sam and Annette's beliefs shaped their lives fundamentally and Faith Chapel provided an outlet for the expression of those beliefs without inhibition. The church was small enough for Sam to get to know people and they him. For the first time since their marriage, Annette saw Sam treated like a real person. Because of this, his ability to converse grew and grew. He felt more comfortable around other people and this in turn gave him the confidence to speak for himself in matters other than hello and goodbye.

★   ★   ★

In the spring of 1974, Annette received notification that Sam would have to make himself available for a further military evaluation of his condition to update his status for insurance and benefits purposes. Since the V.A. in Wichita didn't possess the appropriate facilities, it meant another journey to Fort Riley.

Once again they traveled the hundred or so miles by car the night before with Dick accompanying in a "supervisory capacity." Sam appeared quite calm as he was wheeled into the medical center the following morning. Before he was wheeled away for his examination, Dick drew Annette to one side and informed her that she was to keep quiet and let him do the talking. Not altogether sure what her father-in-law meant by that, she said nothing for the time being.

One hour and three cups of bitter coffee later, the chief medical examiner summoned both Annette and Dick into his office.

"How does Sam behave when he is at home?" the doctor inquired. "How does he conduct himself around other people?"

"Oh, he's really coming on well," Dick declared. "It's amazing how he's taken to the new house. He really is master in his new home. He has few problems around other people; he conducts himself as you would expect a man of his age to," Dick went on, a moderate tone of indignation in his voice.

The doctor cleared his throat before reading aloud a summary of the basic findings of the medical evaluation.

"The patient was oriented to place and person, expressing much pleasure at again being in a military facility. However, his orientation to time was imperfect, in that he knew the month, but not the date or the correct year. His vocabulary was somewhat limited considering his educational background. His thought processes, as in interpretation of proverbs and similarities were coherent. There was no evidence of loose associations, hallucinations or delusions. There was some blocking and vagueness concerning anxiety-provoking subjects such as sexual behavior within the marriage. He showed much vagueness with both recent and remote memory, with recent memory showing the greatest deficit. His spontaneous thought content extended on relatively conservative beliefs and near-cliches of religious and patriotic concerns that appeared important in controlling anxiety. He showed little comprehension or insight into his present condition as far as the purpose for re-evaluation for competency. His best performance in psychological tests is in those areas of information, comprehension, similarity and vocabulary which are based on the previous acquisition of primarily intellectual skills."

Annette was trying to decide what the doctor was actually saying when he came to his conclusion.

"He remains mentally incompetent. He should continue with outpatient physical therapy and contact with the V.A. Hospital."

"Doctor, you have to grade my son as mentally competent," Dick beseeched him. "If you don't, it will ruin his marriage."

Annette could restrain herself no longer. "Wait a minute," she said. "There isn't any kind of evaluation you can give that's going to hurt our relationship. I know all this and I really don't care what kind of evaluation you give. Sam is who he is to me and no one is going to persuade me otherwise."

The doctor sat impassively through the exchange.

As they left the doctor's office, it was clear Dick was fuming but he never said a word. All three were totally exhausted, Sam in particular. He'd been put through a battery of tests and Annette really felt for her husband, who appeared oblivious to why they had come. For Annette, it had been a horrendous day. She prayed they would never have to go through that experience again.

★   ★   ★

Many of Sam's days were centered around visits to the local V.A. Hospital on East Kellog. He loved to be in a military environment and even the V.A. had a military air about it to Sam. It came as a shock, therefore, when Annette received notification later in the spring that Sam was to be phased out of the V.A.'s rehab. program. The letter said there was nothing more they could do for Sam; all the exercises he was doing at the V.A. could be done more than adequately at home, in addition to such occupational therapy as hobbies and crafts.

As far as Annette was concerned, this was a low blow. It was as if they were cutting off a part of Sam's lifeline. Her pleas to the V.A. received only a lukewarm response, although they did consent to have Sam see a specialist for a second opinion. The V.A. set up the appointment with a doctor whom Annette gathered had a very good reputation. As she and Sam were ushered into his office, Annette was optimistic, albeit cautiously, that they might uncover a small ray of hope.

Sam's file lay in the middle of the doctor's desk in front of them. It must have been four inches thick. Without turning over the fly-leaf, the doctor looked directly at Sam. "How long have you been paralyzed, Major Bird?"

The question drew a bewildered look from Sam who turned to his wife for help. She formed the words, "Seven years," with her lips.

"Seven years," Sam replied, looking back at the doctor who nodded with friendly reassurance and continued, "How's the mobility in your limbs, Major?"

310

Sam raised his left arm slowly to his shoulder without extending it, while his left hand hung limply.

"I have full use of my right arm and hand," Sam cited firmly, gesturing with both. "No use of my legs and a loss of balance."

Once again, the doctor looked Sam in the eye, only this time he spoke in a voice devoid of emotion. "For me to put you on a program would be wasting my time and the government's money," he said. "From here on out, it's downhill all the way."

Annette swayed back in her chair and struggled to maintain her composure as she wheeled Sam out of the doctor's office. Once they were in the hallway, she knelt down beside her husband. "Are you okay, Sam?" she asked apologetically. "I'm so sorry for putting you through all this."

Sam's reply echoed the dispassionate tones of the doctor. "It doesn't matter what the doctor says, the good Lord's not going to take me until he wants me; not a day before, not a day after. Why should I worry?"

Annette stared at her husband and saw the depth of peace and calm that had come over his countenance. She yearned to have some of it rub off on her.

However, Annette still wasn't satisfied. They had recently met a young, private family practitioner with a genial disposition named Ray Cook. He suggested Annette contact Craig Rehabilitation Hospital in Denver—a place noted for its striking progress in spinal cord and brain damage rehabilitation. Arrangements were made for Sam and Annette to travel to the hospital in July 1974.

Believing they would need all Sam's medical equipment and accessories, Annette loaded up the Maxivan for a somewhat torturous five hundred mile drive to Denver. However, the drive was not as unsettling for Annette as the sight that greeted her when she wheeled Sam through the large, sliding glass doors at the entrance of the hospital.

Annette had envisaged a generic, antiseptic, regimented hospital environment. Instead, the corridors of the rehabilitation center were filled with people who possessed all the earmarks of the "Woodstock" era. They were dressed in cut-off jeans and

311

sandals and had long hair and beards. Since the hospital rarely used mechanical lifting equipment, the patients quickly learned to ask one of the young orderlies for assistance or do it themselves. An integral part of the hospital's rehabilitation technique was to teach, encourage, cajole and even bully patients to do more for themselves. Further down the corridor, Annette saw a person wearing a neck brace in a wheelchair, whom she assumed was a patient, begging to be left alone. Her mouth opened in amazement as she wondered just what it was she had gotten Sam into. Sam on the other hand, as usual, took it all with a minimum of fuss.

After an initial examination, the hospital recommended some equipment that would help Sam physically, along with several suggestions to help improve his memory. One of the most effective pieces of equipment they advised was a "standing bar" which, with the help of a hydraulic jack, could be used to lift Sam to his feet for a few minutes each day. Using mirrors that enabled him to see himself stand, which at the same time mitigated against loss of balance, the positive effect on Sam's self-esteem was profound.

When the neurosurgeon did a preliminary X-ray to examine the plate in Sam's head, he could hardly believe it. "I thought this kind of prehistoric contraption went out with the Second World War!" he exclaimed. "Look at this!" He pointed to a screw attaching the plate to Sam's skull that had worked its way loose over the years. "If that screw had detached itself, it would have burrowed deep into his brain and nobody would have been able to get at it. I hate to think how he would have died."

The metal plate had been weighing Sam's head down for years. Recently, he'd been having trouble holding it up off his shoulder. The neurosurgeon strongly advised Annette that since Sam was in comparatively good health overall, he should undergo surgery to replace the metal plate with a much lighter plastic one. Annette agreed and notified Dick by phone. Dick and Pauline came out from Wichita, while Pastor Pruitt and his wife took part of their vacation to be with Annette and Sam during the operation and thereafter until Sam was pronounced out of danger.

Just before Sam regained consciousness, the surgeon warned Annette that he might emerge in a semi-delirious state and not to be alarmed if he mentioned old girlfriends or something like that; it would mean nothing.

Annette was at Sam's bedside when his eyes opened slowly. A smile crept across his face when he saw her. "Hi, Honey," he whispered. Sam had never addressed her using this term before.

"Who's Honey?" she glowered.

Somewhat taken aback by his wife's seeming hostility, Sam produced the perfect answer, "Why, you of course!"

It appeared Sam had come through surgery well. The day after the operation, he was wheeled back over to the rehab. unit and Dick, Pauline, Pastor Pruitt and his wife left. The following day, Sam took a dramatic turn for the worse and was rushed back to intensive care. The doctors thought he'd developed an embolism on one lung and the only thing to do was wait while doctors monitored the situation. Already exhausted from days of near-constant vigil, Annette slumped back in her chair. Emotionally spent and void of energy, she started to pray internally. "I love Sam, but I don't know what to do for him now," she prayed. Then she felt a voice from deep within. "I love him more than you do," it said.

This caused Annette to recoil and she first became defensive. "But I've been here from early morning until late at night. I love him so much," her mind implored.

Once again, a voice emanated from deep inside her. "I love him so much that my son died for him and you are not to worry."

At first Annette didn't understand what was happening. Then all of a sudden she sensed a feeling of deep inner peace, as though a great weight had been lifted from her soul. She returned to her sister Dona's in Denver that evening and slept soundly. When she arrived at the hospital the following morning, she was informed Sam had been pronounced out of danger and was ready to be wheeled back to the rehab. unit.

The scar tissue that had built up beneath the metal plate had contributed greatly to the severity of Sam's headaches and seizures. This had been removed along with the plate itself. Sam could now hold his head up straight again. Also, the surgeons had been able to mold the plastic plate more precisely to the contours of Sam's head, thus producing the "normal" appearance Dick had always longed for. Only a patchwork of criss-cross scars remained to indicate what had happened to him.

They left Craig Hospital, perhaps not having received all that Annette originally yearned for, but she was content. At last she could be sure in her own mind that every possible medical avenue had been explored. She told herself that from now on there was no useful purpose to be served in chasing rainbows. No longer was she either optimistic or pessimistic. Her thoughts acquired a strong sense of realism. Now she was going to concentrate on doing everything she could to insure that Sam's body stayed as limber and healthy as possible for as long as possible. From that moment forward, she resolved to enjoy life for what it was. It was a resolution that would soon be put to the test.

★　　★　　★

For the duration of their stay at Craig Hospital, Eric had remained at Brookhollow. Annette had asked a model Christian couple from Faith Chapel to live at the house and look after Eric while she and Sam were away. At that time, Annette's perception of people's goodness was greatly influenced by the degree of apparent fervor with which they glorified the Lord and how much they espoused His will by quoting tracts from the *Bible*. In those respects, the couple appeared to possess the perfect credentials to look after her son.

Shortly after the couple's arrival at Brookhollow, however, the reality of their situation came to the surface. Eric quickly sensed the tension in their own relationship, much of which was directed at him either by treating him with disdain or ignoring him altogether. Eric did the only thing he knew—he retreated to the safe confines of his bedroom. When Annette returned with Sam from Denver, she realized she had made a terrible mistake. For Eric's part, it was simply further evidence of his excommunication from the family unit. He had treated the "intruders" with the same level of disregard he'd built up toward his mother and Sam.

Annette made several attempts to get closer to her son during the next year but rarely made it past first base. Eric's first reaction would usually be to throw up a wall of indifference which Annette took as a sign that he didn't want her around. The contrary was true but she never realized it. Eric was hurting—hurting deeply. The only way he could attract his mother's attention while protecting himself from more hurt was to treat any overture with surly withdrawal. The problem was that Annette could never take the next step and confront the situation—have it out with her son. Instead, she always allowed the issue to be suppressed by both of them, fearing the effect of a full-blown confrontation on Sam. In this, Eric was the perfect psychological co-conspirator, also preferring to drive his own feelings and resentments into deep compartments inside.

The other and perhaps most important determining factor in all this was Sam himself. Whenever Annette sat down to talk to her son alone, it was only a matter of minutes before Sam would call out for her. It developed into a perpetual tug of war for Annette's attention between Sam and Eric. One in which the former would nearly always win.

One day toward the end of summer, all three went shopping together to buy Eric clothes for school. On their way home through the rush-hour and pouring rain, Eric brought up the subject of one of Annette's ex-boyfriends. He spoke of this man in such a way as to obviously be a thinly disguised taunt at Sam. When they returned home, Sam delivered an ultimatum. "You are going to have to choose between your son and me," he pronounced. "Either he goes, or I go!"

Annette gazed sadly at her husband but kept her thoughts to herself. She spent the next couple of days thinking about what she could say to Sam to defuse the situation. Later in the week, she began a delicate explanation. Very soon after she began, she realized that Sam had absolutely no recollection of the incident.

The personality clash between Eric and Sam was profound. Sam insisted on strict rules of behavior for Eric, verging on the military. As far as Sam was concerned, Eric was not allowed to take off his shoes in the house, his hair was to be kept short, and above all, his shirt was to be tucked in at all times. For his part, Eric grew his hair down to his shoulders and always wore his shirts outside his trousers.

One day Eric was unlocking his bike from the rack at school to ride home. At the other end of the rack, two boys were whispering and giggling to one another. As Eric pulled his bike out from the rack, one of the boys whispered in a voice just loud enough for him to hear, "I wonder what it's like living with a cripple?" The boys both giggled.

"Shut up!" cried Eric.

"Make me!" retorted the boy.

Eric threw his bike down and rushed the two boys. A fight ensued.

Half an hour later, Eric walked into the house with mud all over his shoes and trousers, his shirt ripped and hanging out.

"Eric, what have you been doing?" Annette inquired with concern from the kitchen.

"Nothing."

"Come here. Let me see."

"I'm going to my room."

"Come here, young man!" bellowed the stiff, military voice from the living room. "We won't have back-talk in this house. Honor your mother!"

Eric stood there with his arms folded, muttering something under his breath.

"I said, come here!"

Eventually Eric ambled over to where Sam was sitting by the fireplace. Annette watched from the kitchen doorway with a look of foreboding.

"Bend over!" Sam roared. A smirk spread across Eric's face as he dutifully obliged.

With his left arm resting in his lap, Sam, red in the face by now, raised his right arm above his head and opened the palm of his hand. With as much force as he could muster, he plunged the hand down toward the back pockets of Eric's jeans. As it swung into a horizontal plane, Sam's right shoulder lurched forward violently and he completely lost his balance. His right hand finished in his lap, missing Eric completely, as he toppled over to the right, slumping across his wheelchair. Annette rushed across to her husband who had gone all quiet, his face assuming a blank expression.

"Go to your room, Eric!" she cried.

Eric got up quickly and hurried to his bedroom. His smug grin turned into a puzzled, awkward look.

Annette set Sam back up in his chair, bewilderment etched across his face.

Shortly after the incident, Annette tried to talk to Eric again. She also made an appointment for Sam, Eric and herself to see a counselor, but the sessions were little help; she either refused to accept or blocked out of her mind the possibility that Sam could be in any way responsible for Eric's unhappiness.

As for those outside the family like Addie, who saw things in more straightforward terms, the problem was simple: Eric was just a selfish, snotty little brat. "Just you give him to me for a couple of weeks, Honey," she told Annette. "I'll straighten him out for you!"

For good or bad, Annette didn't accept this "generous" offer, preferring instead to behave as if nothing had happened. Above all, she was petrified that discussing the matter with Sam would throw him into a state of consternation. Her biggest fear was that she might end up losing the two most important people in her life. As things turned out, she *was* about to lose one of them.

Eric lived like an exile at Brookhollow, retreating to his bedroom for long periods and immersing himself in the emerging medium of "pulp" television. His allegiances were always to those characters portrayed as rebels, with or without a cause, who, without exception, seemed to prevail against all odds. It wasn't long before the screen images became his reality.

By late spring of 1975, Eric had had enough. On a Friday evening in May, while Sam and Annette were attending a Retired Officers' function, Eric loaded up his mother's little blue

Maverick with all his possessions and then withdrew to his bedroom.

On their return, Sam and Annette went straight to bed. Sam was especially tired that evening. Annette, noticing how quiet things were, assumed her son had already gone to bed.

Once he was sure his mother and Sam were sound asleep, Eric crawled out of his bedroom window with Yogi in his arms and tiptoed across to the car. Yogi obliged by not making a sound. Since Brookhollow Lane sits on a gentle incline, Eric had little trouble pushing the car down the drive and out of earshot. Once he'd made it some 50 yards from the house, he slipped into the driver's seat, started the motor and headed out for his father's home in Colorado. At fourteen, he possessed a Learner's Driving Permit which allowed him to drive to and from school.

The following morning, Annette found a note from Eric in his bedroom. It read:

> *Goodbye, and I'm sorry I have to go like this. I will drop in Monday. I'm staying with friends in Wichita.*
>
> > *Love,*
> > *Eric*

Though a little puzzled by the first sentence, she figured he would have cooled off after spending the weekend at a friend's. Before she could give it a second thought, Sam called to her from the bedroom.

At three o'clock that afternoon, the phone rang. It was the Durango, Colorado, Police Department, saying they had just picked Eric up with only a learner's permit and were holding him at the Wolf Creek Jail. Annette's heart sank.

"Please tell me it isn't true!" she said to herself. It *can't* be true." After working through her own denial and retrieving her composure, she telephoned her ex-husband in Grand Junction. He was no more than two and a half hours north of Durango, so she asked him if he would pick Eric up and return him to Wichita where they could all get to the bottom of the situation. Gene said he would go to the police station and call Annette from there.

When Gene arrived in Wolf Creek, Eric pleaded with his father to allow him to stay with him at Grand Junction. Gene subsequently telephoned Annette and informed her their son's wishes were paramount and easily surpassed her wishes to have him back.

Annette was beside herself. At first she telephoned Grand Junction every night for a week but each time the response was the same, "Lady, your son doesn't want to speak to you. Can't you get that straight?"

Frustrated and angry, Annette went to the juvenile authorities in Wichita the following week. They advised her to contact a lawyer.

The man did not equivocate. "In order to regain custody of your son, Mrs. Bird, you would have to go back to California where your divorce was finalized and custody granted," he said. "But that would just be the beginning. The case would have to be handled by separate attorneys in Kansas, Colorado and California. It could take up to three years to come to court." The lawyer paused briefly. "Have you considered kidnapping?"

Annette rose from her chair, swiftly turned around and left the lawyer's office. She felt utterly helpless, although with the help of friends, notably Pastor Pruitt, she was persuaded to believe that if she did anything to force Eric's return, it would drive him further away. All she could do was wait and pray.

That Christmas 1975, Eric returned home with Yogi and dropped a conciliatory note under the Christmas tree for Sam. A sign perhaps, that at some time in the future, Eric might find it in him to accept Sam. In the meantime, however, it was going to be difficult.

Chapter Nineteen

A Life in the Day of
Sam and Annette Bird

After Tom left in the middle of 1973, Annette felt there was no need for another aide. Dick, on the other hand, was far from convinced. With characteristic insistence, he had made the very reasonable point, under the circumstances, that Annette should have more time to devote exclusively to her son's needs. As a result, several aides were tried—all of whom turned out to be more than satisfactory. The problem was they were at the house during the day when Eric was at school. In the evenings when Eric was at home, Annette was on her own and Sam's demands invariably took precedence.

By the mid-seventies, the estrangement between mother and son had reached a point where Annette decided to cut her losses by letting the aide go. The intimacy of her relationship with Sam had always suffered from the presence of an aide—not to mention the money used to pay him, which claimed the lion's share of the monthly budget. They could put it to better use.

The couple's newly established independence had a significant effect on Sam's behavior. Annette saw the biggest impact in the way he made a greater effort to do things for himself. At times he struggled so hard it made her cringe. An example was the breakfast ritual of putting on his tee shirt. Annette would start breakfast in the kitchen while Sam wheeled himself out onto the patio. There the battle would begin. Time and again Sam would lose his balance and topple sideways to his right, leaving the tee shirt looking like a turtle-neck. Yet by the time Annette had breakfast out on the patio, neck and arms would have found their respective openings and Sam would be brimming over with elation.

Although many tasks had the look of torture, Annette acquired the delicate knowledge of when to step in and when not to; whenever possible she allowed Sam to feel the sense of achievement from doing it himself.

On days when he felt particularly good, it was Sam's desire to wash the dishes, even though they had an automatic dishwasher. Annette would organize the dishes into piles, and Sam would meticulously wash, rinse and stack each one in turn.

In the garden, Sam made use of a three-foot long metal rod with a pincer at one end. He would use it to pick up leaves, pull out weeds—whatever he could reach. His pride in the external appearance of his home matched the pride with which he had worn his uniform. Whether he was in the back garden or the front yard, Sam would drive himself until, often, he quite literally fell out of his chair. Not once did he ask for help and Annette saw, as in the spanking incident with Eric, the precarious balance in which his masculinity hung.

Before their marriage, Annette had watched the interaction between Sam and his parents. Often she found herself cringing when Sam repeated the same question over and over again. She saw how Pauline would ignore the question, acting as though it hadn't been asked; she then would retract herself entirely from the conversation. By the third or fourth repetition, Dick would become visibly irritated. "Sam, I've answered that question before!" he would reply testily, then modify to a more conciliatory tone when he saw the look of dejection unfurl across his son's face, "Don't you remember?"

Sam would then apologize for having asked the question several times and five minutes later, repeat it again. The uneasiness and tension would mount while Sam sat oblivious to it all.

Once they were married, Annette employed a form of running commentary with updates. A couple of minutes after Sam had asked a question, she would try to anticipate its repetition by raising the subject, which generally revolved around people and timing, and try to answer the question in a different way. If Sam continued to repeat himself, without showing any sign of irritation, she would simply answer the question from a different vantage point, always trying to stimulate his memory beyond the threshold of a repeat question. It was not easy, especially when she was otherwise preoccupied, but she realized that by doing this, Sam could carry on a conversation. In time Annette perfected her responses and when she saw a confused expression spread over Sam's face, she could anticipate the question he was about to ask with one of her own. Annette continually strived to place herself in Sam's position. This paid handsome dividends. After 18 months of marriage, Sam had reduced his rate of repetition to once, maybe twice at most. In the meantime, his wife had turned into something of a chatterbox! No doctor or therapist ever suggested she do this—it was a remarkable example of her intuition in providing effective therapy.

While Annette was preparing dinner one evening, Sam wheeled himself into the kitchen to ask an oft-repeated question. "Is there something different about me that makes people shy away?" he inquired, in a confused rather than dejected voice.

"Well, Sam, seeing a man in a wheelchair sometimes does strange things to people," she replied lightly. She knew well that some of their neighbors, renowned for their rigid behavior, could break into the most bizarre departures from normal routine in order to avoid Sam. "If they ever allowed themselves to get to know the Sam I know, they would wonder why they ever kept their distance from you," she affirmed. "Though perhaps we should be glad they're not interested. I'd have to fight them off with a bat!" They both chuckled.

Annette was in no doubt, however, that Sam felt good about himself. He never expressed resentment toward those who shunned him. It was as though, deep down, he understood.

★ ★ ★

In situations where more than one conversation happened to be occurring at the same time, Sam quickly became confused. His concentration would lapse successively like a mechanism continually slipping out of gear until a blank, listless expression took possession of his face. His wounds had left him incapable of latching onto a specific train of thought in the midst of other distractions. Whenever she noticed this happening, Annette would slip her arm under his right elbow and gently clasp his hand. Once he felt his wife's hand in his, a look of assurance would return to Sam's face and he would turn toward her and smile, squeezing her hand tightly. For a short while the two of them would talk together.

It soon became apparent that if Sam didn't encounter a person more than once in the space of a relatively short period of time, he had great difficulty remembering them. Whenever Annette saw someone coming over to speak, she would begin feeding Sam clues pertaining to something he had found striking about that person during their previous encounter: the color of their clothes, the sound of their voice or a distinctive personality trait.

Annette discovered there were some things that left a permanent impression on Sam's memory, like silver-gray hair, brightly colored dresses or someone with a pleasant disposition and a radiant smile. Generally this was all Sam needed to be able to carry on a conversation with that person.

Then there was Sam's customary response after Annette had cooked a particularly big or rich meal. "Uh-oh," he would say, "It's time to get the shillelagh out to beat those calories down." This would always get a smile from Annette, along with a mildly puzzled glance. "Where did you get that thing from, Sam?" she would often ask. Invariably a short pause would occur before he replied, "I don't know, Sweetie-Pie, I just don't seem to be able to remember," he would say with a twinkle in his eye.

Self-deprecating humor had always been a hallmark of Sam's personality. Now it came into play more often than ever—particularly when he fell out of his wheelchair. Gradually, Annette learned to appreciate that Sam wasn't made out of china.

Her greatest fears were never realized, partly because he always appeared to fall with such grace and aplomb. Once he tumbled into a bush beside the planter in the front yard. Annette called out to a neighbor mowing his lawn, while a passer-by stopped his car and rushed over to help. As they were putting him back in his chair, Sam thanked them all and apologized profusely for subjecting them to such inconvenience. Minutes later he wheeled himself back over beside the bush and reassumed the same precarious angle from which he had fallen moments before. Annette's mouth fell open, then she allowed herself to smile.

On another occasion, Sam slid off the tilt table used to regulate his bodily functions by holding him upright for 45 minutes every day. Annette would lift him onto the table, which had the appearance of medieval torture rack, with the hoyer lift. This time, Sam's leg went into spasms while Annette was trying to maneuver him into position and he started to slide off the table. As Annette made a frantic grab for her husband, Sam calmly grabbed hold of the lift with his right hand and gracefully lowered himself to the floor, backside first. The maneuver was executed with such consummate ease, Annette thought it almost balletic.

After enduring years of awkwardness and inconvenience in their respective hospital and twin beds, Sam and Annette finally decided to purchase a double bed. In the beginning, Annette had been led to believe it was essential for Sam to have a single bed equipped with side rails. In the end, they decided to follow their instincts and buy what was known as a "flexi-bed." The flexi-bed came with a push-button hand-control which raised and lowered its head and foot automatically.

The new bed proved a double blessing. Not only could they sleep close together for the first time during their marriage but, in doing so, Annette could relieve Sam's leg cramps without having to get out of bed in the middle of the night. Whenever he let out a moan, which generally occurred two or three times during the night, Annette could feel her husband's leg spasm and hook her foot around the back of his knee to pull his lower leg down before the muscles began to stiffen. All the time, Sam was blissfully unaware of what was happening.

However, there was a certain aspect to life with the flexi-bed that Annette failed to appreciate at first; indeed, she cannot say, with her hand on her heart, that she ever did. Sam would normally be in bed by ten o'clock, which gave Annette a couple of hours to catch up with household chores. It was often midnight before she slipped into bed beside her husband. Every morning at six o'clock sharp, however, she would be wrested from a deep sleep by the buzz, whir and click of the flexi-bed as its top half rose dutifully to the strains of the National Anthem on television as the networks signed on. Within a matter of seconds, the bed and its occupants had been brought to attention, while Sam sang along at the top of his singularly unmelodious voice. Invigorating as it may have been for Sam, this, her husband's most cherished morning ritual, didn't quite strike the same chord with his wife. Begrudgingly though, she had to concede that it did help get her eyes open and start the day. As for Sam, even after a crushing cluster headache the night before, it was simply another day in which to excel. "Praise the Lord! It's another day to be alive," was the daily battle cry.

One of the most frustrating, inconvenient and downright humiliating aspects of paralysis is the loss of the ability to control bowel movements. Either they begin to work at the wrong time, generating acute embarrassment, or they just don't function at all.

Sam's routine for stimulating a bowel movement consisted of a stool softener the night before, accompanied by four ounces of prune juice. The following morning the regime was completed with a Dulcolax suppository and then it was a matter of "sit and wait, and wait," perhaps for an hour, on the wheelchair commode. The same routine was enacted every other day. The more she became aware of what her husband had to endure, the more Annette came to dread this procedure.

Someone once asked Sam if he could have anything in the world, what would it be? "Poop-less food," he replied with a grin.

Up until his visit to Craig Hospital, Sam had always had a wheelchair commode. The hospital recommended a "Shower Chair" which Sam could either use for sitting in the shower or over the toilet stool itself. The first time Sam was able to sit imperiously over the "throne," he was so thrilled he called his godparents to inform them of the tremendous news!

Another innovation was far more effective. A therapist at Craig showed Sam and Annette a way of dilating a paralyzed person's sphincter muscle in order to induce a bowel movement. The hospital taught patients to put on a rubber glove, coat a finger with Vaseline and massage their own sphincter muscle very gently to bring on the bowel movement. Sam's lack of balance meant it was completely out of the question for him to perform the technique on himself. Thus, something that became known good-naturedly as "The Program" was performed every other morning by Annette, who would massage very gently until a bowel movement was induced. The smell was invariably revolting and Sam would often wince with acute embarrassment, "I'm sorry that the odor is not the best right now."

"I don't smell a thing," she'd say softly. "I don't smell a thing."

★　　★　　★

Five consecutive years of turbulence gave Annette a keen appreciation of life's good moments. At 7:30 every morning after the National Anthem, basic hygiene and sanitary honors in the "laboratory," Sam would wheel himself out onto the back patio while Annette prepared breakfast in the kitchen. Breakfast on the patio in warm weather was a lazy affair that included browsing through parts of the newspaper and occasionally catching up on correspondence. Catching up on correspondence had its own little ritual, usually initiated by Annette. "Sam, we really ought to write to Nancy and David," she'd say in the well-intentioned tone that was her way. "It's been a couple of months since we got their letter."

"You're right," would come the purposeful reply. "Let's make it a joint effort." There would then follow a pause of about two

327

minutes while Sam appeared deep in thought. Then he would begin.

"Dear Nancy and David," which was followed by another short pause and then, "Okay, over to you."

Following breakfast, the two of them would putter in the back garden soaking up the early morning sunshine. Sam would carry on conversations with the plants and flowers, inquiring about their well-being and flattering them on their appearance.

Later in the morning, Annette would wheel Sam into the swimming pool room. Six yards by six yards and five feet deep, the indoor pool was built during the latter part of 1976 from the proceeds of Annette's inheritance following the death of her parents. It was completed two days before Christmas and Sam couldn't wait to take a dip. Annette warned him, however, the pool would require three more days to heat to a comfortable temperature. After immersing his toes in the water and seeing them turn blue, he decided that caution was the better part of valor and waited until the day after Christmas for the full baptism.

The pool became both the symbol and the manifestation of freedom—freedom from the wheelchair and freedom from the limitations of paralysis. Released from the forces of gravity with the help of a float beneath his upper body, Sam could experience what it was like to stand without reliance on elaborate lifting paraphernalia. Propelling himself through the water with a flick of his wrist, he breached physical barriers, the primary source of his frustration. Whether he was in motion or still in the clear, blue water the result was pure relaxation and release of tension. At rest in the water, Sam wore an expression of complete inner and outer peace. When asked how it felt, he would invariably reply, "I think this is what Heaven must be like."

Annette, concerned about her husband involuntarily rolling over onto his belly, face down and not being able to right himself, never left the pool when he was in the water. Sam capsized only four times in 10 years.

In the summer, with temperatures climbing into the low 90s by noon, lunch was eaten indoors. Afterward, Sam would lie back in the reclining chair and read. After reaching the end of a paragraph, he would pause to rest his eyes. His right eye provided a narrow tunnel of crisp, clear vision. The view down the tunnel from his left eye was fuzzy and hazy. Sam had no peripheral vision in either eye. Many times he would read the same paragraph over and over. As with conversation, Annette would try to fill each intermission with a series of hints and references in order to help provide the stimulus for Sam to reach the next paragraph. Short stories from the large print editions of *Reader's Digest* proved to be comfortably within his scope. He dearly wanted to read *American Caesar*, William Manchester's 712-page opus on the life of Douglas MacArthur, but he never got beyond page three.

For nine months during 1976, Sam immersed himself in the construction of a grandfather clock. He had signed up for the project as part of an occupational therapy program run by the Wichita Park Board Center. His mentor and collaborator in the project was a retired woodwork teacher by the name of Orrie Jones. Sixty-seven years old, short, round and balding, Orrie Jones did not suffer gladly those with a half-hearted commitment to their projects. In Sam he had a captive, devoted partner. Sam would sand down each piece of cherry wood with obsessive precision before handing it to his tutor for assembly. Long after its completion, the clock chiming in the hallway of 8230 Brookhollow would draw a satisfied smile of approval from its wheelchair bound co-creator.

After a glass of cranberry juice and crackers at four o'clock, Annette would put Sam, who would gradually wilt during the afternoon, down on the bed to sleep for an hour or so. When he awoke around 5:30, it was like the beginning of a new day.

Dinner at Fort Bird was always served at six o'clock sharp and then Sam was ready to venture outside once more. Brookhollow Lane forms half of a horseshoe that connects with the main road on both ends. This provided an ideal circuit for an evening walk. As Annette pushed Sam along the sidewalk, occasionally stopping to speak with neighbors, Yogi would make scurrying sweeps and passes by the wheelchair.

"Do you belong to Yogi?" was the oft-repeated echo of young children playing in their gardens or hurtling up and down the street on their bicycles as Sam and Annette passed them by. Sam adored Yogi.

On returning home, Sam and Annette relaxed with a book or in front of the television. As the clock came around to 9:30, Sam would begin to yield to the rigors of the day, finding it increasingly difficult to keep his eyelids open. Annette would have him in bed by ten o'clock, where he would watch the news. He would be fast asleep before the weather forecast was over. Annette would slip into bed beside him later, only to be greeted by a sustained barrage of loud snores. Instead of keeping her awake, the convulsive, snorting din became a rhapsody of reassurance lulling her to sleep every night.

Some evenings, after returning home from a speaking engagement or a visit, with lights out and the overhead globe producing a warm glow on the water, they would both slip into the pool. About an hour later, Sam's head would hit the pillow and he would fall asleep immediately, a lingering expression of satisfaction on his face.

During the winter, instead of days in the pool, days were spent around the fireplace. Even though Sam experienced very little feeling in his lower extremities, the cold somehow managed to cause him great discomfort. His body's thermostat seemed unable to respond to colder temperatures, a common condition for those suffering from paralysis.

Through it all, without any apparent need for time to herself, Annette was anguished by pangs of conscience during the briefest periods away from her husband. Each week she allotted herself half an hour for a quick trip to the grocery store. With Sam having lost all comprehension of the passage of time, Annette would have to prepare him in advance. Since he was unable to perceive finite periods of time, Annette would get Sam to write her time of departure and E.T.A. on a piece of paper from the clock on the wall. If he ever became anxious for his wife's return, he had only to match the time on the clock with the time he had written down on the paper to figure out how much longer she would be. This worked very well.

When Annette returned to the house, Sam, who had a keen sense of when the door was being opened, would always shout out like a night guard at a border crossing, "Who's there?"

"Oh, it's just me," Annette would reply in a meek and gentle voice.

"It's not just you!" he would admonish her sternly in the closest resemblance to the old booming voice he could muster. "It's the lady of the house and without her, it's only a house and not a home. I missed you, Sweetie-pie."

One afternoon while Annette was at a meeting, Ed Drum, a good friend, himself confined to a wheelchair as a result of polio, came over to keep Sam company. At the meeting a woman sitting opposite leaned across the table. "It's good to see you, Annette. I suppose you've got somebody in to baby-sit for Sam."

"Ed has come to visit for the afternoon," she smiled, suppressing all her indignation at the remark.

★　　★　　★

By the latter half of the '70s, Sam's health had stabilized markedly, despite an occasional seizure. The visit to Craig Hospital had resulted in a more effective and appropriate regimen of medication and preventative therapy. Annette was no longer overwhelmed by the feeling of always having shut the stable door after the horse had bolted. Sam would visit Dr. Cook every six weeks or so to receive treatment for a recurring bladder infection, but that was no more than a minor irritant.

Annette and Sam had become like synchronized swimmers, locked in the same rhythm, side by side, stroke for stroke. She reveled in her femininity as her very presence appeared to ease her husband's pain. She had learned to plan schedules to avoid rush-hours and long delays and she knew which routes to take to avoid bumps in the road. Instead of each dawn heralding yet another daily struggle for survival, it came to represent a continued life of mutual fulfillment.

Medal presentation ceremony, Brooke Army Hospital, Texas.
l to r—Dick, Brigadier General Rhea (commanding officer of the hospital), and Sam.
July 14, 1967

Doris McKibbin with pet samoyed.

B.T. Collins and Sam Bird reunited.
Memphis, Tennessee—March 1968

Annette Okarche Blazier
1957

Mother and Son
1965

335

Ed Blazier—1968

A serene Lois Blazier on her daughter's wedding day.
September 9, 1972

Sam Bird on his wedding day.
September 9, 1972

Wedding day on the patio at 609 Rutland.

The Wedding Party

Bird—Bruce—Oliver—Roberts

Blazier

338

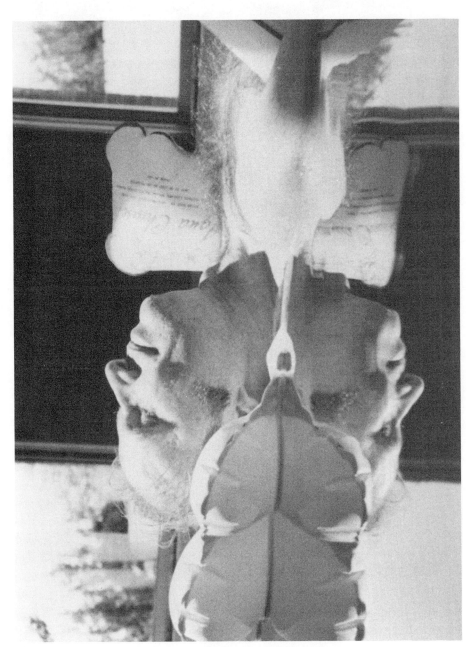

The pool at 8230 Brookhollow.

Sam and Eric—Fort Sill, Oklahoma
May 1981

Paula, Pauline, and Dick at 609 Rutland.
May 1981

Sam and Annette on the day he was given six months to live.
August 1981

Sam, Eric, and Yogi.
May 1982

Fort Bird—July 1982

"Tally Ho!"
July 1982

342

Sam, Annette, and Eric
in Paradise.
1981

Sam in his favorite "room"
at Fort Bird.

Dick and Hazel's wedding.
May 1983

Sam Bird and John White at the Officers' Club.
Fort Myer—January 1984

Dean Parker's Retirement
l to r standing—B.T. Collins, Mark Gatanas, Dave Porecca, Dean Parker.
seated—Sam Bird.

PART VII

AUTUMN SHADES

Chapter Twenty

Negotiating Life's Obstacles

With the exception of Dick and, to a lesser extent, Pauline, visits to Brookhollow during the 1970s from the rest of the family had become about as frequent as a tropical snowstorm. Those who had placed bets on the longevity of the marriage (few exceeding six months) kept away. Paula, who had divorced and remarried, created a legendary reputation for herself in the local advertising/sales community while establishing distance from family, particularly her father, who seemed to rarely miss an opportunity to show his disdain for his eldest child.

When Paula became pregnant for the fourth time, she said, "The stork stepped in and kept me out of the work force again. It took me nine months to get my sense of humor back."

This time, she went straight back to work. When asked what her husband thought about that she replied, "That's a tough one! He knew what he was getting into when he rode up on a white horse one day, picked up my mortgage, three kids and a hail-damaged Vega."

When Sarah was only a few weeks old, a local media representative appeared on her doorstep with plans for a weekly newspaper—*The Wichita Sun*. After struggling to survive for eight months, the magazine folded. At its demise, Paula joined the sales staff of KARD Radio in Wichita. Then came the three years when she was probably at her happiest.

In 1978 a new city magazine called *The Wichitan* was born. Paula became its advertising director.

"I liked her immediately," recounted Pam Porvaznik, the magazine's editor. "She was real bright-faced and engaging, always ready with a smile."

"Her sense of humor was out of this world," said Eileen O'Hara who worked for Paula at the magazine. "She had us in stitches one day, when she referred to a bright young ad man as 'Slicker'n whale shit on a billiard pole!' "

To Eileen, Paula made work fun, though she could be very tough with clients. Eileen couldn't understand how Paula could be so uncompromising and practical when it came to business and yet when it came to men, be so gullible and naive.

Paula quickly established a reputation for energy, creativity and above all, zaniness. She would put crazy glue on everything and once put an attack dog (a German Shepherd) under one of the male editor's desks. When the unfortunate man went to sit down, he all but leaped out of his trousers! She became renowned for Champagne and Egg McMuffin incentive breakfasts for her sales staff. On one occasion she had the mailman join them and had him drunk by 10:00 A.M.

One day, the Doo-Dah Deli, a local eating establishment, called to say they wanted to run a big color advertisement for their salad bar but didn't know what they wanted to do. "Leave it to me," breezed Paula. The following day, she took her staff down to the deli for the shoot. She had a bathtub brought in and filled with warm water. Everyone stood there in amazement as the youngest member of her sales staff, a gorgeous young woman of eighteen, walked out from the restroom, disrobed and climbed into the bath. Paula then had a board placed on the bath in front of her. She had everyone pile lettuce, tomatoes and cucumbers on the board and the shots were taken. The caption on the advertisement read, "A Tasty Treat. Good Enough To Eat!"

After the magazine was published, Paula received a nasty letter from *Ms Magazine* saying they did not appreciate her sticking a woman into a tub and covering her with vegetables; it was demeaning to women.

"I don't understand what they're talking about," she exclaimed. "It was all done in the best possible taste!"

At work, Paula would often sit with the telephone propped on her shoulder, dealing with a big advertising agency while at the same time working on the most minute needlepoint pattern with her hands. Whereas most of us like to be able to concentrate on one thing at a time, she was a multi-talented dynamo who appeared to thrive on "organized chaos."

Paula decided to have her thirty-ninth birthday party at a local mortuary. She mailed out over a hundred fliers and invitations to friends and colleagues. It was a couple of days later before she decided to call the mortuary and let them in on the idea. And this was only after some serious prompting from friends.

"Paula, don't you think you'd better check with them first?" urged a nervous Eileen.

"Why?" replied Paula. "You don't think for a minute they have another party booked, do you?"

"No, Paula. That isn't it. They might object!"

"But why would they object?" she inquired with total innocence. "I'll pay them."

At first the funeral home was so taken aback they didn't know what to think. However, after a few minutes of prodding over the telephone by Paula they were in agreement.

"See," she effused, replacing the receiver, "They think it's a great idea!"

The relatives of the dearly departed didn't think it was such a good idea, though, and letters and telephone calls of protest poured in. Two days later the mortuary called back to cancel.

Eileen looked across at her friend as she replaced the receiver. "Her little bubble was burst," recalls Eileen. "It was as though she was always having to come down off a cloud. But she always bounced back."

★   ★   ★

Dick and Pauline were the only regular visitors to Brookhollow, popping around on a monthly basis. There remained, however, an ever-present current of friction between them and Annette. Pauline's superficial good behavior did little to disguise

351

her powerful feelings of contempt for her daughter-in-law. Sam appeared to be unaware of the strain in their relations.

In autumn of 1974, Sam and Annette made the first of several memorable reunion trips to the Missouri Military Academy during Homecoming. Annette had made reservations at a nearby motel for the night before.

Darkness had fallen when they pulled into the motel parking lot in the maxivan with car-top lift attached. The lot was at the limit of its capacity for cars so Annette was forced to park the van on a gentle incline, across from the main body of rooms.

After checking in at the motel office, Annette returned to the van, unloaded the wheelchair and pushed it around to the passenger side. Because of the gentle incline, the wheelchair sat several inches below the level of the van. Annette slipped the lift's sling beneath Sam, hoisted him from his seat, pulled him out above the wheelchair and began lowering him. The lift reached the downward limit of its extension with Sam dangling four inches above the wheelchair. Annette looked around forlornly, momentarily at a loss for what to do next.

An impromptu alumni party was taking place in the two adjoining rooms directly across from where Annette was trying to transfer Sam into his wheelchair. While she stood perplexed, a man came to the doorway of one of the adjoining rooms with a drink in his hand. He stood still for a moment, contemplating the spectacle on the other side of the parking lot, then turned around and walked back inside to rejoin the other guests. A few minutes later he returned to the doorway with drink in hand and stared across at Sam and Annette once more before turning and walking away.

After about five minutes of standing beside her husband in something of a dither, Annette decided there was only one thing to do. Praying fervently that Sam would land squarely in the wheelchair without pitching forward, she unfastened the sling from beneath him. Dropping abruptly, Sam hit the chair hard but his upper body remained steady. Bracing her husband before he had a chance to pitch forward, Annette strapped him into the chair and wheeled him over to their motel room.

The following day, an alumni luncheon was held in the school's dining hall. Located below ground level, the large, rectangular room had the oppressive feel of an air-raid shelter. It was filled beyond capacity with more than five hundred alumni and their wives—crammed around row upon row of dining tables set with everyday china and silverware but otherwise undecorated. In order to reach the dining room itself, Annette had wheeled Sam down through the kitchen since the steps were prohibitive.

Before the meal began, Colonel Stribling, the school's president, called everyone to order.

"Ladies and Gentlemen!" he announced. "Before we begin, I want to extend a special welcome to one alumnus who has come back to the school by way of Vietnam." He paused briefly. "Ladies and Gentlemen, it is my very special honor and privilege to welcome Sam Bird, Class of 1957, back to school!"

The entire room rose to its feet and the walls echoed to a sustained round of thunderous applause.

When the meal was over, the man from the motel doorway came over to Annette with tears streaming from his eyes.

"I saw you struggling in the parking lot last night," he stammered. "But I just couldn't come out to help you; I just felt too uncomfortable." He paused briefly before continuing. "If only I'd known who Sam was, I'd have come out in an instant."

★   ★   ★

When Sam and Annette first joined the congregation at Faith Chapel, they noticed an open area behind the last pew at the back of the sanctuary. Before the beginning of each service, Annette would secure Sam's chair in that space and sit beside him in a folding chair. By the latter part of the 1970s, the number of those in wheelchairs and their companions positioned there at the back of the sanctuary had swelled to more than a dozen. Their attendance had become a small tradition and constituted a significant presence among the congregation. These people—Ed and Pat Drum, Delbert and Connie Clark, Larry Hudson, Ann and Les Rowland and Ann's mother, Audrie, Mae Fuller and others—became Sam's loyal soulmates.

And then there were those members of the congregation who meant well but had no idea of how to act around Sam. There was one spherical, middle-aged woman with a shrill voice that rose several octaves whenever she saw Sam. Annette cringed each time the lady made a bee-line toward Sam when she spotted them entering the sanctuary. She fought hard to restrain herself as the woman pinched Sam's cheek and spoke to him in a high-pitched warble, as though she were addressing a cute grandchild. "Oh Sam, it's so good to see you," she trilled.

Sam took it all calmly, smiling warmly at the woman. However, he never failed to take the opportunity to sigh with relief on her departure.

Others in the congregation professed empathy and understanding which, in truth, was no more than superficial concern. One day, as Annette was preparing to push Sam up the ramp into the maxivan after church, a member came up to them, "Don't rob me of the blessing, Annette," he urged, "Let me push Sam into the van."

There was a skill involved in pushing Sam up the ramp, and it came in knowing the precise moment to reduce pressure on the wheelchair and allow Sam to glide through the doorway without jamming his legs. Annette, therefore, insisted she could manage. The man waved her aside and grabbed the handles at the back of the wheelchair. He continued talking to Annette and Sam as he guided the wheelchair up the van's ramp, oblivious to when he should release the pressure. Seconds after passing over the threshold, the chair rammed into one of the metal supports inside the van, crushing Sam's feet against a metal stanchion.

Yet, whatever the proclivities of some of the congregation, Faith Chapel was a world away from the cold indifference of Saint Stephen's. The little, red brick church provided Sam and Annette with a fertile environment in which to share and express their faith and, above all, they knew they were welcome there.

On the morning of February 15th, 1977, the day after Valentine's Day, a glowing tribute to Sam under the headline, "A HERO'S BATTLE," appeared as the lead article in the *Wichita Eagle* as part of its contribution to "No Greater Love Day." A result of the article was the suggestion that Sam and Annette should join the speaking circuit. Henceforth, they were invited to speak about their faith and experiences at luncheons and dinner engagements, primarily at Christian Women's Clubs throughout the state of Kansas.

They would undertake maybe half a dozen engagements a year; all of them produced some very special moments. Lifelong friendships appeared to spring from every engagement. Without doubt, the fruits of such trips far outweighed their inconveniences.

After an engagement at the McPherson club, a woman came up to Sam and Annette. "You know," she said, "My husband had a stroke a few years ago and I never really understood what he was going through until I heard the two of you speak."

Sam possessed the disarming knack of making each of the women who came to hear him speak feel as though he were addressing his remarks to her alone. It was difficult to keep the reception lines moving after they spoke. Each member of the audience wanted to share a special thought or anecdote with Sam. On one such occasion, a diminutive eighty-three-year-old lady at the head of the line pulled up a chair in front of him. "Sam," she said in earnest, "I have to tell you about my daughters. I know you'd want to know!" And the rest of the line of women had to make do with Annette.

★   ★   ★

There had been almost a glut of visits to 609 Rutland during the latter part of 1968 from comrades in arms, but during the next decade they began to taper off. The one person who maintained regular contact with Sam, phoning every January 27th and without fail on Sam and Annette's wedding anniversary, was Brien Collins. B.T. had gone on to obtain a law degree at the University of Santa Clara and was carving out a niche in the world of California politics as a celebrated, outspoken maverick.

During one of his visits to Brookhollow, he was accompanied by a lady. When it came to sleeping arrangements for the night, Annette insisted the two of them sleep in separate rooms. B.T.'s thinly veiled displeasure at this arrangement was quite apparent as he took off his prosthetic leg and noisily hopped the full distance from the bathroom to the living room, muttering loudly, "That damn woman would choke the last breath from life itself!"

B.T. had always been a "devout" non-Christian. This was probably the biggest sticking point between him and Annette. Her "puritanical" ways particularly got under B.T.'s skin. "He liked his brown whiskey," as Dean Parker put it. This was anathema to her. He always had a different girl with him whenever he came to visit. *This* really got under Annette's skin. He was often loud and brazen, whereas she was reserved and soft-spoken. To Annette, B.T. was crude—the antithesis of her husband. Their strongest bond was and will always be, Sam.

B.T.'s dialogue over the phone to Sam was always brief and clipped; he was always between planes or going somewhere. He was never able to tell Sam how much he meant to him but he always called.

Over the years, Annette and B.T.'s relationship went from cool to frosty, while paradoxically, a grudging mutual respect, even love, appeared to grow.

★   ★   ★

One early spring evening, Annette received a telephone call from Denver, Colorado. "My name is Company Sergeant Major Dave Bost," the voice said. "I'm coming to Wichita to address a reserve unit. I would like to come and visit my old company commander."

The following week, Annette and Dick took Sam to the airport to greet the sergeant. Dave Bost flew into Wichita's Mid Continent Airport in a small private aircraft on which he was the only passenger. Dick drove the maxivan out across the runway to about 50 yards from where the small aircraft sat. By the time the front door of the aircraft opened, Sam was sitting out in front of the van.

Moments later, the doorway of the aircraft filled up with a huge bear of a man in full dress Army uniform. He held his gaze on Sam as he slowly made his way down the stairs. Once his feet touched ground, he began walking faster and faster until he broke into a trot that quickly turned into a full gallop.

About 10 yards from Sam's wheelchair, he cried out, "How's the old man?" Tears tumbling down his cheeks.

"Just great," Sam replied. "How's the best top sergeant in the Army doing?"

David Bost went to where Sam was sitting and almost squeezed his former company commander out of his wheelchair.

"I can't believe you are really here, Sir," he stammered and continued in a voice full of emotion, "I never thought I'd see you again."

It was as though Dick and Annette were invisible; the two men couldn't keep their eyes off one another.

Dave Bost stayed at Brookhollow for the weekend. Stories and anecdotes flowed the whole time as the two rekindled a bond that had perhaps been the closest one Sam had forged while he was in the Army. On his first evening in Wichita, the company sergeant major stayed up past midnight reading over and over the official Army report detailing the events of January 27th, 1967.

★   ★   ★

After spending most of a decade away from Brookhollow, Eric at age twenty began to exhibit a change in his attitude toward Sam; he viewed him less as a threat and more as a person to be admired. At the same time, the tone Sam used to address Eric had softened considerably. The same could not be said of Eric's hostility toward his mother, however.

Eric held his mother responsible for many of the bad times in his life: divorce from his father, never allowing him to be himself but continually trying to mold him into an image created in her own mind of who he should be and putting Sam's needs above his own. But like his mother, he could be very introverted and very introspective. He liked to bury his hurt deep, in separate compartments within his soul.

One time Annette telephoned Eric on his birthday and he told her he wished he'd never been born. She replied by saying that if he felt that way, then she guessed she felt the same. Eric took this as his mother disowning him—just one more thing to be stored in one of his "compartments." He felt his mother was always putting him down.

They both internalized their pain. Annette always felt things were all right with him—he appeared to be coping. Eric was rarely openly hostile to his mother. He showed his displeasure most by staying away from her; this was the one thing that pained her most, and he knew it.

At the end of February 1981, Eric enlisted in a three-month program as an artillery crewman with the Army at Fort Sill, Oklahoma. During the final week of the course, Eric phoned home to say it would mean a great deal to him if Sam and his mother could make the trip down to Lawton, Oklahoma, for his graduation exercises.

As Eric showed Sam around the base that day, a harmony in the two men's relationship was evident as never before. Eric took great pride in showing Sam the systems that had been updated during the previous 10 years. Sam absorbed every detail. Annette simply looked on as her wish came true—a wish she had expressed to herself during the retirement ceremony in 1972 of Eric having the desire to get to know Sam better.

As Annette wheeled Sam back over to the Pacer at the completion of ceremonies, Eric drew one of his contemporaries to one side and remarked, "If you ever want to see an example of true love; there it goes."

Chapter Twenty-One

Paradise
. . . And Other Predicaments

Several elements combined to provide Sam with a sense of freedom despite his catastrophic physical limitations—a beautiful, spacious home and garden located in a tranquil corner of suburban Wichita. A painted image of an eagle perched above two flags on the side of the mailbox at the entrance to the driveway and a three foot by five foot American flag whipping and flapping over the front yard in the brisk Kansas breeze. There was the indoor swimming pool, shower chair and flexi-bed, and for long-distance travel—the roomy, little, brown AMC Pacer, a versatile gem of a car that might have been designed for the disabled person. In addition, for short trips around town, there was the customized Chevrolet Suburban which looked and rode more like a turn-of-the-century ironclad, although it was a major improvement on the Creepy Coop.

The icing on the cake of Sam's and Annette's lives arrived in the form of four consecutive winter trips to Hawaii between January 1980 and January 1983. They came about as a result of a seemingly innocuous conversation between Sam, Dick and Annette in the summer of 1979.

"Oh, how great it would be to get away somewhere," Annette mused aloud. "Anywhere, even for a short while." Sam looked at his wife with wistful approval.

"Where would you even think of going?" Dick retorted sarcastically, showing open disdain for the notion.

The thinly veiled rebuttal appeared to catch Annette momentarily off guard, as though she had been in the middle of a daydream. Snapping back into the conversation with unusual impulsiveness, she blurted out, "Hawaii would be a lovely place to visit."

"That's impossible!" Dick replied, seizing on the remark. "You couldn't possibly do that."

What had been little more than a throwaway suggestion immediately assumed cause *celebre* proportions in Annette's mind as she set about making inquiries through local travel agents.

'What difference is there in traveling five hundred miles or five thousand?' she thought as she made reservations for Sam, Eric and herself to fly out of Wichita on January 10th, 1980.

Any remaining doubts she might have had concerning the sanity of the idea were dispelled by Sam's air of eager anticipation, which built steadily during the months prior to the trip, especially as cold winter nights began to draw in.

On the morning of January 11th, they flew into one of the worst storms to hit Hawaii for years. The aircraft spent 45 minutes circling the airport in heavy turbulence. They had to wait for a temporary control tower to be erected to replace the one that had just blown down.

Sam remained calm through it all, despite slowly slipping down out of his seat belt. Eric unbuckled himself and crossed the aisle to pull Sam up, incurring the wrath of a panicky stewardess. Annette, meanwhile, was turning paler and paler, her head pressed against the window, yearning for the whole awful merry-go-round to stop. It was all she could do to hold down the contents of her stomach. When the aircraft eventually touched down, they took a "handicab" wheelchair taxi from the airport to the majestic Kohala Hilton on Diamond Head Beach.

Annette awoke the following day before dawn and drew the curtains back slightly to peer bleary-eyed out the window. They appeared to be surrounded by an ocean with several palm trees and small flags sticking out of it. The bizarre weather tantrum of the previous day had flooded the entire area. An hour later, as the sun came up, the realization dawned that they were surrounded by a golf course.

While Eric rented a car and explored the island, Sam and Annette unwound from life's problems by sitting out on the beach in front of the hotel, soaking up the sun and marveling at the abundance and variety of natural beauty all around them. The stark mountainous outcrops, shrouded by dark, heavy clouds, played host to rushing waterfalls and lush, green valleys; perhaps the scene offered Sam a reminder of another time and place. If so, he never let on.

Throughout the trip, Sam was able to indulge his passion for food, eating at a different restaurant each day. Despite gaining weight, he'd never looked so healthy. Eric proved a bulwark of reliability. The maid at their hotel was constantly saying what a wonderful son they had. More than anything, this made Annette glow with pride. It was such an unlooked-for reward. At last they were functioning as a family.

The highlight of the trip for Sam was tracking down an old Citadel classmate at Schofield Army Barracks. He gave Sam a guided tour of the post and Sam came alive. The entire trip to Hawaii proved an unmitigated success on all fronts. They resolved to repeat it the following year.

★   ★   ★

In August of 1980, Sam's cousin, Margaret Louise, the daughter of Dick's older sister, Margaret, died from a ruptured appendix. Long since ostracized by Dick, Pauline and other members of the family because of her homosexuality, she had withdrawn from the mainstream of Wichita society with her lover. Both her parents were dead and she had stayed away from doctors and hospitals for as long as possible because of lack of money. When her condition worsened to the point the pain became unbearable, her lover phoned Dick and begged him for the money to admit Margaret Louise to the hospital. Reluctantly he acquiesced, but not before letting his thoughts on the subject of unconventional sexual preference be known. By then it was too late.

361

Margaret Louise was laid to rest in the Bird family plot at Maple Grove Cemetery on North Hillside Avenue. Before the funeral, which Dick paid for, he left explicit instructions at the entrance to the cemetery that "family members only" were to be admitted to the burial service. There was no headstone to mark the gravesite.

Margaret's brother, Chip, flew in from California for the funeral and stayed for a week at Brookhollow. Chip was an intellectual atheist who was heavily into cryogenics. Chip's view of Christianity as a myth and Annette's fundamental beliefs caused a certain level of tension between them—especially in the beginning, when Chip conducted a time-and-motion-study of Annette's movements around the house.

"Annette, why do you keep going back and forth between the living room and kitchen? If you thought about it, you could save time by just making one journey," was one of his observations.

By the end of the week, however, each had largely adjusted to the other's foibles. So when Paula suggested they all meet for lunch at a local Mexican restaurant before Chip's flight back to California, Annette did not object.

During lunch, Paula bubbled, punctuating much of the conversation with humorous asides. When her brother hiccupped during dessert, she roared, Sam laughed and even Annette cracked a smile, though somewhat uncomfortably. At the end of the meal, Paula took Chip to the airport and Annette took Sam home to lie down in an attempt to rid him of the hiccups that refused to subside.

Indeed, they continued through the evening with Sam experiencing great difficulty eating. When it came time for bed, Annette, becoming increasingly concerned, phoned Dr. Cook. He told her it was a matter of getting Sam's diaphragm to relax; once he was asleep, they would probably go away. But Sam never slept. He lay awake all night hiccupping. The next day there was still no let up. In the days that followed, Dr. Ray Cook, their G.P., went through his full repertoire of remedies, to no avail. Finally, after 11 days of torment, Sam began spitting up blood. Dr. Cook admitted him to Wesley Hospital, telling Annette they would have to put him under an anesthetic in the hopes of forcing Sam's diaphragm to relax. There were no guarantees of success.

By now Annette was fraught with anxiety. She knew her husband's body couldn't take such punishment much longer.

Once in the hospital, Sam, now in an unconscious state, was connected to various IV's. Annette was sent home to rest but couldn't, so she returned to the hospital to sit beside her husband's bed. The weather seemed to parallel Annette's feelings; it rained constantly for the next 36 hours while Sam slept.

Shortly after midday on his second full day of sedation, the skies began to clear, lighting up the room as the sun tried to break through the clouds. As a shaft of sunlight shone through the big picture window opposite his bed, Sam began to come round. The hiccups had stopped. He smiled as he opened his eyelids. "My angel," he said, staring across at his wife who was sitting with her back to the window.

"No Sam, it's just me, your wife," Annette replied.

"No!" he insisted. "You are my angel and you have the wings to prove it."

'Oh dear,' she thought. 'It must be the effects of the anesthetic.'

"Sam, it's me, your wife, Annette," she repeated.

"No, look behind you," he urged. She turned around to see the sun peaking out between two huge, billowy, white clouds and realized her body had been silhouetted against them.

'I must have been a vision indeed,' she thought to herself and smiled at her husband. She didn't want to argue the point since he was still far too weak. In any case, she was so utterly relieved the hiccups had subsided she accepted her temporary divine status and went home to catch up on some much-needed sleep.

Shortly after Sam returned home from the hospital, it was apparent that his strength had been greatly depleted. Changes in lifestyle at Brookhollow began to appear as the couple began to spend more time together in the same room. Sam would stay in the kitchen until Annette had finished the dishes. While he was in his "laboratory" (the bathroom) brushing his teeth and shaving, she would tidy and rearrange things in the bedroom. In the afternoons while Sam sat back in the recliner, Annette was always at his side with her embroidering. He began to tire more quickly in the pool, not managing the same number of "laps" as he had in the past. His head was leaning markedly to the right again, as it used to before the surgery at Craig. During times of acute exhaustion, it would come to rest on his shoulder. Annette had never seen this before, but she realized the strength she had tried so hard to preserve was starting to ebb away. Bouts of hiccups, lasting no more than 30 minutes and finishing as abruptly as they began, became a regular occurrence.

Little things Annette had grown accustomed to and taken for granted—"as part of their daily rhythm"—like Sam's snoring in his sleep, became ever sweeter music to her ears. The warmth of her husband's body came to represent the ultimate in reassurance.

Nothing, however, would deter Sam from returning to Hawaii the following January and by the fall of 1980, plans were well underway.

Ed Drum, their good friend from the Kansas Paralysis Chapter, who often visited Sam when Annette went out, had recently lost both parents in quick succession and was feeling melancholy. Sam and Annette agreed a trip to Hawaii could be just the tonic Ed needed. After a period of arm twisting, Ed eventually gave in and the three of them flew out of a frigid Wichita on Monday, February 2nd, 1981. The sight of Annette traveling with two men in wheelchairs drew strange looks on the flight to Dallas.

This time, all was calm as they flew into Honolulu International Airport. They stayed at a hotel in the Waikiki area.

Sam began his first full day in Hawaii by biting his lower lip hard and drawing a good deal of blood. "I hope and pray we have no more of those meals!" he quipped laconically, and then carried on with his breakfast.

Meanwhile, Ed emerged from the bathroom.

"Hey, Ed, go out on the lanai and take a good look at Hawaii," said Annette.

"Er, I don't think I like it out here," he muttered.

"Gee, Ed, you're cranky this morning. What's the matter?" Annette replied.

"There's a man peeing off his balcony over there. That's what!" he shouted back.

"Oh dear! Oh my goodness!" cried Annette.

"Better make sure you've got your hat on then!" Sam chimed in from the table with a grin.

The three of them shared the same room and it worked to perfection. Ed would be up and out early, allowing Annette the opportunity to take care of "the program" and other personal hygiene. In the afternoon, he'd return for a nap while Sam and Annette went for a walk along the shore. Waikiki Beach gave them a greater outreach than they'd had the previous year, since the beach itself was wheelchair accessible. Then they would all rendezvous in the evening for supper. Ed left for home a week before Sam and Annette but he enjoyed himself tremendously.

The question arose from certain Bird quarters whether money should be spent on taking such grand excursions. Sam was now markedly thinner and had developed a deep sallowness to his complexion. Annette didn't know what the future held but she knew she'd rather have the memory of seeing Sam have a good time than a large checking account to spend when he was gone.

As far as Annette was concerned, the little inconveniences of the trips were nothing compared to the benefits. She gave Sam a bed bath every day and he had her all to himself. The friends they made in Hawaii helped Sam stand up for a few minutes each day, so even the standing bar wasn't missed. Everywhere they went it seemed people went out of their way to treat them with care and understanding. And they were able to visit a different restaurant every day; well, Sam was in clover! Hawaii was paradise. Having left all their problems at home, they were able to enjoy each other and the moment to the utmost.

Annette was prompted to ask her husband if he would consider moving to Hawaii on a permanent basis since everything, particularly the climate, was so beneficial.

"No," he said. "I was born in Kansas. That's my home."

★   ★   ★

By the spring of 1981, Sam's cluster headaches, which could be accurately described as a whole series of mini-migraines, were becoming more frequent and ferocious in their intensity. Bright lights and loud noises of any kind were devastating to Sam at such times. The only physical signs that he was in the throes of a cluster headache, however, were the tears streaming down the right side of his face and the profuse draining of his right nostril. If Annette asked if there was anything wrong, he might say, "This isn't one of my better days," but that would be all. He never complained.

Then about a month later, Sam became stricken by a severe cramping sensation in his left leg. These cramps failed to respond to Annette's regimen of stretching and rubbing exercises. When the pain became extremely severe, she would lift Sam out of his wheelchair as quickly as possible and transfer him onto the bed, trying to make him more comfortable by changing his position, but this had little effect. By August, the symptoms concerned Dr. Cook so much that he sent Sam to see a neurologist for a series of tests.

The specialist informed Annette that the nerve endings surrounding the damaged area of Sam's brain were showing marked signs of deterioration. These "rogue" nerve endings were primarily responsible for the pain in his left leg and other parts of his body. He made it clear that the only way to relieve Sam's pain was an operation to remove some scar tissue that had built up following the 1974 operation at Craig Hospital. He was reluctant to recommend this course of action, however, for fear it would result in the removal of brain tissue as well. Annette was in no doubt. Following the operation at Craig, the surgeon had informed her that under no circumstances should any further incisions be made on Sam's head. Quite simply, there was no place left to cut.

Taking a deep breath, Annette asked the specialist for a prognosis.

"With the nerve endings continuing to deteriorate at the same rate; no more, no less," he said, "Sam has approximately six months to live."

Annette thanked the doctor for his frankness. Once the implication of the prognosis had sunk in, she found herself facing another dilemma. 'Should I tell Sam? Can I tell Sam?' she wondered. After agonizing over the decision for several sleepless nights, she resolved that if he asked her what the doctor said, she would tell him. If he didn't ask, she would say nothing about it.

★　　★　　★

On September 10th, the day after Sam and Annette's ninth wedding anniversary, Paula went into the hospital for a biopsy. Throughout June and July she'd been dogged by a flu that refused to respond to antibiotics and she'd become quite run down. A family shower had already been organized for the 10th by Annette and Sam to celebrate the forthcoming wedding of Paula's only son, Bruce. Paula, now divorced from Jim Oliver, told Annette to go ahead with the plans.

"Kid, this biopsy's nothing," she said with typical verve. "I'll be out as soon as it's finished and come over to the party."

The following day at five o'clock, Paula called from the hospital. "Sorry, Kid, I can't make it. I feel too sick." The diagnosis was cervical cancer.

By this time, Dick had long since been taking full-time care of Pauline—her condition was worsening by the day. She had had heart trouble for the past 20 years. After being confined to bed for six months, Sam's mother died on October 7th, 1981. She was seventy-four. Sam said he envied her; she was no longer in pain.

Paula's friend, Claudine Talbott, decided to pay her last respects to Pauline at the mortuary the night before the funeral. As she was entering through the main door, she saw Paula and her daughter, Sarah, leaving the "slumber room" and coming toward her.

Paula, now quite recovered from her biopsy, was wearing a striking, white suede dress with a bodice patterned with leaves in an Indian style. She had a huge squash blossom necklace around her neck. She looked electric. She'd stopped at the mortuary on her way to a function at the Mid American Center, of which she was now the director.

Claudine flashed a sympathetic look at her long-time friend, half expecting something along the lines of, "Thanks for coming."

"She looks pretty good!" Paula exclaimed, before breezing past her and out of the door. Claudine stood there dumbfounded for a couple of seconds before proceeding into the slumber room.

"Actually, she did look great," Claudine recounted later.

★   ★   ★

The episode with the hiccups in 1980 and its aftermath marked the beginning of the deterioration of Sam's overall condition. Annette's first reaction was panic, followed by a fragile calm that grew stronger in the belief that if this was the beginning of the end, the ultimate responsibility for Sam's life now lay in God's hands. On many nights, however, she found herself quietly crying herself to sleep.

While the two of them were eating breakfast one day during the late summer of 1982, a year after the brain scan, Sam asked his wife the question she had long been dreading. "What did the doctors tell you about my condition, Sweetie-pie?"

"Sam, do you really want to know?" Annette replied haltingly, the question having taken her completely by surprise.

"Yes," he replied firmly, fixing his eyes on Annette's.

"They told me that you had approximately six months to live, and there was nothing more they could do," she answered as calmly as she could.

"Thanks for telling me, Sweetie-pie," he replied softly. Without betraying a flicker of emotion he continued eating his cornflakes.

PART VIII

SUNSET

Chapter Twenty-Two

A Premature Ending and Some New Beginnings

Paula was great at initiating things: projects, newspapers, marriages and families. She would hurl herself with gusto into whatever caught her imagination at the time—whether it was an advertising promotion, her children or a "cure" for Sam's brain damage. That would then become her cause *celebre* until she tired of it or something more appealing took its place on the horizon. She was an over-achiever, yet she never quite managed to follow through on her short-run triumphs. The formula for sustained success always seemed to elude her.

Two months after the cervical cancer diagnosis, Paula went to the M.D. Anderson Clinic and Tumor Institute in Houston, Texas, to have a hysterectomy. Ever since the diagnosis in early September 1981, family and friends had become very concerned because the growth had been found to be at a fairly advanced stage.

Following the operation, Paula telephoned Annette and Sam. "Well, Kid, they say they got it all," Paula said, sounding very upbeat.

"Oh, Paula, that's great news," Annette replied, visibly relieved. Her reaction mirrored that of Paula's many friends who had feared the worst.

Paula returned to Wichita at the end of November. She was looking forward to returning to her job of the past nine months

371

as Director of the Mid American Indian Center, after a short convalescence.

She sent bouquets of flowers to all her close friends thanking them for "being there for her."

"I feel like this is springtime all over again," she said to her close friend, Pam, upon her return. Pam did her best to return a cheery smile, but Paula looked so thin.

Two weeks before Christmas, she was informed the cancer had returned with a vengeance, having spread throughout a kidney, and she returned to the hospital. A medicine man from one of the local tribes came to drive away the evil spirits and close friends prayed.

After agonizing for a month over the decision, the board of directors "fired" Paula from her post at the end of January 1982. The final meeting was described as "tearful" by all those in attendance. "I don't think I've ever been in a situation where there was so much compassion—and yet not seem to be able to do anything about what was before you," said Bill Jones, one of the trustees. During her term as director, the center's debt had been reduced from $110,000 to less than $20,000.

"Paula's done a good job for us—she's brought in money and in these past months has, at times, worked from bed working telephones, trying to keep things going," said the chairman of the board of trustees. "But we are at a point where there is a need for that position of leadership to be filled. We're at a critical time when we must have someone there."

The center did agree to extend Paula's medical benefits for another six months. But things were unraveling. Paula had two children—Laurie, sixteen and Sarah, seven—at home and no money to support them with. She'd been left with nothing except a second mortgage and a profusion of unpaid bills when Jim Oliver left her. For years she had kept up a front about her financial problems, not wanting to expose any avenue of vulnerability in a tough business world. But now she started opening up.

Her friends came up with the idea of a "We Love You Paula" party at the Broadview Hotel in Wichita to raise money. Appropriately the party was set for Valentine's Day. Paula helped write the copy for the fliers and plan the day.

More than a hundred pairs of clapping hands were waiting as she came in flanked by her four children that Sunday afternoon. Bruce pushed the wheelchair. She was wearing a bright pink dress and a Valentine's Day corsage. Eileen O'Hara had bought her an Afghan blanket to cover her legs so no one could see how thin she was. The smile on her face lit up the room as the band struck up with "You Are My Sunshine."

Long tables were topped with fancy food and a pink cream-cheese heart filled with cherries bore the inscription, "We Love You, Paula."

"I feel terrific," she laughed. "This is the first time I've been upright in a month."

Paula was aglow. She had mustered just enough strength for one last performance.

The party raised $5,310, including a $1,000 donation from Senator Bob Dole, who read about Paula's plight in the newspaper. Sam and Annette were in Hawaii at the time (it was their third trip) and, in fact, had not been told about it. Dick did not attend. He was most conspicuous by his absence.

'Where is Dick Bird when his daughter needs him most?' was the unspoken thought dominating the party. Everyone knew how much money Dick had. They couldn't believe he hadn't offered to help her out at any time over the past six months.

In a special thank you letter to her friends, Paula told them it made her recall the words of a Mac Davis song: "Life ain't no easy freeway, just some gravel on the ground; And you pay for every mile you go; And you spread some dust around . . ."

"I think I've done that," she said. "And I've always hoped that when the dust settled, somehow things would be better for everyone. The 'We Love You Paula' party was the happiest day of my life."

Two and a half months later, at 2:45 in the morning of May 5th, 1982, Paula's bittersweet life, like so many of her original ideas, came to its premature end. Seconds before her death, she opened her eyes and murmured, "Hello, Mama, I'm coming."

As she would have it, her death made front page headlines in the *Wichita Eagle-Beacon.*

Several years after his daughter's death, Dick was asked why he spoke so little about her. "She had her chances," was all he would say.

When pressed about why he didn't come through with financial aid in his daughter's hour of need, he replied simply that he did not know she was ill.

★　　★　　★

By summer of 1982, Dick was gradually piecing his life back together after Pauline's death the previous October. Inevitable as it had been, it had still come as a body blow. "Mrs. Bird" had always been the dominant force, both financially and emotionally, though the latter had not always seemed a positive force to those close to the family. Many thought the union that had produced Sam and Paula had always been something of an enigma.

In August, Dick enrolled in a one-week elder hostel program at the University of Kansas at Lawrence. It was designed to provide a source of "cultural stimulation and reorientation." The week had barely begun before he struck up a friendship with a vivacious widow named Hazel Merritt who had lived much of her life in Ellis (in western Kansas) raising four sons. After her husband, a railroad engineer, died, she went back to school and then spent three years teaching in Papua, New Guinea.

Dick didn't waste time with elaborate subtleties during their initial period of acquaintance. Hazel was somewhat unnerved and recoiled at first. Undaunted, after the week at the hostel, Dick continued to pursue Hazel with increasing ardor bombarding her with letters and phone calls. Hazel, in turn, went on to hand Dick a series of rebuffs, refusing to answer his phone calls and letters. By Christmas he'd become quite despondent at his lack of progress and began to turn inward in deep depression.

In a gesture designed to elevate Dick's spirits, Annette asked him if he would like to accompany her and Sam to Hawaii that winter of early 1983, not thinking for a minute he would say yes. Sam, who'd been looking forward to the trip for some time, thought it a wonderful idea. He didn't perceive the invitation in quite the same terms as his wife. At first, Dick said no, then he said he didn't know and finally he said yes. His response see-sawed for several weeks; one minute he wanted to go and the next he didn't. At last, he said yes and left it at that. Sam was thrilled, Annette was less so; though she persuaded herself that if she could manage two men in wheelchairs, she could surely cope with Sam and his father. Several factors combined to ensure that this was not to be.

The friction between Dick and Annette was evident right from the start. It intensified at Honolulu International Airport when they couldn't agree on what sort of transport to take between the arrival lounge and the luggage collection area. Since neither would give in, they both ended up walking with Annette pushing Sam in the wheelchair. As Sam was being helped up into the handicab, Dick became adamant that Annette had forgotten something and insisted she go back and check. She paid no attention to her father-in-law and climbed into the cab.

At their condominium, it was apparent that the image of their rooms portrayed in the glossy brochure was a significant departure from reality. Since all three were exhausted, Annette decided to wait until morning to take the matter up with the travel agent and get them transferred to a different hotel. Unfortunately, that night Dick took every item of clothing out of all three suitcases and meticulously hung or placed them in closets, drawers and cupboards.

The next day proved difficult, though a move was eventually made to the Ilikai Hotel across the street. After a week at the Ilikai, they transferred again to the Twin Towers, an imposing block of condominiums nearby.

The accommodation at the Twin Towers was comprised of one separate bedroom and a living room with a hide-a-bed. Before Annette and Dick had a chance to enter into a discussion about who should take the bedroom, Sam announced that his father should have it. "Dad has made many sacrifices on my behalf," he declared. "Not least, providing me with a military education.

375

It shall be my privilege therefore, to provide him with the best possible accommodation."

"But Sam," Annette pleaded, "The hide-a-bed . . ."

"But nothing, Sweetie-pie. Dad will have the bedroom."

★　　　★　　　★

Prior to the trip, Dick had booked a week in a Hawaiian elder hostel, so Annette steeled herself to hang on until she and Sam had the condominium to themselves.

When Dick returned from his week away, he announced he was returning to Wichita a week early to take care of paperwork. Annette sighed with relief. Coping with Sam and his father had not been the tolerable burden she'd envisaged back in Wichita. Dick was well aware of this. It was the main reason he decided to return home.

The remainder of the trip turned out to be a journey into paradise. Sam was in slow motion, which in the past might have frustrated both of them, but now it seemed completely natural. The routine of bathing and dressing Sam was finished by midday and they would go for a short excursion around the hotel and perhaps take in lunch. By three o'clock, Sam would be ready for a nap. They didn't venture out as much as they had on previous trips, but it was enough to revel in each other's company, watching the sun set behind the big ships crossing the horizon and the catamarans skipping across the water nearby. They both liked to be in the hotel lobby, picking up the atmosphere and circulating on the periphery of the groups of people congregating in the bars and restaurants.

On reading the local newspaper one morning, Sam saw that the movie, *The Lords of Discipline*, was showing at the theater opposite their condominium. He was keen to see it. It was the movie of Pat Conroy's controversial, million-copy, best selling novel about life at a military academy in the sixties. The author had attended The Citadel between 1963 and 1967.

Annette writhed in her seat throughout the movie. She never got over the shock of hearing people in a military environment swear. Sam was the only example of a person from a military environment to whom she had been exposed for any length of time, and he never swore.

Critics called the movie "a tough and often shocking film." It was certainly an indictment of Sam's school. Afterward, he commented simply that it didn't resemble The Citadel he remembered.

Late that night, Sam's hiccups made an unwelcome return. Annette lay beside her husband, almost too scared to breath. "Please, dear God, not the hiccups again," she prayed.

When they subsided the following morning, she felt a keen appreciation for Sam's oft-quoted remark, "The best thing about pain is when it goes away. It feels so good." She could say the same for acute anxiety.

They spent the last week of their vacation at the Kui Lima on the north shore of Oahu. The imposing structure designed by Frank Lloyd Wright straddled the peninsula on pillars and gave the impression of being on an island, surrounded by water. The hotel was nestled in the semi-seclusion of quiet beaches. The only interruption to the peace came when high winds blew the palm trees back and forth.

Annette yearned for time to stand still. She had the distinct feeling this would be their last time in Hawaii together. From the arching palms to the moonlight on the water, she wanted to soak up every last moment.

★   ★   ★

On returning home, they discovered Hazel had had a change of heart and had made contact with Dick. The cloud of depression that had hung over Dick for months had lifted and the change in his demeanor was remarkable. A few weeks later, Dick proposed and Hazel accepted.

Dick and Hazel were married on May 14th, 1983, in Kansas City. Sam, who was overjoyed his father had found someone to spend the rest of his life with, was best man and Annette was matron of honor. Or, as Paula's youngest daughter, Sarah, put it, "Best Woman." At the wedding, Eric, now twenty-two, announced that he too was getting married—in July. He had met

377

his wife-to-be, Tammy, at school in Springfield, Missouri. Now it was Annette's turn to glow with pride.

Eric and Tammy's wedding took place at Faith Chapel on a hot summer's day when the temperature reached 105 degrees. Sam wore a dark suit and quickly became exhausted. His head leaned over onto his right shoulder, but he still insisted on playing the full part of the father of the groom. Alas, Annette's thoughts were deflected from her son on his day and dominated by concern for her husband's well-being. She was relieved when it was all over. The day ended with a terrible thunderstorm.

The fall of 1983 saw their yard resplendent with color. American Beauty roses arched out in huge tentacles of color and continued to bloom right through autumn. Matched in their splendor by the golden-brown sycamores and bright yellow chrysanthemums, the garden was a kaleidoscope of color. Despite his sensitivity to bright lights, the combination seemed to have a soothing effect on Sam.

Christmas was unique. The cold weather set in and Sam's circulation problems were pronounced, so Annette decided they would do little in the way of entertaining. Instead, they volunteered to look after two extra dogs besides Yogi. The two canine visitors were exemplary and it was a relief to have the kind of visitors you don't have to entertain.

In early January, Yogi slipped out of the house and disappeared. Four days later the vet called to say someone had brought him in and it looked as though he'd been involved in a fight with another dog. He had a broken leg and several puncture wounds. After the vet set his leg, Annette brought him home to Brookhollow where he took up residence by the fireplace on a rug Sam had knitted himself. The rug was normally a restricted area but Sam was prepared to make a concession in this special case. Annette's concession came in carrying Yogi outdoors periodically. After a couple of months' convalescence, Yogi recovered almost completely—except for a slight limp. The following year, while staying at Tammy and Eric's house, he disappeared mysteriously while Eric, now a cross-country truck driver, was on the road. Yogi was never seen again.

Chapter Twenty-Three

The Last Curtain Call

On New Year's Day, 1984, Sam and Annette received a communication from Major General John Ballantyne, the commanding officer of the Military District of Washington. They were cordially invited to a special retirement reunion in honor of Dean Parker. The ceremony was to be held at the Ceremonial Hall, Fort Myer, Virginia, at four o'clock on the 30th of January.

"Do you want to send a telegram, Sam?" inquired his wife.

"No," he replied, in a matter-of-fact tone of voice.

Mildly puzzled at her husband's response, Annette went on to ask Sam if he wanted to send a gift. Again he said no. By now Annette was completely baffled; there had always seemed to be an unbreakable bond between the two men.

"Is there anything you want to do?" Annette asked.

"Yes. I want to go!" he declared.

Her heart sank. She looked at Sam's feeble frame, the pallor of his skin and the dark, penetrating circles that ringed his eyes. 'How can he possibly survive, let alone endure such a trip?' she thought to herself. There were urinary problems, digestive problems and the incessant headaches that came over him, wave after wave. Worst of all, it was the coldest part of the year in Washington, bitter and clammy. Sam would brook no further discussion of the matter.

In her search for allies, Annette even called her old antagonist, B.T. Collins. "Surely you don't expect Sam to be there," she entreated.

"We're counting on it," he retorted.

Finally, she turned to Dr. Cook.

"Do you want my advice?" the doctor said softly.

"Yes, of course," she replied.

"Do what Sam wants—even if it means bringing him back in a pine box."

On January 12th, Annette telephoned Dean Parker at work in Washington. "Sam is coming—with or without me," she said.

This was Dean's cue to set in motion a series of special events. On putting down the phone, he went to the Ceremonies and Special Events Office where a sergeant major, who had been a young PFC in Sam's company back in 1964, was sitting at his desk.

"Sar'nt Major Brown."

"Yes, Sir?"

"Sam Bird is coming in for my retirement. What can we do?"

"Leave it to me, Sir. I know just the thing—the only thing."

A week later, Annette received in the mail a five-day itinerary for their stay from the Military District of Washington.

As the day of their flight to Washington came closer, Annette grew more anxious. She was just plain scared that Sam wouldn't survive the trip. For the past eleven and a half years, she had devoted every sinew of her being to maintaining his comfort and upholding his dignity. Now these instincts were being supplanted by a more selfish motive—the fear of losing him.

They flew into Washington International Airport on TWA Flight 844 at seventeen minutes past four on the afternoon of Saturday, January 28th. David Porreca was there to greet them at the airport. He had made sure a handicab was there to take them to the Quality Inn, Pentagon City. Colonel Joe Conmy went straight to the hotel to welcome them. Sam was completely exhausted by the flight and subsequent journey to the hotel, but the sight of the colonel infused him with a fresh shot of energy and anticipation.

The following day, a Sunday, a trip had been organized to the Tomb of the Unknown Soldier to watch the changing of the guard at one o'clock. Sam had always maintained that if ever there was sacred ground in America, it was at Arlington National Cemetery at the Tomb of the Unknown Soldier.

As their handicab drew up on Memorial Drive, a hundred yards or so from the tomb, Annette was aware of two soldiers standing on the sidewalk opposite. After the cab came to rest beside the curb, the two soldiers, dressed immaculately in dark-blue great coats and wearing white gloves, walked over and opened the door.

"Major Bird, Sir," one of them announced. "We are your military escorts, Sir."

Annette was somewhat taken by surprise at this. 'It must have been Dean Parker,' she thought to herself. 'He must have let someone know there was going to be a disabled person at the cemetery. How considerate of him.'

The two escorts wheeled Sam to the edge of the cordoned-off area in front of the tomb where about two hundred people were gathered to witness the guard change on this bitterly cold day. CSM Brown came over to where Sam was sitting and whispered quietly in his ear. "Sir, I'm pleased to inform you that you have the honor of laying a wreath at the Tomb of the Unknown Soldier," he said.

This was an honor normally reserved only for the president and foreign heads of state.

For a moment Sam was speechless, then he replied, "Oh, thank you," in a voice overflowing with emotion. A solemn expression came over his face and then suddenly, he sat bolt upright in his wheelchair.

The two escorts gently pushed Sam to the foot of the tomb, one of them carrying the wreath on his arm. On reaching the tomb, there was a short pause before the soldier handed the wreath down to Sam. Sam leaned forward and momentarily lost his balance. Swiftly, imperceptively, one of the escorts reached across and steadied Sam's arm. After laying the wreath, Sam straightened up in his chair before executing the most rigid of salutes. After allowing Sam to savor the occasion for a moment, the two escorts drew the chair back eight inches, turned it around on its axis and wheeled its occupant to the steps. Taps sounded and the off-duty guardsman made his way off the area.

Throughout the ceremony, Annette had been almost beside herself. She worried about the effect of the bitter cold on Sam, unable to properly appreciate the sheer joy and sense of fulfillment her husband was experiencing during that solemn 20 minutes.

After the ceremony, a dark-haired man of average build wearing a black leather coat and sunglasses approached Annette and drew her to one side. "My name's Gatanas," he said. "I served with your husband in Vietnam. There are only four words that come to mind when I think of Sam Bird," he continued. "The epitome of decency."

★　　★　　★

Monday, the 30th of January, was the day of the retirement ceremony itself. Sam couldn't have been happier to be inside the ceremonial hall at Fort Myer. This was where he had once organized nationally televised pageants involving intricate maneuvers before capacity audiences. Now listening to his favorite fife and drum corps and watching two platoons from the Old Guard—perfectly groomed soldiers executing every maneuver with faultless precision—Sam's pride was matched by Annette's awe.

After the formal retirement ceremonies, there were several speeches. The keynote speaker was B.T. Collins, representing the "band of brothers" from Vietnam in 1966:

"Eighteen years ago there were four of us, who have not been together since that time in 1966, Bravo Company, 12th Cavalry, 1st Cavalry Division.

"On my right, in the wheelchair, is our old man, Captain Samuel Bird, who, as member of the Old Guard in 1963, was the officer in charge of John F. Kennedy's casket. He was the one who provided us in 1966 and later on in 1967 with the leadership in how to train and act in front of young men regardless of the circumstances.

"The three of us, of course, are eternally grateful for what Sam Bird taught us. Particularly in his love of country and the Old Guard of the United States Army.

"And there is a man, who puts it far better than I can. His name is William Manchester who wrote about Sam Bird in a book called *The Death of a President*. He spoke of a lean, sinewy Kansan. Sam Bird was the kind of American youth congressmen deeply praised each Fourth of July, and whose existence many, grown jaded by years on the hill, secretly doubt. Lieutenant Bird was a square, unsophisticated patriot. The strains of the National Anthem still thrilled him. He had joined the regular Army because he wanted to serve his country, and he considered it an honor to be stationed at the nation's capital . . ."

The retirement ceremony for Dean Parker had turned into a tribute to Sam Bird, yet no one seemed to mind, least of all Dean, who looked across at his former company commander. 'Sam has come home,' he thought to himself.

★   ★   ★

The following afternoon at half past one, Sam and Annette visited the Vietnam Memorial. The temperature was 38 degrees, although it felt much colder because of the biting wind off the Potomac. Annette wrapped Sam up as best she could and George Brydie, their handicab driver, gave them a condensed history of the memorial on the way there.

Soon after they arrived, Annette realized they were the only ones there. The grass was dead, the trees were bare and the sky was gray. The statue depicting the three soldiers of the war had yet to be erected. There seemed to be a place for a flagpole, but at the time Annette did not notice a flag. The scene was stark and eerie as she wheeled her husband toward the Wall, in the face of the chill wind blowing off the river.

"What do you think of it, Sam?" she asked. They didn't go all the way to the end of it or up close enough to touch it.

At first, the question seemed too much for him to take in, as he said nothing. And then he uttered his reply, seemingly bewildered by it all. "It's not enough," he stammered and Annette turned the chair around and wheeled him away.

They returned to their hotel at Pentagon City where Annette experienced great difficulty warming Sam up. She put him to bed knowing rest was the only thing that would enable him to get through the evening.

Sam and Annette had been invited to dinner at the Fort Myer's Officers' Club that evening by Colonel and Mrs. Conmy. They were to be joined by Dean Parker, John White, a close friend from Sam's years at Fort Myer, and his wife, Mary. Throughout the trip Sam had been looking forward particularly to this evening. Physically, however, the four days in Washington had begun to exact a toll on Sam that caused Annette to have strong misgivings about the dinner.

Half an hour before George Brydie and his handicab were due to arrive, as Annette was applying the finishing touches to her make-up, Sam called out from the bed, "Do you love me, Sweetie-pie?"

"Yes," she replied.

"Do you love me a lot?"

"Yes, you know I do. What's wrong?"

There was a short pause before Sam replied, "I think I detect a foul odor."

Annette went over to the bed where she saw that Sam had indeed suffered a bout of diarrhea. She had already dressed him in his suit for the evening.

Within 20 minutes, Annette had completely undressed, washed and dressed her husband again with a jacket and clean pair of slacks. When she finished, she begged him to allow her to phone and cancel the evening.

"I'll be fine," he assured her firmly.

As Annette was wheeling Sam down the hallway, he paid her his own special tribute, "On behalf of the Congress of the United States, they thank you!" he declared. "On behalf of the citizens of Washington, D.C., they thank you. On behalf of the president, he thanks you and on behalf of myself," he affirmed softly, "I thank you."

"Oh, Sam," she replied.

On their way to Fort Myer, Annette made Sam promise to let her know immediately if there were any problems; she would make the excuses so they could return to the hotel.

"Yes, Sweetie," he replied obediently.

As soon as they arrived at the club, Colonel Conmy and John White insisted that Annette allow Sam to sit between them and would brook no argument in the matter. This made Annette very uncomfortable. When she looked across at her husband, though, her anxious look was greeted by a mischievous grin that said, "I'll never tell."

John White cut Sam's meat for him and Colonel Conmy made sure he was passed everything he needed as the men reminisced. Annette didn't think she had ever seen Sam so pleasantly preoccupied and for the first time during the trip, she allowed herself to relax. The dinner turned out to be the perfect ending to a journey "home" that in itself consistently elevated Sam above his pain and fatigue.

At the airport the following day, Sam was exhausted but content. The flight home passed without incident and he returned to Brookhollow physically spent but spiritually boosted beyond words.

The return from Washington heralded a new phase in the battle to preserve Sam's strength. He was now much weaker, despite his uplifted spirits. More alarmingly, his head would lurch to the right at the slightest sign of fatigue; his need for prolonged periods of rest was becoming more and more evident.

In February, there were Christian Women's Club meetings in Dodge City and Garden City. Annette prayed for good weather and it appeared her prayers had been answered when the temperature rose above 50 degrees on both days. On February 13th and 14th, both luncheons presented Sam and Annette as the sweetheart couple who had come to share their story with them. It turned out to be a very good trip all the way around. They finished with a speech at Ulysses and slowly made their way back to Wichita. On the way home, Sam appeared to eye the stark, barren plains with particular relish.

In May, they traveled to Junction City for another engagement with the Christian Women's Club. They drove up in the afternoon and spent the night, allowing Sam the opportunity to rest and muster his strength. Annette spoke alone the next day. Sam was too weak to speak but he was there to greet the ladies afterwards.

On their way back to Wichita, Annette noticed for the first time a black and blue bruise spreading across the top of Sam's left hand. Dark circles had set in more deeply than ever around his eyes and he had become fidgety to the point of distraction, rolling up little balls of tissue paper in his right hand and flicking them out the window. Annette had never seen him this way and she realized this had been their last speaking engagement.

By the beginning of June, Dr. Cook had become so concerned about Sam's internal problems that he had arranged for a visit to a urologist, accompanied by a kidney scan. This time, he didn't go into great detail with Annette about the procedure. It was clear to her on viewing the scan, however, that things weren't as they should be. Sam was beginning to collect fluid in his abdomen. No sooner had he taken a couple of bites of food at mealtimes, than he would say he was full. Coming from a man who had loved to eat all of his life, this was an ominous sign.

That same month, Dr. Cook suggested a nursing service pay regular visits to take Sam's vital signs. Annette welcomed the suggestion, relieved she no longer had to shoulder the whole burden alone. In addition, Sam really took to the nurse and looked forward to her visits.

Toward the end of summer, Sam started pestering Annette to make reservations for Hawaii. She was reluctant to do it, but finally, at Sam's insistence, they picked out a date in January together. After the reservations had been made, Sam spent many hours talking and reminiscing about Hawaii's wondrous beauty. Annette had the feeling he had some other place in mind.

Despite his increasing debilitation, Sam never became depressed, although one day Annette found herself caught off-guard by a particular remark he made. "I hope I haven't disappointed you as a husband," he said earnestly. "Have you heard any complaints?" she replied, not altogether sure whether it was one of Sam's characteristic wisecracks, or if he meant something else by it.

Sam continued to endeavor to fill each day with as much physical activity as his fragile frame would allow. He refused pointblank to take his breakfast in bed. Occasionally, he would have lunch in bed if he felt particularly weak, but only because he was satisfied that he'd been up during the day.

Afternoons were spent reclining and dozing in the electrical Niagara Chair in the family room. The two of them would sit together, not saying much, maybe listening to some gospel music. Sam's appetite for prayer seemed to become greater by the day as he became more earnest in his talks with God. He spoke with the Lord as though He were right there in the room, still addressing him as "Sir," his commanding officer above, but it had a greater intimacy now.

He had a desire to call old friends and did call a few, but for the most part he was reluctant, saying he didn't have anything important to tell them and he knew they had busy lives.

It had reached the point for Annette that she just wanted to soak up everything about Sam—from his earth-shattering snores to the warmth of his body next to hers. Filled with a sense of abject helplessness in the face of the inevitable, she prayed silently. Deep down, her feelings of desperation at the thought of losing Sam were immense, but she also could not bear the thought of watching him linger in suffering.

Annette prayed that *she* would live precisely five minutes longer than Sam in good health. She prayed her husband's mind wouldn't go before his body and that when the hour came, he would go rapidly.

★   ★   ★

That summer was difficult. It was a constant labor of love to keep Sam comfortable. His right leg was swollen like a ripe watermelon. He felt no pain but it looked as though sores were about to begin breaking out across his right ankle. The fluid build-up in his abdomen was not so much a problem of pain as one of constant discomfort. The cluster headaches, however, were a different story; they came on him in wave upon wave of unforgiving intensity. But not once did he complain. Annette dimmed the lights and tried to muffle harsh sounds as much as possible in an attempt to maintain a soothing environment.

Sunday, September 9th, was their 12th wedding anniversary. Since Sam had been unable to make it to church for some time, a group of the church elders paid a special visit to Brookhollow. It was customary for all anniversaries at Faith Chapel to be celebrated with a song. Sam asked the elders if they would mind singing at his home. Immediately, the eight men struck up with "Sweeter As the Years Go By."

Just over a month later, on Sunday, the 14th of October, Sam decided he really wanted to go to church. They arrived 10 minutes late to avoid the commotion before the service began, slipping in through the door at the back.

During the service, Annette noticed Sam surveying everything around him, looking up toward the ceiling, up and down the aisles and fixing his gaze on different individuals for short intervals. She wheeled her husband out of the sanctuary several minutes before the conclusion of the service to avoid the crowds once again. When they returned home, Annette saw that Sam was completely drained of energy. In the days that followed, he spent very little time up—just long enough to eat breakfast before returning to bed.

Chapter Twenty-Four

'Til We Meet Again

Annette awoke slowly that Thursday morning, October 18th. She sensed the dampness of the sheets to her right as she opened her eyes. Looking over at Sam, she saw his pajamas were soaked with perspiration and realized he had been awake all night.

"Why didn't you wake me, Sam?" she asked softly.

"It just felt so good to lie here and watch you sleep, Sweetie-pie," he replied with a smile. "What a marvelous gift it is, to be able to rest so peacefully."

They both lay in bed motionless for a short while before Sam spoke up again. "Would you help me with a bath in the tub, Sweetie?"

Her husband's request invoked tremors of disquiet which intensified as she surveyed the frailty of his frame, swollen abdomen and right leg.

"Are you sure you feel up to it, Sam?" she asked, failing to conceal her apprehension at the thought of resurrecting an activity they had discontinued six weeks earlier because of his failing strength.

"Yes!" he replied.

As always, her doubts proved to be no match for his insistence and she wheeled the hoyer lift from the bathroom over to the side of the bed.

With gentle dexterity born of 12 year's experience, she slid the lift's sling underneath him as he lay on the bed. Taking her husband in her arms in a tender embrace, she raised him to the sitting position and with slow, deliberate strokes pumped up the lift with one hand while bracing his back with the other. Once he was in position, she wheeled him over beside the bathtub where she lowered him carefully into the warm water. After moving the lift away, she dipped the sponge into the water and held it just above her husband, squeezing gently to allow a gradual trickle over the exposed portions of his body.

"Oh, that feels so good," Sam warbled ecstatically as his wife interspersed the squeeze of the sponge with gentle dabs of his chest and shoulders.

Following the bath, Annette laid her husband back down on the bed and rubbed oil into his body, after which he insisted on being dressed and placed in his wheelchair so he could eat breakfast at the table.

Sam took no more than two or three bites before indicating he was full. Annette wheeled him back into the bedroom and laid him down once again.

Around two o'clock that afternoon, Pastor Pruitt and his wife, Ruth, stopped by for a visit. Sam came alive in the presence of the pastor and his wife. He was visibly attentive and alert, lacing his own contribution to the conversation with characteristic sprinklings of self-deprecating humor.

When the opportunity presented itself, Annette interposed a question she had been bottling up inside for a long time. "Sam, are you afraid of dying?" she asked.

"No," he replied, "Sweetie-pie, could you get me a glass of apple cider?"

Annette returned from the kitchen with the cider and Sam took a couple of sips. "That tastes good," he said, "Maybe I'll have some more a bit later, I feel kind'a full."

Sam's unequivocal answer to her question had not satisfied Annette and she sat preoccupied with the notion that he had only answered her in such a way because it was expected of him. Five minutes later, she could restrain herself no longer and probed again, "Sam, are you afraid of dying?" She posed the question with a look in her eye that said—have you really thought about it?

"No," he replied, more insistently this time.

The pastor took all this as a cue for a prayer and prayed that God would send his angels to protect and guard over Sam. As the pastor and his wife got up to leave, Annette repeated the question a third time.

"No!" Sam replied, this time with an indignant look that said—why do you have to ask me three times?

The Pruitts left Brookhollow at half past three and Annette spent the remainder of the afternoon sitting in a chair next to Sam, sewing while he drifted in and out of sleep. They spent his waking moments chatting about the future and holding each other by the hand.

"My only regret," said Annette, "is that I won't be able to see the expression on your face when you meet the Lord."

He looked his wife directly in the eye. "I've already seen Him," he declared, with profound assurance.

"What do you mean?" she asked, somewhat taken aback.

"Every time my Sweetie-pie does something for me, I see the Lord's expression in her face."

They went on to compare their visions of what Heaven must be like; they talked about Paula, allowed themselves to bask for a while in the warm glow of reminiscence and Sam talked about his mother. They were scrupulous with every detail as though it were the last, yet they talked as though they had forever.

At six o'clock, Annette asked her husband if he was hungry.

"I will be by the time you've fixed something," he quipped. He lay watching the evening news as she prepared dinner in the kitchen. She returned with a tray for both of them. Sam took one bite from each item on his plate and said it tasted very good and perhaps he would save some for later.

As the evening wore on, each intake of breath became more labored, although Sam did not complain of any pain. Neither of them wanted to watch more television so Annette dimmed the lights, put one of their favorite Gospel recordings on the record player and pulled a chair up beside her husband. She slipped her right hand into the palm of his, dispensing with words—the last obstacle to the completion of a perfect union.

Seeing that Sam appeared to be getting sleepy, Annette prepared things so they could both go to bed early. She slipped into the dark Hawaiian robe emblazoned with big red and pink roses and tulips on green stems that Sam had bought her for Christmas two years ago.

It was approaching nine o'clock when Sam asked his wife how long it had been since they had seen George and Pam, his favorite nephew and his wife. George was the eldest son of Sam's half-brother, Bill.

"Oh, quite some time," Annette replied. "Would you like to see them?"

"Yes," he said.

"When would you like me to make the arrangements?" she asked.

"Right now!" he exclaimed, with the same insistence he'd answered her repeated questions earlier in the afternoon.

Annette made the call immediately. "Pam, is there any way that you and George can come over, right now?"

Pam telephoned her father to come over and stay with their young children and she and her husband were on the doorstep at Brookhollow within the half-hour.

George walked into the bedroom ahead of his wife and greeted his uncle cheerily. "How're you doing, Sam?"

"Tell me about brother Bill," Sam demanded in earnest, without returning his nephew's greeting.

"Well, Sam, he's in bad shape," George replied frankly. The truth about Bill's alcoholism had been concealed behind a loyal wife's meticulously embroidered veil of denial for some time, and now following her death it had become clear it was killing him.

It was as though Sam had already rehearsed what he was going to say next. "Let's pray for brother Bill," he said, and the four of them linked hands and bowed their heads.

After the prayer, Sam took everyone by surprise once again by becoming extraordinarily talkative and dominating the conversation.

The clock had just finished striking ten when Sam's chest began to reverberate with a grotesque gurgling and rattling sound. "That sounds terrible," he remarked with surprise. "Is that me?"

"Yes," Annette replied softly.

"How strange," he said. "I don't feel any different."

George helped Annette sit Sam up in bed to try to ease the cacophony. As they began to lift, Sam jerked forward vomiting forth a mixture of blood particles and food.

George volunteered to phone Dr. Cook while Annette held her husband's hand. Once Dr. Cook was on the line, Annette picked up the receiver.

"We need to clear his lungs of fluid," was the doctor's first imperative.

"That sounds like hospital," Annette replied.

"Yes," said the doctor.

"Does that also imply life supports?"

Once again his reply was in the affirmative.

"Is there anything that can be done for Sam's headaches?" she asked with greater insistence.

"No," he said softly.

"Then that will not be the route we shall take."

"Okay," the doctor replied, "I'll be out in a little bit with some medication to relieve Sam's pain."

After replacing the receiver, Annette returned to her husband's bedside, climbed onto the bed and knelt down beside him. She took his hand and clasped it tightly with both of her own.

"Sam, Dr. Cook is on the way over with some medication for your pain," she stated calmly.

"But I really don't feel any," he replied, and they talked some more. Annette was in the middle of a conversation with George when Sam interrupted.

"The fingers on my left hand hurt," he said.

"But Sam, they're right here," Annette replied in a kind of non sequitur.

He reiterated that he could feel something in his fingers.

"What does it feel like, Sam?" she asked.

"As though they're trying to wake up," he said, going on to utter something that was quite unintelligible. Then Sam turned his head to the left—something he normally would have found uncomfortable—and fixed his eyes intently on those of his wife for an instant before lifting his gaze above her. She looked on as years of pain made an imperceptible departure from her husband's countenance.

At that moment, Dr. Cook entered the bedroom, while Sam's lungs sucked in two giant gulps of air. The doctor walked over to the bed. "Sam is gone," he pronounced quietly.

"No! He's still breathing," Annette protested.

The doctor took out his stethoscope, placed it upon Sam's chest and listened intently for about 10 seconds. He shook his head. Annette leaned over and put her ear against Sam's chest where the stethoscope had been. There was no sound. She rose once more and knelt beside her love, clasping his left hand. The doctor took her left hand and gripped it gently with his own.

"Let's say the Lord's Prayer," he said quietly. The four of them bowed their heads.

"This is a very special bed," the doctor announced following the prayer. Annette looked at him quizzically.

"This is where Sam Bird rested, knew his wife and met his Lord," the doctor proclaimed softly. From that moment, the value of the bed soared in Annette's estimation.

George offered to call Sam's father. Annette nodded her consent from the bed. It was almost midnight by now and Dick and Hazel were both asleep when the phone rang. Hazel took the call and thanked George for taking the trouble to let them know. Dick remained asleep, so she got up from her twin bed and walked across to where he lay. Gently pulling back the covers, she slipped into bed next to her husband, taking him in her arms.

"Dick, did you hear the telephone?" she whispered, cradling her husband's head close to her. Dick came round slowly. "Honey, that was George Bruce. He called to tell us Sam has just died."

Dick shuffled uneasily for a moment and turned away as Hazel loosened her embrace. There was a short pause.

"Thank you, Lord," he said quietly.

Hazel held her husband in her arms until he fell asleep once more—or possibly pretended to do so.

Meanwhile, at Brookhollow Dr. Cook suggested calling the funeral home. The suggestion produced a surge of panic in Annette; Sam was still wearing his catheter.

'Sam's going to leave here as a whole person,' she thought to herself. Dr. Cook offered to remove the catheter. Annette declined. It was something she had to do alone before letting go.

Dr. Cook turned and left the room and Annette wiped away the remaining perspiration from Sam's body, delicately removing the catheter. As she dressed her husband in his pajamas, Annette sensed for the first time that he was no longer there. From the time Sam took his last two breaths she had been aware of a pervasive presence that had appeared to move from the core of his being to engulf the entire room. Now only the body remained.

It was two o'clock in the morning before everyone had left the house after Annette insisted she would be fine. Suddenly, displacing the numb fatigue that had overtaken her body, she felt a yearning to get out of the house and run. By the time she had made it to the corner of the street, the chilly October air was slicing through her. She turned and walked briskly back to the house. After a warm shower, she curled up on the damp patch where Sam had lain.

"Lord, this is where I want to meet you when the time comes," she prayed.

She drifted in and out of restless sleep before being wakened by the ring of the telephone shortly before six o'clock the following morning.

★　　★　　★

Sam was laid to rest following services at Faith Chapel on Monday, October 22nd. The church was packed to the rafters. The "band of brothers" flew in for the funeral and B.T. Collins delivered the eulogy.

A friend, Ann Rowland, wrote to Annette following the funeral:

> *B.T.'s remembrance was beautiful; reflective of Sam's*
> *love and humor . . . and your own sharing with us warmed*

395

my heart and made me quite happy for you, but, something quite unexpectedly touched me deeply in a different way.

As the procession passed the mini-mall on Harry Street, an old man in shabby clothes stood at attention, leaning on a cane, eyes blurred behind thick cataract lenses, his old hat held across his heart.

'Now that,' I said to myself, 'is a tribute Sam Bird would appreciate.'

Epilogue

On several occasions following Sam's death, it was mentioned to Annette that her husband's name should be added to the Vietnam Memorial in Washington, D.C.

In the summer of 1987, the "Moving Wall" came to Wichita. A half-size replica of the original, it was on display for four days on the north lawn at the campus of Wichita State University. Prompted mainly by curiosity, Annette decided to attend the opening ceremony and dedications while vaguely recalling Sam's indifferent reaction at the memorial itself on that late January day in 1984. Joining the five hundred or so people gathered together on the lawn, she sensed an overpowering surge of emotion which she had not felt on that barren, frigid day.

Even though the replica was only half the size of the original, the sight of all those names, the enormity of them, struck her for the first time. There was great power in seeing it up close. But it was the line upon line of Vietnam Veterans—a peculiar assortment, clad in everything from denim jackets to business suits, short haircuts and American Legion headgear, straggly hair and beards, men in wheelchairs, men on crutches, teenage daughters, wives remarried—that left the deepest impression with her.

'Sam's name should be with them,' she thought to herself. He might not have died in Vietnam but as B.T. had often said, it was a direct result of the wounds he had incurred; it just took him 18 years to die, that's all.

After going through much bureaucracy and with the eventual help of Senator Bob Dole, Annette was told the application had been approved and Sam's name would be dedicated along with 23 others on Veterans' Day, November 1987. Annette invited her ten-year-old nephew, her sister Carol's son, Seth, to accompany her on the trip.

Annette and Seth flew into Washington on the evening of November 9th. The Marlboro Cigarette Company had organized accommodations at the Embassy Suites Hotel for the families of the 24 whose names were to be dedicated on the 11th. The company had also organized a fund-raising concert starring the country music recording artists, The Judds and Alabama, for the evening before in Constitution Hall. Each new engraving cost approximately $1,800. They were met at the hotel by Dick and Hazel who'd brought Paula's third daughter, Sarah, with them for the occasion.

For the 12 years of her marriage to Sam, Annette had thought of Dick as a thorn in her side. Now, she viewed him differently. Dick would always be "Dick," but now she accepted the fact that he really loved his son, and it was his all-powerful protective instincts that had governed many of his actions. And now Dick was much more charitably disposed toward his daughter-in-law. From the days following Sam and Annette's engagement, when he had been at the forefront of the chorus of cynical reaction, he'd observed closely everything that had transpired between his son and daughter-in-law. He had noted every last detail and now was ready to repay his debt of gratitude with genuine affection and more. As for Annette, she now referred to her father-in-law as "Dad" instead of "Dick."

During their four years of marriage, Hazel saw a different side of Dick emerge. She saw a man who genuinely regretted the way he had treated people in the past—but more than that—he wanted to change; he was really trying to be the person who had been lost in an unhappy childhood. Hazel may have been the catalyst but others were appreciating too; there was a good man inside Dick Bird.

★　　★　　★

The benefit concert that evening produced a variety of emotions in Annette. The cocktail party beforehand left her feeling somewhat empty. The room was filled with people, elbow to elbow, nibbling at small, fancy bites of food that might have been better left on display. The same could have been said for the majority of the conversations—awash in a sea of platitudes. The only people who seemed totally at ease were Sarah and Seth, who amused themselves by circling the room and pointing out the faces they recognized from television.

The evening was relatively balmy and the air hung heavy around them, depressing Annette as she hailed a cab outside the concert hall for herself and Seth. She recalled some advice she'd had suggesting it would be wise to visit Sam's name on the Wall before the ceremony. Annette asked the driver of their cab to take them to the memorial. It was approaching ten o'clock when the cab drew up to the north of the Wall. Not being familiar with the Washington, D.C., area, she asked the cab driver to wait for them.

As she and Seth made their way southeastward down over the small rise, her eyes lit upon a group of four men dressed in combat fatigues sitting cross-legged on the ground, facing the east end of the Wall. The men were talking quietly among themselves as Annette and Seth almost brushed by them while making their way toward the center of the memorial. Apart from these four men, the entire area was deserted.

The floodlights positioned along the bottom of the Wall shone over the names, causing them to stand out in the darkness. At first the row upon row of engraving had the appearance of a generically aligned mass of letters. Then they reached E-14, line 90, and the letters became the person. Annette felt instinctively drawn to their touch. The stone was warm and substantial against the soft palm of her hand. She felt tears welling up deep within, but never making it to the surface, as though reinforcing the perception that the pain of Vietnam will never subside, but it's too late to grieve.

Seth eyed the scene with dutiful reverence, although it fell beyond the scope of his comprehension. After an extended moment of silence, they returned to the cab where they found the four men inquiring whether it was available.

"If you're going our way, you're welcome to share a ride with us," she said.

All six bundled into the station wagon and they set out for the hotel.

During the journey, the four men told Annette they were from Connecticut; every Veterans' Day, 30 of them traveled to the Wall for two days to be with the friends they had lost during the war. They recounted stories, drank a little, laughed a little and cried a little before returning home for another year. Then they asked Annette why she and Seth were there. She told them about Sam, that his name was to be dedicated the following day.

As the station wagon pulled into the hotel driveway, Annette reached for her purse. The man beside her reached across and gently laid his hand on her arm. "No one pays for this cab who has helped one of us," he announced softly.

Annette and Seth stepped out of the cab and she thanked the men for their generosity before bidding them good night. By the time the cab had driven off into the night, Seth's eyes were wide with amazement.

"Wow!" he exclaimed. "We rode for free!"

★   ★   ★

The morning of the 11th, everybody awoke to discover Washington had been smothered by a blanket of snow that had fallen during the night. Eric, who, unbeknownst to his mother, had managed to route his semi to be able to attend the ceremony, found himself cut off 20 miles outside the city. The early morning traffic lurched into full swing and conditions became increasingly hazardous as all across the city cars became stranded. Annette felt sure the ceremonies would be canceled, but they weren't. As someone said later, no one ever called off a war because of bad weather.

Everyone arrived at the Wall by bus. They stepped down into a carpet of snow six inches deep in places. The combined blast of frigid air and driving sleet tore into the exposed faces of these latter-day pilgrims as they made their way along the path toward the Wall. The area around and above was littered with reporters, television crews and a handful of so-called dignitaries and congressmen—many of whom had sent their representatives. Chairs had been arranged for the families and a vocal group of veterans who had made the pilgrimage despite the weather. Dick made it to the Wall's approach but he could scarcely catch his breath. His emphysema made the intake of ice-cold air a torture he could no longer withstand and he had to return to the bus. At the Wall, Annette met Pam, George and his younger brother, Bill. They were joined by B.T. Collins and a news crew from Sacramento.

The snow began to fall more heavily as the proceedings were called to attention. An unaccompanied version of the National Anthem was rendered by Alabama from the top of the Wall. Annette thought she had never heard it sung so beautifully. That was followed by The Judds with their own rendition of "God Bless America." If the trip to Washington in 1984 had been one for Sam to relish and savor, it was now his widow's turn. The presence of the snow and wind became insignificant.

★　　★　　★

"To see his name . . . it's a milestone to me." Brien Thomas Collins lowered his head. A layer of mushy snow had solidified across the top of his green beret. He brought up his index finger to stroke away the moisture beneath his eye. "It's good for his father too." Sniffing, he swung his chin round into the driving sleet and snow, shooting an intent glance at the immense granite span. "But for all of us who-who-uh . . ." He took a second to recover his composure. ". . . It's something, it's really something. When I'm eighty-five years old, I'm gonna be able to go here, and I'm gonna tell people . . ."

Leaning forward, with all his weight on his one good leg, he replaced the note that accompanied a photograph taken in

October 1966 of a tall, slender, twenty-six-year-old man gazing down—softly, assuredly. His beloved olive green, jungle sweater was unbuttoned to the chest. A close-shaved crop of golden hair highlighted the warmth of a natural smile as the clear blue morning sky came down to meet lush, green hills in a country far away.

Gossamer flakes of snow settled on the photograph's plastic cover. A white carnation partially concealed the message written on the note alongside, although it was possible to make out the words—"I love you, I love you, I love you."

Collins straightened slowly. "I'm gonna be able to point to his name." He ran his finger over the freshly engraved inscription on the middle of the Wall. "I will be able to say that I served with that man."

Index

403

Give the Gift of Inspiration to Your Friends and Colleagues!

ORDER FORM

YES, I want ___ copies of *So Proudly He Served: The Sam Bird Story* at $24.95 each, plus $3 shipping per book. (Kansas residents please include $1.47 state sales tax per book.) Canadian orders must be accompanied by a postal money order in U.S. funds. Allow 30 days for delivery.

Name _____ Phone_____

Organization _____

Address _____

City/State/Zip _____

Please make your check payable and return to:

Okarche Books
P.O. Box 782076
Wichita, Kansas 67278-2076

or call

(316) 687-0049